INTERVENTION

INTERVENTION

GUIDES & PERILS

Leonard W. Doob

Yale
University
Press

New Haven
and
London

Designed by Deborah Dutton
Set in Sabon text and Gill Sans display types by The
Composing Room of Michigan, Inc.
Printed in the United States of America by BookCrafters,
Inc., Chelsea, Michigan.

Library of Congress Cataloging-in-Publication Data

Doob, Leonard William, 1909–
    Intervention : guides and perils / Leonard W. Doob.
        p.   cm.
    Includes bibliographical references and index.
    ISBN 0–300-05571–4 (alk. paper)
    1. Helping behavior.   2. Problem solving.   I. Title.
BF637.H4D67   1993
302'.14–dc20   93–9716
                                                        CIP

A catalogue record for this book is available from the British
Library.

The paper in this book meets the guidelines for
permanence and durability of the Committee on Production
Guidelines for Book Longevity of the Council on Library
Resources.
10 9 8 7 6 5 4 3 2 1

To a very small number of friends alive at Yale University
and elsewhere

CONTENTS

FOREGROUND

Chapter One

Human beings constantly interact as equals or unequals
and in pairs or in groups. The content, timing, and morality of their interactions are perplexingly varied. Here
one kind of interaction comes to the fore that—without
apology and abruptly in an introductory paragraph—is
quickly defined: "Intervention refers to the efforts of
one or more persons to affect one or more other persons
when after an event the former, the latter, or both perceive a problem requiring resolution." This definition
performs no intellectual miracle, yet at least the broad
character of the present analysis is bluntly suggested at
the outset.

A mother observes her child playing with matches;
she intervenes and removes the matches, whether or not
she explains her intervention to the child. A devout individual who believes he has committed a sin seeks forgiveness from a deity and thus requests that deity to
intervene in his behalf. An ill person consults a physician and asks him or her to ease the pain by diagnosing
and then curing the illness. Factory workers threaten to
strike for higher wages or for safer working conditions;

a designated person intervenes and persuades both their representatives and those of management to discuss their differences, to try to find a solution, perhaps a compromise, and thus to avert the strike that might damage both parties. In 1938 Hitler intervened in the affairs of Austria by moving his army into that country and annexing it; obviously and tragically he thus initiated a series of actions that subsequently affected Austrians and Germans as well as millions of other persons in World War II. Common themes pervade these interventions, whether they be baby's play, a prayer, a medical challenge, a threatened strike, or a military incursion. It is useful, therefore, to employ intervention as the significant common denominator and then eventually to decide whether such interference (one of the frequently employed synonyms) has been effective or justified.

The concept of intervention is often used in a more restricted sense to refer to the attempt of a stronger nation or organization to impose its "will" on a weaker one.[1] Certainly the challenge to comprehend international relations is staggering in its own right. The more general aim here, however, is to stress that resolving or coping with unresolved problems of all kinds involves individuals and consequently can, must, or should be embraced within a unified form of reference. It is unavoidable not to be involved in interventions. Directly upon birth, in fact, infants, though utterly dependent upon others, are able to respond to persons and thus elicit responses from them. Their actions may not be intentional in an adult sense, yet the effect on their parents *is* noteworthy.[2]

Of course there is nothing magical about the term *intervention*. Other words—intercession, interposition, or control, or even influence, propaganda communication, or meddle—could and do serve a similar function. Important only is that the term *intervention* can be employed in so many different contexts and hence heuristically alerts us, like the German word Weltanschauung, to a universal attribute of human relationships, including their moral implications. Yes, a nation's leaders may intervene by declaring war on another country or by seeking to prevent that country from engaging in warfare; the concept is deliberately all-embracing.

Intervention thus defined has implications for human beings even when an ostensible nonhuman objective is specified. Some of us intervene or try to intervene to preserve a forest, an endangered species, or the "uninhabited" continent of Antarctica. Our intervention, however, is opposed not by the trees, the animals, or the land mass but by other persons who seek timber or tourists; who would use the animals for food or their hides, entrails, or tusks for clothing or symbols; or who would prospect for oil or expand the territory they control. To achieve or not to achieve such human goals, consequently, persons intervene and curb other persons and thereby affect nonhuman events.

The scope of the all-embracing definition and ensuing mode of analysis, nevertheless, must be narrowed a trifle. Perhaps it is self-evident both metaphorically and biologically that animals intervene to protect themselves against other animals and people, to obtain food, and to perpetuate their relations among members of their own species. The topic is intriguing but carries us far afield, for then such anthropomorphism might also have to be extended to include plants that "intervene" in behalf of their own seed as well as inanimate forces like the weather or the hours of daylight that "intervene" in human planning. Next, although it is true that almost any communication, whether it be a shoulder shrug or an advertising campaign to promote the sale of a brand of lipstick or tractors, stems from a person who intervenes or tries to intervene in the purchasing decisions of potential customers, the details of what transpires in such contexts must be considered in detail by specialists: historians of individuals (psychiatrists, psychologists), of groups (political scientists, sociologists), or of societies (anthropologists, historians).

Finally, let it be clear that unresolved problems may not give rise to intervention. An individual resolves or tries to resolve his own problems: he finds a solution by recalling a similar experience in the past, through trial and error, or by consulting an acquaintance. Two or more persons or groups may hesitate to bargain with each other in the absence of a third party or intervener,[3] yet even then one of the individuals may eventually intervene independently in his own behalf.

The opposite of intervention, *nonintervention,* must also be confronted in order to explain a failure to intervene when intervention may be judged either possible or desirable. A passerby knows he cannot swim; although a child seems to be drowning after falling into a lake, the adult stands hopelessly by. Believers in what is called precognition, "the prediction or knowledge of random future events"[4] without the basis of "inference or reasoning," may believe that deliberate intervention is ultimately futile, even when they are also convinced that they themselves can prevent such events from occurring. A person skilled in intervention refuses to intervene in a conflict that has been called to his attention because he judges it would be futile to do so; no other third party is immediately available, so the conflict then becomes more intense. Both in its charter and in many but not all of its actions the Organization of African Unity has proclaimed a doctrine of nonintervention in each nation's affairs since its members and peoples have experienced unwelcome interventions in the past by colonial and other intruding forces.[5] The League of Nations and the United Nations (UN) have followed or tried to follow a policy of intervention with reference to conflicts between states but one of nonintervention for civil wars (except for "rebellions") within a state. In theory, therefore, these international organizations adhere to nonintervention in the domestic affairs of other states lest national sovereignty be violated, although the policy is not followed when the leaders of one state convince themselves—as did President Kennedy and his advisers during the so-called Cuban missile crisis of 1961— that their own security is threatened by events in a foreign country.[6] The Secretary-General of the UN in 1991 to 1992 used his good offices to send Cyrus Vance and then a group of peacekeepers to Yugoslavia in an effort to end the tragic fighting between the Serbs and other regions of that ethnically diverse country and then later to try to relieve the suffering of the peoples there.

Events and Problems

An event with its problem is the point in time at which both the analysis and the contemplation of an intervention begin. The assumption must be that the precipitating factor for the problem, any problem, must be an event, which is clearly any change that affects and consequently is perceived by one or more human beings. A change in a distant galaxy becomes an event only when it is observed by an astronomer or if it produces a change that is perceived by someone on earth. Whether that change also creates a problem for the astronomer or the earth dweller depends upon him or her as well as upon its impact. An event with a problem resulting in a crisis or dispute is likely to challenge somebody to participate in order to seek a resolution.

In analyzing interventions, therefore, the precipitating event and the ensuing problem must be specified. A definitive listing of the events leading to interventions need not be attempted, indeed should not and cannot be attempted because all human activity would then have to be cataloged and pigeonholed. To suggest the awesome scope of interventions, however, it must be sufficient only to remind ourselves of the varied changes that do occur and hence inspire or provoke interventions. The changes are or can be:[7]

1. *Environmental:* momentary or enduring over which human beings have little or no control (climates, weather, erosion) or over which they have some or considerable control (pollution, erosion, utilization of forests, plants, animals, minerals).
2. *Individual:* the human body (disease, dying, dangers), the human psychic (personality tendencies, pathologies).
3. *Social:* every kind of human relationship (family, neighborhood, class, clique, caste, club, education, industry).
4. *National:* the larger social groups (ethnicity, politics, community).
5. *International:* relations between nations (trade, treaties, war).

Merely naming a particular intervention immediately indicates the nature of the problem confronting individuals after an event has occurred.

Variables

The variables to be contemplated in analyzing or planning interventions are offered in one bulky question in the manner once cogently proposed for the study of communication:[8] "After an event giving rise to an unresolved problem, who initiates an intervention with whom; why, when, where, and how; may, must, or should there be an intervention; and then what actually occurs during and after the intervention?" That bulky, clumsy sentence serves as an introduction to the eight chapters of this book; slightly elaborated and labeled, the contents consist of the following steps:

1. *Foreground:* after which event and unresolved problem is there a possibility of an intervention?
2. *Participants:* who initiates the intervention with whom?
3. *Rationale:* why is an intervention contemplated and why are participants selected by whom?
4. *Timing:* when does or must the intervention begin?
5. *Method:* where and how will the principals interact?
6. *Morality:* may, must, or should there be an intervention?
7. *Reality:* what actually occurs during the intervention?
8. *Evaluation:* how is the outcome of the intervention subsequently viewed?

Steps 1 through 6 are taken before the intervention occurs, at least from the standpoint of one or more of the participants; from a historical standpoint that would reconstruct the steps leading to an intervention, these are steps for which information is sought after the fact. Steps 7 and 8 involve the actual intervention both when and after it occurs.

The vocabulary can and must be selected as these eight steps are analyzed, inasmuch as jargon is rife and confusing. First, the role of individuals in an intervention is specified:

1. *Intervener:* the person or persons who alone or in representing a group seek to resolve the problem of another person or persons who belong to the same or different groups.
2. *Principal:* the person, persons, or groups with an unresolved problem.
3. *Bystanders:* person or persons who, though not participants, may affect an intervention by their presence, actions, or absence. Included may be spectators in a Western courtroom in their assigned seats: they are supposed to be quiet, yet they are interveners because their very presence and number as well as the sounds coming from them can affect the proceedings.[9]

The word *participants* is used when reference is made simultaneously both to the intervener and the principal.

Next, the number and relation of the participants is indicated:

1. *Dual intervention:* one or more interveners and one or several principals in the same group with similar objectives regarding the unresolved problem. A drowning child is rescued by a passerby. There is a person-to-person interaction; the intervener tries to assist the principal.
2. *Multiple intervention:* one or more interveners with one or more principals belonging to different groups in conflict; the intervener is frequently called a *third party,* and principals may be known as *disputants* or *adversaries.*[10] The groups are in conflict either because they disagree (a wage settlement between management and workers) or because they agree concerning an objective that cannot be shared (opponents in a game or a war).[11]

For *timing,* the intervention's onset may be:

1. *Preactive:* a problem looms but has not yet arisen or become acute. Officials make certain that nuclear wastes are removed so that principals' health will not be threatened.
2. *Reactive:* a problem has arisen and is apparent. Officials or-

der nuclear wastes to be removed after principals complain that their health is being impaired.

This temporal distinction is admittedly not clear-cut because, like any temporal boundary, it depends upon the participant's or the observer's subjective judgment. Consider the moment at which leaders of the United States intervened in the Gulf War of 1991; were they actively intervening to prevent some future action by Iraq, were they reacting to the invasion of Kuwait by Iraq, were they responding to concerns about oil coming from Iraq, or were all three goals or options prominent at the time?

Finally, the *methodological procedure* is highlighted:

1. *Consultation:* interveners provide information or advice sought by principals and have no authority to enforce a resolution. An ill person visits a physician and subsequently agrees or does not agree to follow his prescription.

2. *Domination:* interveners arbitrarily intervene and impose a resolution not necessarily sought by principals. Police arrest persons selling illegal drugs.

3. *Consent:* interveners arbitrarily intervene and propose a resolution satisfying to principals even when they have not been consulted. A scholar or a citizen suggests how teachers can improve their pupils' morale; the teachers voluntarily agree.

The above methods may be utilized either in a dual or in a multiple intervention; the following are variants when the interventions are multiple and when a third party plays a role:

4. *Adjudication:* interveners have the legal authority to propose and enforce a resolution, whether or not they or the principals have initiated the intervention but after the principals have indicated their problem. One side goes to court and sues the other for damages.

5. *Mediation:* interveners facilitate a resolution to a problem by inducing principals to interact or by eliciting information from them and offering general or specific suggestions during the interaction, but without authority to impose or enforce a

resolution. A friend, clergyman, or therapist suggests that a married couple discuss their difficulties with him or her before filing for a divorce.

6. *Arbitration:* interveners have the nonlegal authority, originally or momentarily granted by the principals, to require principals to participate in the intervention and to have the interveners propose an arbitrary or binding resolution. In many countries arbitrators or arbitration boards settle or seek to settle disputes between labor and management.

The terminology concerning these procedures is particularly confusing because it has not been standardized.[12] When consultants' advice or counsel is followed, they may be considered interveners. Mediators may encourage principals to express their feelings, to indicate their objectives, and to be guided by suggestions they may offer;[13] the resolution may come from the principals with or without the assistance of the intervener.[14] In arbitration the resolution, whether recommended or binding, is the responsibility of the intervener.[15] Both in mediation and arbitration somewhat informal interventions over an extended period of time may be called *workshops.* Adjudicating interveners impose and may also enforce their own resolutions, but principals may be consulted.

Ordinarily as well as in the present analysis, two concepts are excluded from the category of intervention, although they are closely related to it. *Bargaining* and *negotiation* between two or more persons usually take place in the absence of a third person, the intervener; the resolution of the conflict is sought by the principals themselves as they interact. Interveners in the role of mediators, however, may propose that there be bargaining or negotiation to resolve the apparent differences and then withdraw; or they may in fact organize the intervention before withdrawing. Also while bargaining or negotiating, the individuals may affect one another: at any moment one may seize the initiative and thus become, in this limiting context, the intervener. In the midst of a multiple intervention the intervener may step aside as the principals bargain or negotiate with one another.

Sequence of Decisions

Both the elongated question concerning intervention and the listing of chapters in this book, as unveiled in the previous section, give the impression that the analysis and planning of interventions follows a sequence of decisions beginning with a foreground (Step 1) and ending with evaluation (Step 8). At both ends of the sequence that ordering is valid. We begin, as already mentioned, with an event that produces a problem, as a result of which participants (whether interveners, principals, or both) select themselves or are selected (Step 2); and eventually there is interaction between or among the participants (Step 7). Retrospectively, however, the historian or the social scientist may observe first of all an intervention that has already occurred and that is thought to be a success or a failure (Step 8), to account for which some or all of the preceding steps (Steps 2–7) must be charted. Throughout the analysis, especially in the first six chapters, much of the exposition is phrased in terms of planning rather than accounting for interventions that are occurring or have already occurred. This procedure does not deprecate the latter but avoids cluttering sentences with a reference to both tasks and having to use verbs in the past as well as in the present or future tense.

After the event with its ensuing problem and after locating potential participants (Steps 1 and 2), the ordering of the intermediate decisions is never rigid and therefore any ordering of these decisions (Steps 3, 4, 5, 6) is possible. Hypothetical but not unrealistic illustrations indicate possibilities for each of the decisions:

3. *Rationale:* the child seems to be drowning, the passerby knows that he must be saved immediately (Step 4) and that he himself can effect the rescue by diving into the pond and pulling him out (Step 5); saving a life is surely desirable (Step 6).

4. *Timing:* one foreign office believes that trouble is brewing between two countries and hence seeks to arrange a conference (Step 5) in order to prevent a war between them (Step 3) be-

cause such a war would have disastrous consequences (Step 6).

5. *Method:* an arbitration board stands ready to consider a dispute within its jurisdiction but, whether or not it has legal authority to intervene (Step 6), it must first investigate the facts in the dispute (Step 4) and accept or select the principals (Step 3).

6. *Morality:* a missionary or crusader believes he must convert the unconverted and at first carefully selects principals likely to respond favorably (Step 3); he realizes that conversion is a long process (Step 4) which requires converts to appreciate the rewards awaiting them when they accept and act upon his message (Step 5).

The principals themselves stress the importance of the sequence and the risks of intervening or nonintervening. In general and after a particular event, are participants willing and able to run risks in connection with the problem at hand? Are the risks considered less important when the need for a solution seems urgent? Which method seems more or less risky with reference to the current problem? Isn't it desirable to tolerate a great risk to intervene in behalf of a precious value? Somehow the risks at each step are combined and the overall risk from intervening or nonintervening is determined or intuited by the participants.

Guides and Perils

Tons of relevant data, information, and viewpoints have been published and left unpublished in the past on the subject of intervention. A computer terminal in a Yale University library recently indicated 102 books with the word itself in the title and 1,077 books dealing with the topic in the last decade or so. Let us not depress ourselves by imagining the number of general and scholarly articles devoted to the same problem. Simply saying "international relations" immediately suggests the shelves in any library devoted to the conditions under which one country intervenes in the affairs of another or in which selfish or generous bystanders seek to prevent or augment interventions between one country and another. From another relevant viewpoint are attempts to discover the conditions under which persons do or do not intervene in order to help other persons; thus an entire volume is devoted largely to experiments in which American students do or do not intervene helpfully.[16] Somehow in the present finite analysis a selection must be made.

Within the last two decades one technique, that of meta-analysis, has sought to rescue theoreticians and practitioners alike from being discouraged or misled by the large number of studies concerning a particular topic and by their inconsistent and often contradictory generalizations. The studies employ various methods ranging from laboratory experiments to reports and observations under real-life conditions. Discarded are studies methodologically deficient as a result of sample size, faulty sampling, incorrect statistical methodology, or inept reporting.[17] When a meta-analysis was once made of eighty-eight studies concerning the effects of ratees' ethnic group on the performance ratings given them by sixty white and fourteen black American raters, the "issues" or critical variables required in an overall conclusion were the study's location (laboratory or "real" life), the previous training of the raters, the type of rating (behavior or trait), the actual purpose of the study (administrative or research), and the ethnic composition of the group. The studies surviving these strict criteria of selection were differentially weighted and finally combined statistically to produce an overall generalization.[18] Meta-analyses may emit well-founded but modest conclusions; thus in a meta-analysis of 443 studies—yes, 443—of intervention in behalf of the rehabilitation of juvenile delinquents, the finding is reported to have been that "there was an approximately 10 percent decrease in recidivism among treated juveniles as compared to untreated juveniles."[19] One more example: among the 157 studies of multiple interventions aiming at ethnic desegregation in the United States a decade or more ago, proponents of this policy could certainly find research substantiating their view that this policy had been beneficial to black children; yet only nineteen of these studies satisfied the strict meta-analytic criteria for inclusion, and based on those studies, it was found overall that the black students had made only "slight gains in reading when . . . taught in desegregated schools and their gains in mathematics were near zero."[20]

Unfortunately meta-analysis cannot be utilized to sift through the voluminous literature devoted, related, or relatable to intervention. As here defined, intervention occurs in varied situations ranging, as already indicated, from environmental to international events. Interveners who describe their own efforts, whether limited or numerous, may be prone to exaggerate a trifle the nature or significance of the outcome. Many laboratory experiments, especially when they employ university students as subjects, are so far removed from reality that it often seems insulting both to them and "real" life in this instance to use their sites or even the nature of the subjects and their culture as one of the variables. Most important of all, immediate or far-flung standards of the success and failures of interventions are not standardized and are also variable, so that a meta-analysis would have no reliable dependent variable to measure or determine.

In place of an unattainable meta-analysis of intervention, a less lofty procedure is being followed: proposed are guides to that subject. These guides are substitutes for the kinds of generalizations or hypotheses to which meta-analyses might conceivably give rise. Their imperfections—the deviations from the central tendencies they purport to indicate—are called perils, and frequently the adverb *perilously* appears to reinforce the possible qualification. The perils include not only the objective risks as viewed by the neutral, allegedly detached observer but also the subjective reactions and experiences of those formulating and attempting to utilize the guides both in theory and in practice. In every section of succeeding chapters italics are used to call attention to the principal guides.

Guides, with or without perils, however, must overcome precisely the same difficulties that give rise to meta-analyses. An official of the foundation that has been encouraging meta-analytic research has suggested the kind of research his method would remedy; his observation is also too true of research on intervention:

> The [United States] federal government spends millions of dollars annually to evaluate the effectiveness of social programs such as job training, drug rehabilitation, adolescent pregnancy prevention, or remedial treatment of juvenile delinquents. To the despair of policymakers, this research often yields conflicting results: some studies show positive effects; others, negative or inconclusive effects.[21]

In one significant respect guides may be more useful to potential participants than meta-analytic generalizations. When deciding whether to participate as interveners or principals, their interest centers not on overall generalizations that meta-analysts might be able to squeeze out of admirable statistical analyses but on much more specific clues to the event and the participants' situation at hand. If meta-analytic conclusions indicate the probable outcome in only a percentage of cases under the strictly stated conditions, guides would indicate what might be anticipated in the very specific situation at hand, a situation that might not even satisfy the criteria for inclusion in a meta-analysis. Meta-analysis may indicate that only 10 percent, more or less, will be affected whereas a guide may indicate marked success in a situation resembling the one at hand; let us, therefore, intervene or become principals in this particular intervention.

Guides, then, are salvaged epistemologically from the past because they appear to be promising, if limited, generalizations and hence may be useful right now and in the future. A more respectable name for the guides, hypotheses, is not employed for a methodological reason. Hypotheses must and can be validated or invalidated—if not forever, then at least for laudable periods of time. Interventions, on the other hand, may be complicated and so deliberately diverse that they cannot be encompassed in a rigorous sense. Instead an effort is made to squeeze out of selected materials modest guides that may possibly prove useful even if fallible and perilous. A single intervention, deliberately reported in its own right, is rarely repeated in detail, but at the very least it may suggest items to be observed in the future.

Here again is an ancient challenge for historians and all of us: why study the past if history is seldom repeated, yet how else can one profit from what is learned in the past? Is it not true, as a geographer has emphasized, that the "past is gone; its parity with things now seen, recalled, or read about can never be proved" and hence the past "cannot be verified through observation or experiment"?[22] Guides at least offer checklists of phenomena that may be critical in the present. Inasmuch as the relation of academic and scholarly research to policy-makers in government is most complicated and therefore, according to one survey of relevant studies, more frequently than not policy is not guided by research,[23] it would be presumptuous to insist that such research has more to offer than the hints suggested by guides. The analysis here is purposefully though not utterly dissimilar from others within the prevailing literature, especially those concentrating on so-cial conflict.[24]

In the spirit if not the letter of meta-analysis and social science, the literature on intervention merits general criticisms that, lest they be forgotten, will be subtly and unsubtly repeated here and there throughout this book. Being human, many progenitors of theories concerning intervention utilize their own experience as the basis for their claims. Although perforce that experience may be explicitly or implicitly limited, usually to less than a half dozen instances, their reports are likely to be written in the present tense and thus give the misleading impression that their proclaimed truths are applicable throughout eternity.[25] Without naming names, let it be said that some writers are not modest concerning their achievements, which they cite as the only, the best, or the better method to utilize in similar or dissimilar interventions. Ethnocentrism is another defect in most of this literature. An excellent workbook on mediation derived from the author's "own experience as a marital and divorce mediator" at only one American university and from thirty interviews with "mediators around the country" unhesitatingly proclaims that it is useful to probe the "real issues" in a conflict and desirable to "increase informality whenever possible (addressing each other by first name, no parliamentary procedure)" because thereby the "tone" of mediation is established.[26]

Then laboratory experiments systematically attempt to simulate real-life conditions by subjecting individuals to controlled manipulation by means of "vignettes" or contrived scenarios;[27] most of these subjects have been college students, usually in the United States, without or with additional subjects from other countries, who cooperate with the experimenters because they must do so as a requirement of the course they are attending or because they are offered a small monetary pittance as compensation. Very little information is generally provided about their milieus, so the struggling reader cannot even imagine whether their reactions have been influenced by their ethnic, religious, political, or economic backgrounds. Social scientists who conduct experiments under these artificial conditions or who review such studies usually or eventually wonder whether the findings are valid in "real life;" some are overjoyed when the findings appear or are guessed to be similar or complimentary, or they blast the approach when they believe otherwise.[28]

Of course, in pursuit of fame, profit, or self-expression there are also books targeted to a popular audience, written in the first person, overflowing with boasts concerning the author's achievements and offering advice to readers who would also be similarly successful; from some of them, like one written by an attorney with impressive experience,[29] sagacious and even systematic guidance is obtainable. Negotiations may furnish valuable clues to some aspects of intervention[30] since, as already indicated, the participants may intervene with one another at the outset or during their interaction. We have at our disposal, in short, an embarrassment of riches and semi-riches from which, prejudice or no prejudice, there is no escape.

Specific studies that are linked somehow to interventions are constantly cited or summarized in the present volume. They illustrate and perhaps enliven the discussion, even as there are frequent references to a hypothetical child in danger of drowning in a hypothetical lake. For earthly or moral reasons any reference to such a topic as the United

Nations or the sustainability of our planet is of practical, compelling interest. A study that is well designed and analyzed at least suggests a guide, whether in the meta-analytic sense or not. Apparently unique interventions in the past may be useful in the present. The ascent of a balloon or airplane above the ground without visible support at first glance may convince an observer that the "law" of gravity is invalid or that another principle must be usefully evoked to explain this apparent exception to a generalization derived from gravity; the "exception" is of keen interest to persons who fly. In the affairs of human beings very, very few generalizations survive without being punctured by "exceptions." What do we learn from history? we must ask again in a slightly different form. Only one principle emerges: every event has a historical background. All other historical generalizations must admit exceptions that, like the principles they contradict or challenge, are valuable in their own right. Persons who have not eaten for forty-eight hours are hungry and find food to eat. Yes, they are likely to be hungry and to seek food, but . . . The exceptions are numerous and useful; references may then also be made to illness, crop failures, wandering in a desert or near the top of a mountain, or a hunger strike. Historical references are essential as tentative if perilous guides, both to understand and anticipate some aspects of an intervention such as the metaphors employed by participants as well as the folklore and tradition that are likely to be salient for them during their interactions. When a geneticist humbly states and offers evidence that "the fruits of scientific injury . . . are best described as tentative truths" and that "scientific explanations of the natural world are necessarily fragmentary,"[31] his reservations are applicable many times over to intervention.

The use of guides and perils deliberately avoids a Great Debate, one that has grown most intense in recent years, concerning the nature of social science. Libraries are overflowing with competent, stimulating treatises on whether social science should or should not follow the pattern of natural science in seeking to achieve overpowering generalizations, a "grand strategy" that transcends the research being reported, the cultural restraints, the zeitgeist, and even the investigators responsible for the findings and the research. Can we possibly "take into account . . . both the meanings and the causes of social phenomena"?

Disagreements, moreover, persist even concerning the best or the most appropriate terminology to be employed and trumpeted in attacking each problem. Consider a few of the labels: rationalism, Marxism, form of life, hermeneutics, freedom, flapdoodle, and more recently "impairment."[32] The combatants are almost always able to trace their best thoughts or theories back to the respectable, classical philosophers in ancient Greece and thus to heap credit upon themselves and to discredit their opponents. With the modest terms of guides and perils, no dogmatic position, therefore, is being defended here except to assert, like anyone approaching a puzzling subject (whether a philosopher, a social scientist, or a layperson), that the discussion of a challenging subject of intervention may possibly increase our sagacity when attention is paid to guides and perils. Yes, we are all solipsistically encased, and having admitted our predicament, we do the best we can to select and communicate what we discover and believe. As many scientists and philosophers now state, we are confronted with "chaotic behavior"; that is, the "behavior of a system whose final state depends so sensitively on the system's precise initial state that the behavior is in effect unpredictable and cannot be distinguished from a random process, even though it is strictly determinate in a mathematical sense."[33] With knowledge and theory from the past, we go as far as we can. We do not reach perfection; surprises occur.*

---

* A few stylistic devices have already been employed without warning or explanation in the present chapter, and they will continually appear throughout this book. Some notes at the end of the book begin with "see" to suggest that the cited study or the generalization being utilized has given rise to what appears in the text but differs slightly or greatly from what the original author may have intended; hence that author is thanked but absolved of some responsibility. The perilous attribute of guides is suggested by the frequent, boring, and repetitious use of the adverbs *once, possibly,* and *probably,* and especially of the auxiliaries *may* and *tend* in order thus to suggest that at least some qualification is essential.

As this introductory chapter concludes, the decided advantage of employing the concept of intervention so broadly is claimed and admitted without the trace of an apology. The concept as here defined embraces a significant aspect of human behavior even as other diverse concepts and approaches would grasp aspects of behavior: theology, cognition, authority, history, culture. The list goes on and on. Here it is simply claimed or asserted that forever and ever some persons affect others, deliberately or not, successfully or not. Whenever there are contracts, some aspect of intervention may be involved. Then if we can comprehend how intervention functions, and if we have the verbal apparatus and at least a tentative guide to grasp what occurs, we may obtain another significant and necessary insight into all of us. Let's see.

PARTICIPANTS

Chapter Two

Regardless of the sequence of stages in interventions, the participants must be identified or identify themselves. Before and immediately after an event with its accompanying problem, both interveners and principals have been existing as human beings. Their reactions to the event, whether or not an intervention occurs, stem from their personalities as developed as a result of their genetic structure, their culture and society, and their distinctive life histories during and after socialization. If there is to be or has been an intervention, interveners and principals, whether dual or multiple, interact. Their characteristics that are directly relevant to interventions constitute the guide in this chapter.

Interventionists

Without violating the sacred distinctions previously advanced, it is necessary to note that when confronted with problems to be resolved, some interveners must be included or include themselves among the principals as they would resolve problems. They are not disinterested in the intervention's outcome but, like other principals, are also its dominating beneficiary or victim. A citizen intervenes between two gangs whose rivalry is disturbing the neighborhood not only to restore and establish peace between them but also to make the community safer for himself, his family, and his associates. Through his dominating interventions in other European countries immediately prior to World War II Hitler hoped he would affect those countries, himself, and all persons of German stock who would benefit from his diplomatic and military incursions. More or less in accord with the Oxford University Dictionary and with a handful of English-language speakers who have been informally consulted, such persons may be called *interventionists;* for them the intervention might be classified as indigenous rather than exogenous.

Perhaps the most illustrious and elusive dual interventionists are artists: poets, composers, sculptors, painters, and dramatists. At the outset, so they tell us or so we tell ourselves, they have private thoughts, feelings, insights, elations, frustrations, or experiences. They are thus their own principals. And they intervene in order to perpetuate these internal events by expressing or seeking to express what they are or have been experiencing. They themselves evaluate the final product and judge whether their interventions have been successful or unsuccessful. Of course some interventionism may be less solipsistic. Artists may be commissioned by outsiders to produce or compose, and while creating they may also consider potential or active audiences from whom they anticipate or would gain earthly or spiritual applause and favor.

Artists may originally satisfy themselves as principals and may affect contemporary principals who read, hear, or view their creations; thereby they create monetary or enduring joy or fury. If their creations are preserved and somehow endure, their interventions affect principals in ways difficult or impossible to anticipate. Did the followers of Jesus and Muhammad, of Dante and Shakespeare, of Bach and Beethoven, believe that centuries later masses of principals would be responding to these original creators or their creations? Thus principals may now or later be affected by interventions in which they themselves have not been participants. Citizens are eventually influenced by the ways in which their leaders resolve problems. In secret diplomacy almost all principals are deliberately excluded during the interaction so that the negotiation can occur more efficiently from the standpoint of the interveners; but eventually they may be affected by the decision or resolution allegedly made in their behalf. Absolutistic assessments of interventions are to be avoided, a guide that will be emphasized again in chapter 8: *changes in judgment and reactions over time are usually to be anticipated.*

The use of contraceptives to prevent conception is a very private form of interventionism. Either a female or a male or both decide beforehand to prevent pregnancy by not having intercourse, by confining the sexual act to periods when the female is not likely to conceive, by using mechanical devices, or by having the female ingest drugs that curb pregnancy. Women in this role are always the interventionists unless they are at variance with the male and, contrary to his view, seek thereby to become or not to become pregnant; men are interveners when their view differs from that of the woman, when they force the female to employ or not to employ a contraceptive, or when they rape her. The motive for interventionism here has deep psychological and social roots, especially perhaps among females and in particular religious beliefs; intervention may spring from a variety of motives including the desire to avoid the responsibility of raising a child and the restrictions therefrom, economic considerations when a family already has children, the avoidance of interference with sexual activity, and—more recently—the fear of acquired immunity deficiency syndrome (AIDS). This form of interventionism is likely to be related to socioeconomic status in Western societies, to the availability and knowledge of contraceptive methods, and to attributes of the interventionists such as—once suggested in a survey of white American females—temporal and value orientations.[1] The avoidance of giving birth to a child by aborting the embryo may be similarly appraised except when the health of the mother or the malformation of the embryo is involved.

Dreams are a form of interventionism: their content at the moment depends completely upon us (except for external noises or disturbances), and we or our unconscious intervenes to convey some kind of symbolic message to ourselves. A person who prevents himself from carrying out an impulse when awake for reasons of conscience or philosophy is certainly an interventionist: his "better self" dominates by intervening in his own behalf. A "creative, aggressive, well-educated, highly intelligent" person may undertake very specific measures to prevent herself from committing "professional suicide" in her occupation.[2] Any individual who is in conflict not with other persons but with himself concerning incompatible goals (selecting a vocation or a spouse)[3] is also an interventionist: he intervenes as he decides what to do. Many—too many—books and articles as well as radio and television programs that flood the American market and that usually have the mercenary motive of increasing their creator's own sales or popularity provide advice concerning how the distressed or ambitious can intervene in their own behalf. "Any intelligent person, I believe, can readily convince himself that he would do well to learn something toward emotions control," an author modestly claims in a book whose jacket indicates that thereby it is possible to "Avoid Heart Attacks, Ulcers, Breakdowns," to "Lessen Fatigue, Absenteeism . . . Breakdowns, Constipation," and to "Gain Increased Productivity . . . Clearer Thinking . . . Longer Life."[4]

A peril: the distinction between intervener and interventionist is seldom as sharp as such self-helpers suggest. An intervening parent who protects her child is also a dominating interventionist since by doing so she preserves her own happiness and that of her family; however, her primary and conscious objective during the intervention concerns the child's welfare. Probably any intervener, unless he is a supreme masochist, derives some satisfaction from being a successful interventionist; if he happens to be a sadist, then a failed intervention will bring him joy. The choice of the label, then, depends upon an analysis of the gratification admitted by or ascribed to whoever conducts the intervention.

Power

Power is used here in the broadest possible sense to refer to all the relations between potential participants before interventions begin or are even contemplated. For mandatory arbitration in labor disputes the principals may not have the power to decide whether to participate but, whether or not they originally have an agreement to submit their dispute to a designated intervener, that intervener has the power to propose a solution or to impose one that is binding. Individuals or groups that voluntarily participate in an intervention know they will have the power to withdraw when they feel they are not attaining their objective or when the interaction appears futile. The source of power varies from cultural or traditional customs to wealth or physical strength. The Secretary-General of the United Nations functions as an intervener in behalf of peace and human rights, as new problems concerned therewith arise, only when he has been authorized in general terms by the UN Charter and when the Security Council grants him permission to do so. But according to Article 99 of that charter, he may always call the councils' "attention" to a new problem or event: in this capacity he has at least the power to initiate an intervention and he uses his good offices toward that end. All the mass media, unless restricted by regulations within their own society, may exercise a similar privilege, even as concerned citizens alert the police when they hear cries of distress or suspect abuse or criminal activity in the premises of their neighbors. In addition, the outcome of interventions may favor the individual or group with power in the society. In theory, nobody objects to providing adequate housing to everyone within a society, but in the United States, although interventions by various organizations including government have sought to improve housing accommodations, much less has been accomplished for groups possessing weak political and economic power such as Afro-Americans, Hispanics, American Indians, and Asian-Americans.[5]

In a much broader sense, *participants, especially interveners, must be convinced they have the power not only to intervene but also to produce a resolution through intervention.* Here arises the very general and compelling problem of inevitability that includes questions pertaining to determinism, fatalism, and destiny.[6] Although interventions may be facilitated by the belief of principals that intervening in human affairs itself is inevitable, more generally there is likely to be a negative relation between the belief in some inevitability doctrine and the inclination to participate in interventions. Whatever will be must be—and you and I are powerless to interfere with the inevitable. Explicit or implicit in all religions is a doctrine ascribing not only power to one or more gods but also relative powerlessness to disciples; human intervention, therefore, is ultimately useless or futile. Noteworthy, however, is that the god or gods are all-powerful only to some degree: human beings, including even devout believers, are always assigned some responsibility to obey divine principles, to demonstrate their faith by deeds and in prayers.

Whenever the concept of freedom is applied to individuals, the assumption must also be made that they do or would possess the ability, opportunity, and power of intervention in some respect. Unquestionably, particular persons do not and cannot refrain from intervening in some situations even when they believe that major events in the foreground are inevitable or unavoidable: they brush off the insect that is stinging them. And the most enthusiastic advocate of human freedom acknowledges inevitable limitations upon that freedom: all men—and women—are mortal, and the weather will always keep changing, yet health measures may be undertaken to prolong life and some adaptation to anticipated changes in sunshine, rainfall, and temperature is usually feasible.

Experience

The fact that all human beings inevitably participate in interventions, as here defined, throughout their existence means that they always acquire experience both as interveners and as principals. These previous experiences, being gratifying or frustrating to some degree, influence them whether or not renouncing a present goal for the sake of one in the future is found to be desirable. The need to renounce

is culturally acknowledged, so that it becomes part of one's guiding expectations. Two proverbs, translated from Hausa society in
Nigeria, proclaim: "Slave during the rains, lord in the dry season";
"A hare is not caught by sitting down."[7] Similar guides appear in the
West: "A penny saved is a penny earned" and "But lay up for your-
selves treasures in heaven." Many persons, particularly those living in
a changing society or experiencing profound failures, have "ideas of
what they might become, what they would like to become, and what
they are afraid of becoming";[8] and then they may intervene to achieve
or not achieve such possible selves.

Experience with all kinds of interventions indicates that renunciation of the present has been essential after certain events. Participants
know they must abandon a momentary activity or value in order to
participate in give-and-take. The burden upon interveners is usually
clear. At the very least intruding in a conflict between two friends or
strangers requires an expenditure and hence a loss of energy. Protesting against the status quo may lead to a variety of punishments ranging from alienating some bystanders (whose esteem may or may not
be prized) to a crucifixion either figuratively or literally. The sacrifice,
however, may also gratify interveners who believe that thereby they
are following their moral principles. The energy being expended,
however, may not be easily measurable or experienced. Writing a
letter of protest surely requires less physical exertion than parading in
front of authorities in order to protest their policies or actions; yet the
ability to compose the letter stems from expenditures in the past that
have induced the protest and may result in further expenditures in the
future. Also, drafting a statement may require more effort and consul-
tations than joining fellow sympathizers in a well-organized parade.
One ultimate sacrifice, advocated by Gandhi and sometimes practiced
by him, involves self-suffering that may be deliberate or the consequence of renunciation: not only the belief in the "law" of Karma—
behavior is a function of one's own previous experiences and the
determiner of future incarnations—which suggests nonintervention,
but likewise a belief in "human endeavour" so that one attains "salva-

tion through Karma by annihilating its effects by detachment," which is a form of intervention.[9]

Experience involves one or more of the following actions during past events: initiating the intervention, actual behavior during the interaction, and the role followed in reaching a decision concerning the resolution or nonresolution of the problem at hand. The intervener's part in all three may vary from slight to extremely significant. Some interveners are in a state of readiness to play a prominent role during particular kinds of interventions and actual decision-making. Such persons are usually *professionals* who have been trained or train themselves to achieve certain specific or general goals:

1. Therapists having the goal of physical, mental, or metaphysical health: psychiatrists, psychologists, physicians, social workers, clergymen, cult leaders.
2. Authorities having the goal of preserving society or public order: leaders, judges, attorneys, police, soldiers.
3. Official diplomats having the goal of improving relations between nations: leaders, foreign-office personnel, consultants.
4. Unofficial diplomats having the goal of promoting international understanding and functioning with or without "the blessing or at least the knowledge of officials or governments or international organizations":[10] private or endowed foundations, scholarly and scientific organizations, the Club of Rome.
5. Neutrals having the goal of settling actual or potential disputes between individuals or groups: umpires or referees, chairpersons.

In contrast, *lay interveners* have received no formal training and may spontaneously intervene or be requested to do so. They support a cause, humanitarian or otherwise. They intrude when two other persons are arguing because they think their intervention will induce the principals to see the light. As passersby they seek to prevent trouble and to uphold what they consider to be righteousness. Parents present a special problem of classification: are they professional or lay interveners as they intervene obligatorily to safeguard their offspring and give them a proper upbringing? Their training may be informal, but it becomes lengthy and rigorous as their children mature; and they are ever and conscientiously ready to intervene presumably—or usually?—on behalf of those children, who may or may not seek their assistance.

Professional interveners with incomes derived from their interventions are likely to be highly motivated to increase their professional standing by the successes they achieve or by the ways in which they behave during interventions. Success brings clients. A gentle or firm technique or a just or unjust decision later attracts or repels principals with particular tastes or needs. To some extent all interveners are interventionists: their egos (defined however you wish) gain or lose as a consequence of the outcome. Leaders of countries who intervene in the affairs of another country may do so in self-defense, or so they claim: they affect principals in that other country and benefit themselves as principals. In a multiple intervention the interventionist as principal may derive personal satisfaction or increased prestige as a mediator or arbitrator if the intervention is successful.

The distinction between professional and lay interveners is certainly never absolute, but its utility becomes evident when a classification of principals is attempted. Unavoidably every individual is or becomes a principal now and again, as a snap reference to infancy and childhood immediately suggests, and hence "anyone can participate in mediation and be a mediator."[11] Although it is true that the role of being interveners or principals shifts as children mature, individual differences become more apparent. Some persons have a greater tendency to lead or to follow, to intervene or to be the target of interventions. The difference results in large part from a series of experiences so that later, after an event with its accompanying problem, some of them intervene in order to try to resolve the problem; others as principals seek assistance toward the same end.

The platitudinous guide that *past experience is useful in the present and the future* must be carefully examined. Although such experience may frequently determine the participants who initiate the intervention as interveners or principals, and hence whether some persons routinely do or do not anticipate that intervention may be useful in resolving present problems, other attributes besides experience can be more salient. You must have confidence in the physician's skill if you are to consult him or her again and again. Are professional interveners more competent than lay interveners because their experience may be more extensive and focused? No, it is self-evident that some experienced diplomats fail and give way to less experienced colleagues and that some parents influence the socialization of their children more skillfully than professional experts devoted to child guidance. The status and titles of professionals, however, communicate their experience to principals who then perilously or erroneously equate that experience with skill. Potential interveners may be acquainted with the techniques employed in labor-management disputes in the past; they may have read the relevant literature on the subject; they may have written wise or foolish words on the subject or delivered an acclaimed or unpopular speech. But actually plunging into a dispute, whether as manager, union organizer, negotiator, or mediator, is another matter: they may be nervous and insecure; they may be unable to establish contact with the critical persons in the dispute; they may not utilize relevant information during the give-and-take of the interaction.

Utilizing past experience as a guide, in short, is somewhat perilous. Psychologists and others have manufactured fancy terms to refer to the tendency for past successes and failures to reinforce or extinguish judgments and behavior regarding the present or future, but the old-fashioned word *habit* conveys the relevant meaning, provided the qualification of "other things being equal" is attached to it. Individuals who take the lead in a conversation or dominate a meeting of friendly or hostile peers have learned that their dual or multiple interventions bring them satisfaction and seem successful; other people in the same situation have learned to function as principals by being quiet and then later, when they are with more congenial persons, to behave as they jolly well please. Philanthropically inclined individuals believe that their contributions to noble causes have benefited the less fortunate, or if they require evidence that this is so and the evidence seems convincing, they then continue to contribute. Mediators and arbitrators reenact their past techniques, but only when they are convinced that by doing so they probably or just possibly will be successful once more. Sometimes, moreover, past experience is not the best guide, or it is lacking or irrelevant. So-called common sense or the ability to size up a situation, such as knowing how to calm persons after the natural catastrophes of cyclones, earthquakes, or windswept fires, may suddenly become the reason for intervening to produce order and relief. Principals may believe they have formulated an efficacious guide for themselves—ask for more than you expect and then eventually you will get what you want—yet the experience guide may turn out to be self-defeating. In spite of such wisdom from the past principals may be compelled to respond quickly and adapt themselves to the situation at hand. *Each intervention is somewhat unique,* and though ostensibly similar experiences are recalled vividly or faintly, participants may mislead themselves when they fail to note that past situations have been dissimilar, slightly or markedly, from the new one now confronting them. *Experience can be as perilous as inexperience.*

Participants also use the experience of others as their guides. Vicariously interveners learn from a friend of an acquaintance or from a document that interventions of a particular sort have been successful or unsuccessful and consequently they believe, rightly or wrongly, that they themselves can or cannot repeat the technique. National leaders may formulate their interventional policies on the basis of historical events.[12] In the early 1990s the destructive, dominating role of Germany in the two World Wars was recalled again and again both before and after the unification of the two Germanys and during discussions concerning future plans for Europe. Literary and other aesthetic models serve as guides not only to contemporary and succeeding artists but also to their present and future audiences.

The experience of others need not be in the present or even codified from the past; like any current language it may be derived from other generations and gradually or quickly be embodied in traditions or actions that function unwittingly as precedents. Foreign offices are prone to repeat the past. Over decades most of the original thirteen colonies that became the United States intervened in (conquered or subdued) lands occupied by Indians, Spaniards, and French in a westward push to extend their territories. Later, American leaders used that precedent of "manifest destiny" to intervene in the affairs of Cuba and other Caribbean and Central American countries as well as the Philippines. The Monroe Doctrine proclaimed nonintervention for European states tempted to intervene in the Americas. The United States, however, has repeatedly intervened not only in Central and South America but also in Asia and Africa. At the end of World War II such intervention was based upon another dominating policy: the actions were described and praised as a "defense against communist expansion." Past experience became less of a guide than the assertion that American leaders "best understood the needs of newly emerging areas" rather than the leaders and the peoples themselves in those areas;[13] another precedent was thus established that justified intervention in Korea and Vietnam. Still later, when Iraq invaded Kuwait, a doctrine stressing the need to protect the sovereignty of nations like Kuwait justified the dispatch of armed forces, but this time the executive branch of the American government, which may well have had other motives, managed to obtain the consent and active if token cooperation of the UN Security Council, including the then Soviet Union and other nations in the Middle East.

Planning

Participants' past experience may be utilized as the basis for plans deliberately anticipating future interventions in situations that may or may not be similar to those in the past. A future orientation is necessary as well as a tendency to renounce alternatives in the immediate present for the sake of a goal to be attained in a specified manner. In sports umpires and referees have learned or been taught and hence know in advance when and why they must intervene to uphold the codified rules of the game: they have a plan based on those rules that in turn have been formulated as the games evolved. Planning is considered to be "the discovery of means to achieve a goal for particular people in a specific environment" in order to anticipate and foster interventions that have not previously taken place.[14] For the moment let attention be concentrated again on that hypothetical situation in which a child, who has been and will be drowning sporadically throughout this book, is in a lake and will presumably perish unless someone intervenes and rescues him:

1. A child, though silent, is rescued by a passerby who observes him struggling to stay afloat.
2. A child cries for help and is rescued by a passerby who hears his cry.
3. A child, though silent, is rescued by a lifeguard who observes him struggling to stay afloat.
4. A child cries for help and is rescued by a lifeguard who hears his cry and observes him struggling to stay afloat.

The four situations stem from the same event, the child in the lake who is in trouble; then a dual intervention occurs. As the principal the child does not initiate an intervention or a plan when he is silent (numbers 1 and 3: domination but praiseworthy); he does so when he cries for help and hence reveals previous learning and a primitive plan for the emergency (numbers 2 and 4: compliance). When the child is silent, the passerby or the lifeguard initiates a plan either as a lay intervener presumably without previous deliberation (numbers 1 and 2) or as a professional with a plan (numbers 3 and 4): he responds similarly whether or not the initiative comes from the crying child. In any of these four situations the intervener must be motivated either to come to the rescue of anyone in trouble (numbers 1 and 2) or in his planned professional role at the moment (numbers 3 and 4). The decision-making and the activity during the intervention of domination or compliance is obviously one-sided: the adult realizes that the child must be rescued, and since he presumably knows how to swim and to carry a body ashore, he decides to effect the rescue. But obviously the lifeguard deliberately anticipated the event in a general sense and hence had planned his own reaction; not so the passerby. The response of the guard is probably more rapid and skillful than that of the layman.

Consider an equally profound dual intervention to serve as a guide between planning and motivation. A hiker who sees that her companion will tumble off the cliff on which the two have been climbing if he takes another step or two forward quickly intervenes and pulls him back onto a safe path. A moment earlier this intervener did not intend to intervene but then, immediately and without hesitation or premeditation, she intervened and prevented a tragedy. In fact, without quibbling it is clear that the motive to intervene, however spontaneous, originated within the hiker: instantly she perceived the cliff and her companions' proximity thereto, she had positive feelings toward the other person, she "knew" she would be able to pull him to safety. The hiker's dominating intervention, consequently, can be considered unplanned in comparison with, let us say, a police officer who carefully observes that a motorist is exceeding the posted speed limit and then authoritatively intervenes by sounding a siren, thus causing the culprit to pull off the road and be ticketed. In each instance the intervener is motivated to alleviate a problem and is able to do so, but it is clear that the hiker's action can be called a form of planning only by making a vague humanitarian assumption concerning the value of helping people in distress.

The distinction between the rescuer and the child as well as between the hiker and the police officer is clear-cut, but frequently the boundary between planning and not planning an interaction is fuzzy. The mother who as a dominating custodian prevents her child from playing with matches is like the hiker at the spur of the moment but also like the police officer: she intends to observe her child constantly to prevent him from hurting himself. She has a general dominating plan always to protect or defend the child under all conceivable circumstances, whereas the hiker is motivated only to reach the top and is not seeking to become a hero. Busybodies who intrude and affect other persons in a variety of situations function according to a plan also derived from past experience unrelated directly to their own welfare. Happily the historical explanation of planning interventions need not be settled here, except to note that individual differences complicate ensuing actions; thus the police officer who has a legal responsibility to intervene in specified situations may step back or at least hesitate to do so when his or her own life is in danger.

The discussion of hypothetical events leads to a guide: *Expectations or anticipations are a form of informal or formal planning.* Without forethought the driver of a car knows on which side of the road he must drive if he is to reach his destination safely; only when he is in a country with a rule different from his own, as when a North American is in Britain, is some planning essential. In multiple interventions and also in bargaining, principals enter into the actual interaction with views concerning their opponents and with plans they themselves will or will not propose.[15]

Guides to planned interventions must be adapted to each individual. Women's concern about their own children has deep biological and social origins that include their gender and constitutions as well as the pressures associated with motherhood in their society. Some mothers, however, are more watchful than others; hence the entire syndrome of motives becomes relevant. Political leaders execute an intervening plan not only to try to resolve a problem at hand but also for other reasons: as intervening principals they would bolster their reputation, popularity, or egos.

A noble and nonpsychological possibility, however rare, is that intervening activities can originate in interveners' central values, relegating personal motives to a secondary role. Religious leaders intervene in the earthly affairs of their fellow human beings because they believe they are thus fostering divine guides like those expressed in the New Testament. Quakers try to subscribe to this view in their personal lives as well as in international affairs. In modern times, therefore, they have followed their tradition and have attempted to mediate international conflicts, such as the India-Pakistan War of 1865 and the civil war in Nigeria during 1967 to 1970.[16] Quakers who feel impelled to "put God's love into action" in a particular situation, however, do not immediately spring into action, although they have a distinctive plan to help principals in international and other conflict situations to resolve conflicts. Before actually intervening they call a meeting at which the practical details are discussed; at this stage relevant facts may have to be collected and even a proposed settlement tentatively drafted.[17]

Mediators, arbitrators, and social scientists have well or hazily formulated plans and principles derived from previous experience to guide them as future interventions are anticipated or analyzed. Once it was asserted that "people are likely to change rapidly (1) when they are transplanted out of their usual milieu; (2) when their view of an old or a new milieu is transformed as a result of a new or sudden insight; and (3) when they are converted to a new view of their old or new milieu as a result of a change in a significant part of their central philosophy."[18] For transplantation the intervener with such a guide may enable principals to interact in a novel location (their intervener's office, a foreign country); transformation and conversion require a prolonged intervention during which the principals are jolted by one another or by means of semi-unconventional procedures to be described in chapters 5 and 7. Two quick comments are essential. The guide purports to be useful when rapid change is to be induced; hence it is probably not useful for minor interventions, such as settling specific disputes between persons or between labor and management. Then it may have to be modified or rejected for practical or theoretical reasons; transplantation can be too costly, too time-consuming, or too great a departure from principals' expectations. It is useful, nevertheless, for potential interveners at least to scan such a guiding plan and determine or guess whether any of its prescriptions are applicable to the situation at hand. One peril to the guide arises when adequate information is not available or attainable. In planning a complicated dual intervention such as a coup, interveners may be unable to determine precisely why sufficiently similar interventions in the past have succeeded or failed.

Some plans may also include a procedure enabling a potential intervener to decide whether a particular intervention should be undertaken. Professional mediators and arbitrators, who almost always

favor intervention to resolve conflicts and who for idealistic or mercenary reasons are usually eager to intervene, must first decide whether
a given conflict is one that is in keeping with their philosophy, that
they feel competent to deal with, or that seems to involve potentially
greater benefits than risks. Even individuals who believe they have a
plan to bring understanding or tolerance to two quarreling persons
may hesitate: do they wish to be branded busybodies, will they make
matters worse by trying to help? As ever, hesitation is—or should
be?—greatest when the leaders of one nation hesitate to engage in
warfare even when they are convinced they can win, as was evident in
late 1990 as the American president and his staff reached a decision
regarding intervention in Iraq.

The concept of intervention is not being overstretched again when
attention is called to the possibility of unintentional and hence unplanned intervention. The mere presence of another person may affect
an individual's own self-conception: he may feel more confident when
confronted with a depressed person than when he has contact with
someone who is overbearing.[19] A police officer in uniform, returning
home from a day's duty and anticipating hours of rest, may not realize
at the moment that he is interfering with dual, dominating intervention: the sight of himself inhibits someone about to commit violence.
Mothers, fathers, and relatives intervene in the lives of their children
without a detailed blueprint for creating normal, sensible, caring persons: they perform rituals on holidays, relate stories at bedtime, teach
children how to behave, and indicate what they believe to be the best
ways to cope with the problems of existence.[20] Two specialists argue
that in African countries "government conservation and rural economic development" have been "applied without an awareness of the
broader social implications they embody" and hence have had unintended, damaging consequences: these policies have had "little rele-
vance to the realities of the environmental changes experienced by
most Africans since colonisation."[21] Repeated must be the impressive
fact that the moral philosophies of notable personages continue to
affect the planning of future generations in ways that might not have
met originally with their approval. Unintentionality, in short, is attri-

buted to individuals when apparently they have no other alternative, for psychological or realistic reasons, to think or act as they do or when socially or philosophically it may be assumed that they have no responsibility for what has occurred.[22]

Almost by definition interventionists plan their actions: they think they know the principal, that is, themselves; they know, too, what they wish to accomplish and the method to employ; and they may also be highly motivated. This guide, however, is a bit perilous inasmuch as relatively disinterested persons often intervene in behalf of values of direct benefit not to themselves but to others. Someone seems to be lost in a busy city street when a passerby offers to assist him, though she has nothing to gain from the action. Of course the bewildered person may take the initiative and request help from the stranger. In either case the intervener rendering assistance pleases herself by thus effectively and altruistically executing a humanitarian principle.

Attributes

Since a Supreme God almost by definition is considered to be the most imaginably powerful intervener, it is useful to consider the attributes that it or he or she or He or She is supposed to possess. Let William James be the guide to some of the attributes he believed to be a "specimen of the orthodox philosophical theology of both Catholics and Protestants";

> [God] must be both *necessary* and *absolute,* cannot not be, and cannot in any way be determined by anything else. . . . He has *intelligence* and *will* and every other creature perfection. . . . He cannot *need* to create, being perfect in being and happiness already. . . . He is *omniscient,* for in knowing himself as Cause He knows all creative things and events by implication. . . . God of course is holy, good, and just.[23]

Human interveners, it is clear, never quite demand or acquire all such divine attributes, yet they must have at least one or some of them.

Contrast the way in which a modern social psychologist specifies and postulates the ideal attributes of an intervening consultant in multiple interventions: he or she must be "a skilled knowledgeable scientist/practitioner whose background, attitudes, and behavior engender impartiality and whose understanding and expertise enable the facilitation of productive confrontation, that is, the open and direct discussion of the contentious perceptions, attitudes, and issues separating the parties."[24] Both gods and human interveners have highly desirable attributes, therefore, but are the postulated attributes more than platitudinous guides to comprehending interveners? Or if the ideal focus may be shifted back in historical time for a single sentence, suppose that potential participants were to be selected on the basis of whether or not they can confront themselves with the alternatives once provided by Aristotle in his *Metaphysics:* "Of things that come to be, some come to be by nature, some by art, some spontaneously."

Two empirical challenges must accompany the postulation of participants' attributes. In the first place, they themselves may not agree whether a given person can be so characterized; the competence of an individual to be an intervener or a principal may be appraised differently by different people. Related to such differences is the ever-present peril of attributing any predisposition to another person. Therefore what has been called a "risky stimulus inference" must be made;[25] we seldom know enough about others and hence our judgments are risky, especially because the precise motives of participants usually can be inferred only perilously from their actions. Violent and aggressive interveners, a philosophically inclined psychiatrist once suggested, may attack other persons for reasons that include the "playful" ("the Zen Buddhist art of sword fighting") as well as "blood thirst" ("a passion for killing as a way to transcend life").[26] Murder, the gentle act of intervening by disposing of a principal forever, stems from a wide range of motives (perhaps from personal gain to relieving the victim's suffering), yet it is challenging to note, according to a British psychiatrist, that "murderers who kill themselves, compared with murderers in general, form a less socially deviant group, and . . . their relationships to their victims are more often close and intimate."[27] When one individual intervenes unofficially suddenly in the conversation of two other persons, his or her apparent impoliteness may be either self-seeking or altruistic. The true rationale behind official diplomatic interventions is usually concealed from outsiders and stems from a variety of conflicting motives among officials that finally do or do not result in unified action.

Attributes can be located with a high degree of certainty when it is possible to specify the event and its problem for which the intervention is designed. The intervener must be able to swim if he is to rescue the child; the principal must be powerless if she is to be murdered; the foreign audience must understand the language in which the broadcast is transmitted if they are to be affected; the missionary must be self-reliant if he is to convert the heathen in an unfriendly land. Elementary, yes, but consider the practical difficulties when interveners are unable to anticipate the situations in which they will actually intervene. During World War II the Assessment Stations of the Office of Strategic Services (oss) of the United States examined and tested potential interveners for a range of positions before they were accepted for duty. Psychologists, psychiatrists, and other experts designed and administered a very impressive and heterogeneous set of interviews, schedules, tasks, and observations that enabled them— they hoped—to weed out the generally unfit and to select men and women who appeared stable and sufficiently secure. These professionals, however, possessed "intimate knowledge" of only "a small number of oss activities" that ranged from being a medical technician or clerk to being a saboteur or undercover agent.[28] The assessments, therefore, could be only very general: the assessors and many of the men and women being assessed could not foresee, certainly not in detail, the situations in which the applicants would function. A guide can be forced to emerge: *The salience of traits and information of individuals depends both upon their utilization and reinforcement in the past (the components of experience) as well as upon the stimuli and demands of the situation at hand.* Most of the time you are outspoken or shy, well or poorly informed, but when you are seeking to impress someone you are . . . what?

It would be foolhardy to reject guides provided by investigators concerning the attributes of experienced participants. An ex post facto effort has been made to locate the factors accounting for the high morale of a British battalion which fought so valiantly in one battle against the Germans in World War I that of the roughly 700 men who went into combat, only 143 emerged "fit and able"; the rest were either killed or wounded or missing (their German opponents suffered similar casualties). This group, it is said, revealed pride in their unit, excellent rapport between officers and the other ranks, self- and imposed discipline, a sense of duty developed through training on the basis of their own backgrounds, and of course adequate rations and ammunition.[29] Although in such a battle all members of the battalion participated and although in other interventions it is leaders who are the interveners, the morale of a group must be considered more than a useful metaphor calling attention to such a relationship between leaders and followers.

Or consider lay interveners who volunteer to counsel criminals and others experiencing difficulties with the legal system; who assist organizations like the Red Cross; who actively support a cause such as Planned Parenthood in the United States or advising victims of AIDS; or who pour their energies into councils associated with the theater or the arts. A survey of such consultative interveners in North America once revealed "little consistency" in their personality characteristics except perhaps for tendencies toward "interpersonal sensitivity and tolerance." On a sociological level, however, it was concluded that "the majority appear to be middle-class females from urban centers who hold white-collar jobs and have a higher than average level of education."[30] A tidbit, yes, but at least the glimmering of another guide.

By shifting to a situation that he could control and by squeezing the ensuing data, the same investigator also reports more positive findings with Canadian undergraduates who did or did not volunteer to help others in their spare time. As a group, those volunteering to aid persons accused of breaking the law revealed "tendencies toward compromise, concreteness, and political nonconfrontativeness" to a greater degree than the nonvolunteers; and they also tended more frequently to seek and be involved in conflict situations rather than to perform nonoppositional roles than those volunteering for general social service.[31] In this situation, the students who volunteered were inclined to engage in an activity more or less in accord with their own preferences. If such a generalization were true in other areas, could one expect to find that interveners in politics likewise differ from those pursuing religious objectives and that therefore politicians thus differ from clergymen? Careful research of this kind, it appears, is necessarily limited to the problems and the participants at hand; yet again at least questions are raised that may serve in the formulation of guides.

The specific nature of an intervention largely determines many of the attributes that potential interveners should possess: they must know something about the culture and background of the principals, they must be able to speak their language or be dependent upon a competent interpreter, they must be acquainted to an unspecified extent with the rewards or punishments of participating. Again there is no guide without obvious exceptions. In short, *desirable or necessary attributes and previous experiences of participants are so varied that generalizations and guides are exceedingly difficult to discover and hence perilous to use.* Education or training may be essential to become a skilled therapist or diplomat, yet that factor alone does not guarantee notable achievements. Additional proclivities, including even genetic factors, may be relevant. Aspects of maternal behavior regarding an infant have biological roots, but the precise care and mode of socializing the child reflect the mother's experiences and training in the society where she lives. Cultural factors play a role; the tendency, for example, in many Western societies for interveners in service organizations (social workers) to be women and those in industry and foreign offices to be males may affect the process of selecting interveners at this point in historical time, even though the policy may be modified or abandoned as the experience of the two genders and stereotypes concerning their proclivities change. Finally, some traits may seem intuitively, yet without evidence, to be desirable attributes, especially for interveners, such as an overall tendency to be empathic regarding other persons: "I often have tender, concerned feelings for people less fortunate than I," as an item on one questionnaire for American students stated.[32] But under what circumstances are interventions more efficient or "better"?

In the remainder of this chapter, a not too strenuous effort is made, fruitlessly or not, to enumerate the principal attributes of participants, a most perilous enterprise because differences peculiar to each person always intrude.

Confidence

Confidence is singled out as an essential attribute of many interveners because, it must be assumed, they will not or do not function in that role unless they are convinced that they can be successful or at least not bring too much damage upon themselves. Interventions always involve some degree of risk; thus in modern societies there are interveners who would diminish the risks inherent in some industries such as nuclear power plants, and others who either minimize the risks or else argue that the benefits outweigh the risks.[33] The rescuer of the child in the lake is confident that he can reach him and bring him ashore. The courage that comes from self-confidence is especially necessary when multiple interventions are contemplated and when the principals believe or at least claim that their differences cannot be negotiated or are irreconcilable.[34] Interveners who think, realistically or not, that the odds are stacked against them require confidence to carry on. Even though juvenile delinquency cannot be anticipated with complete accuracy and even though early interventions may possibly stigmatize the child,[35] probably enough is known to risk intervening by assuming that in spite of ignorance and the risk, some action is needed to avoid damage to the child, his or her family, his or her peers, and possible victims.

Confidence may reflect a general character trait. For reasons to be found in their life history, some but not all interveners usually feel confident concerning almost whatever problem confronts them. In school they may have believed they would never fail an examination; they have felt fairly certain that they would have satisfactory personal relations and would marry the person to whom they were attracted; and they may have anticipated that they would solve the everyday tasks of their occupation. More specifically, professional interveners appreciate the fact that they have been useful or successful when intervening in situations resembling to some degree the challenges of the present. Perhaps on earlier occasions they have been less confident, but their successes have increased their overall confidence.

Any belief strongly supporting a positive view concerning the inevitability of future events is likely to affect the confidence of potential interveners. If you think that whatever will be, certainly must be, then your projection can encourage or discourage you. Why not intervene if success seems certain; or why bother to intervene when failure is probably unavoidable? Close examination, however, reveals, as indicated previously in connection with participants' power, that all doctrines of inevitability permit some intervention, so that confidence to intervene is thereby increased, or the wish not to intervene is thus diminished. Until the late 1980s and the 1990s Marxists could believe, and certainly their elders and teachers did believe in the inevitability of revolution: capitalism would be overthrown and centralized authorities would direct the economies of nations. Marx, however, in frequently quoted statements did not subscribe to such a doctrine; he himself modified the Marxist view when he asserted that "men make their own history, but do not make it just as they please,"[36] and in the *Communist Manifesto* itself the last line urges, "Working men of all countries unite." Similarly other doctrines that appear to imply nonintervention do not completely exclude intervention. Darwin and Darwinism, though suggesting that evolution will continue as it had in the past, have never inspired all peoples confidently to step aside and not seek to improve their lot through intervention; and later evolutionists can perhaps find consolation in the evolutionary theory that changes in the past have occurred at irregular temporal intervals—and hence may have been affected by interventions. One scholar who has examined over fifty societies throughout history suggests that slavery reveals intervention and nonintervention by both the slaves and their masters: "Those who most denied freedom, as well as those to whom it was denied, were the very persons most alive to it."[37]

Within recent years, especially after being operationalized in questionnaires that are reasonably reliable and valid, the concept of "locus of control" has appeared to tap a general trait relating to the belief that on the whole, with the usual exceptions of course, individuals can or cannot control the events to which they respond. Those believing they do exercise control are said to be internally oriented, the others externally oriented. Promising is the guide that *persons with an internal orientation are more likely to have been or to seek to be participants in interventions,* whether as interveners or principals, than those externally oriented: the internals think they can change events by intervening, the externals that the effort is likely to be futile or unsuccessful.[38] A frequently employed questionnaire provides two subscores, one that refers to "Personal Control," the other to "Political Control." There may or may not be a relation between these two subscales. When a sample of a hundred students in Poland was measured in 1985, the two were indeed closely related. But in 1991, after significant political changes had occurred there, another sample of a hundred students indicated different beliefs: their scores concerning Personal Control were on the average very similar to those in the earlier sample, but in the later sample they were more internally oriented on the Political Control scale than on the earlier one, probably because with a less rigid government in power they believed that events could be to a greater extent controlled by individuals.[39] Their feelings about themselves with respect to intervention thus remained unchanged, but their confidence in a possible political role increased.

The confidence of interveners may increase when they are aware of the objectives they would attain. Physicians would preserve or restore the health of their patients, and therefore their problem is to find ways to achieve that meaningful objective. Nature lovers and other environmentalists would preserve endangered species of plants and animals as well as forests and wilderness areas, and hence they have the energy and will to seek these objectives through the organizations which they establish or to which they belong. Interveners in the unhappy affairs of a married pair may know that they cannot restore the purity and sweetness of the love that once characterized the relationship, but they may be confident that they can achieve certain limited objectives for those seeking a divorce: minimizing intervention by the state, protecting the best interests of the pair's children, or managing if not resolving the conflict.[40] Mediators and arbitrators in the area of industrial relations may have ultimate general goals such as increased productivity or amicable relations between labor and management, but they are less certain concerning the subgoals necessary to achieve such objectives. An academic writer with considerable practical experience suggests how policies concerning interventions in American companies have shifted over time. One of a dozen guides is "based on a fair day's pay for a fair day's work," another more recent one has reinforced "group achievements."[41]

Interveners must be not only confident but also courageous when they contemplate intervening in an effort to solve some major problems. According to a clinical psychologist, all available evidence from psychiatry, psychology, the social sciences, and animal ethology appears to validate the guide that "the child is father to the man" or "the hand that rocks the cradle rules the world" and that therefore, in his brave words, "there is no problem of the world that could not *readily* be solved by good will all around."[42] One word, "readily," has been italicized here. Readily? Then why do all the problems persist and why do some of them even multiply? What is done under this condition of uncertainty is not to delay intervening until even more evidence is accumulated and until more techniques have been tried and achieved varying degrees of success and failure. No, many interveners in such areas courageously drive themselves, for praiseworthy or other reasons, to do what they can, however imperfectly.

Whether or not interveners are confident, the progress of an intervention depends also on the self-confidence attributed to them by the principals. At the least the interveners must display confidence so that their appearance or reputation and therefore their prestige and credi-

bility attract potential principals at the outset.[43] Confidence in interveners, moreover, increases or decreases as the intervention proceeds,
a judgment that is affected not only by the interveners themselves but
also by the context in which they function. Thus principals who are
not privileged to select an intervener—every young child and his
parents, or a patient in a small community having only one physician
immediately available—must judge that intervener to be competent
in the absence of any realistic alternative. When dominated principals
have no choice except to participate—they are confronted with a
bully or are citizens of a country being invaded—they probably do
not question the intervener's confidence and hence submit or rebel.
Persons in the West who are in distress may consult a psychiatrist only
when they believe that his personal competence is comparable to that
of the physician who tends their physical ills; psychiatry, though a
branch of medicine, has not achieved the same status as surgery or
gynecology, as some psychiatrists have been reluctantly admitting.

Adaptability

Adaptability is often a prized attribute in interventions. Even that
rescuer of the drowning child does not follow a rigid pattern: he must
react not only to whatever current flows through the lake but also to
the struggling principal. Interventions are likely to contain somewhat
unique principals or problems. During the interaction, changing conditions may require interveners to modify their ongoing technique.
When principals in multiple interventions or in workshops speak up
too frequently or seek to monopolize the interaction, interveners then
must have the courage or tenacity to silence those who dominate the
enterprise or at least to curb their flow.

Likewise interveners may have to curb themselves so that principals have the opportunity adequately to express their viewpoints and
feelings. They must not be "caught up in the turmoil of emotions that
usually beset the participating parties to a quarrel,"[44] or at least they
must control whatever inclination they may have to favor one group
rather than the other. During mediations, interveners may have to sit

back and listen even when they believe that what is being communicated is nonsensical or that they themselves have a more sensible
proposal to make; for some persons keeping quiet in most social
situations requires almost more restraint or patience than they possess. In many multiple interventions, however, when interveners
would assist principals, they first establish rapport by expressing sympathy or understanding. Perhaps *the most useful guide for interveners, therefore, is patience;* thus the techniques of peacekeeping
forces have been "those of negotiation, mediation, quiet diplomacy
and reasoning, tact and the patience of a Job—*not* the self-loading
rifle."[45] Indeed Job's pattern must be followed when one hears principals begin sentences with "I would argue," "I believe," "It seems to
me," "Everybody knows that," "Experience teaches us," and other
verbal clothing that would conceal but inevitably reveal a prejudice
that must be analyzed or taken into account before the problem at
hand can be resolved. Metaphors and other figures of speech must be
similarly confronted, perhaps subtly if not decisively.

A Quaker who tried to intervene unofficially in the Indo-Pakistan
war over Kashmir in 1965 suggests generally that interveners not only
must be acquainted with the situation at hand and must have the
reputation of being impartial, independent, and experienced in the
region of conflict, they must be willing to listen to the contending
principals, they must carry messages to each side, they must assess and
evaluate evidence, and then and only then may they make proposals
to try to resolve the conflict. But in this particular international conflict the interveners' praiseworthy restraint produced "no break-
through," although the evidence they provided gave "support . . . to
the position of moderates on each side."[46]

Self-confidence, though important as a mediating factor, may be
perilous when it leads interveners to believe that they themselves are
infallible. Instead, if they are to be successful in resolving a conflict,
*the technique to be employed must be adjusted to the situation at
hand.* This guide is neglected when the interveners' successful experiences in the past lead them to believe that they can similarly resolve all
future disputes. Such adaptability is essential as the number of con-

ceivable solutions to problems increases. Therapists in an organization concerned with the prevention of potential suicides attempt to resolve a variety of problems, such as marital and other family difficulties, chronic alcoholism, personal loneliness or alienation, and the need for medical attention.[47] Although a scholarly, experienced, and skilled social worker was once convinced that there was "as yet no well-developed treatment methodology in crisis-oriented brief treatment, any more than there is in any other casework approach,"[48] she could successfully suggest to her students in various centers in the United States and Israel that they intervene and adapt their approach to the particular crisis at hand. In some interventions, interveners must aim not to propose a solution or a resolution but to have the principals learn something about themselves or, in intergroup interventions, about other principals: again patience and self-control are essential, a bloated ego that must ever speak up is counterproductive.[49] Without attributing godlike or omniscient attributes to interveners, it is necessary to note in passing that in some interventions they must be able to pierce the chatter of principals and discover what they "really" seek to achieve or intend to say. Do the advocates of nonintervention in fact favor the status quo or do they happen to be suspicious concerning the proposed intervention? Interveners must be both tactful and forceful, and it is not simple to know which stance to adopt.

There are limits to interveners' adaptability, particularly when they themselves recognize their own areas of competence and incompetence. The dermatologist, in spite of her medical degree, does not accept patients who are experiencing psychiatric difficulties; nor is the psychiatrist likely to deal with someone having dermatological problems unless he convinces himself that the condition of the human skin may be dramatically affected by the individual's psychological difficulties. Even when the problem resides in their area of specialization, interveners may feel incompetent to deal with the variant at hand; they may specialize in conflicts within industries concerned with manufacturing but exclude themselves from those arising in the oil industry.

Whether or not the original initiative for an intervention comes from themselves, principals must be able or may have to be willing to adapt to whatever takes place during the interaction. By definition, choice, or compulsion they have been functioning prior to the event that leads to the problem. Then they decide or it is decided for them that interveners must or should change or assist them. Even when they are accustomed to be principals in certain specified interventions, at the critical moment of contact they must be willing to conform to yet another intruder. At the very least they hear, see, or read what that outsider proposes. In essence their adaptability consists of having what is loosely but appropriately called an open mind.

Knowledge

Interveners require knowledge relevant to the problem and the principals at hand. A principle has been hurt in an accident and seeks first aid. Adequate knowledge exists concerning how to deal with him, how to stop his bleeding, how to bandage him, and whether hospitalization is necessary. Intervention can be quick and effective, provided of course someone with the necessary skill is close by. Even when knowledge is less certain or uniform concerning other ills, such as reducing drug addiction or smoking or dealing with serious mental disturbances, risky and perilous interventions can be and are attempted. The aim of diagnosis, as a psychiatrist once wrote, "is not the collecting and sorting of pebbles . . . rather to provide a sound basis for formulating a treatment program, a planned ameliorative intervention."[50] Consider the host of specialists employed by the military and foreign offices of every government as they attempt to assess the strength and intentions of other countries, particularly those considered unfriendly.

It is also essential for interveners to possess relevant knowledge about the judgments and attitudes of principals, whether the intervention is to be brief or prolonged. Both common sense and scholarly research suggest that human beings have more or less distinctive ways of "coping with ambiguity" which are especially important when political decisions are to be made. It may be useful to know whether potential principals have had similar experience in the past in resolving unresolved problems: they are likely to be inclined to avoid interveners with dissimilar attributes, such as those who are extroverted or highly educated. Even these days in the West they may retain prejudice with respect to skin color or gender. The guide can come from historical accounts; perhaps interveners or citizens believe that interventions in civil wars have seldom been successful and hence it would be foolish for their foreign office to attempt to be a peace mediator in a distant country. Useful too is insight into the strength of principals' beliefs and attitudes as well as some of the resulting problems. A basic belief concerns the ultimate power attributed to the state or to a church, an issue still prevalent in some Western countries. If interveners are to employ television in a campaign to win mass approval, do they think their audiences are passive and seek to enjoy themselves or are they, in the words of an English psychologist who has conducted extensive research on the reactions of British viewers to soap operas, to be "regarded as active, knowledgeable, and skilled in their role of interpretation"?[51] Whose knowledge, moreover, is to be considered more relevant or important, that of interveners or principals? Hospital patients constantly crave a drug that will enable them to sleep and thus make them no longer conscious of pain, but doctors hesitate or refuse to intervene by means of the drug whenever patients request relief because they know or believe that addiction can be the consequence.[52]

The knowledge of interveners is more likely to be useful and effective when it is incorporated into a theoretical system. Even a venerable sociological concept like "functional groups" that refers to the slightly or markedly different feelings and attitudes people have regarding their family, ethnic group, neighborhood, and country[53] alerts interveners to problems that may be relevant to the intervention being contemplated. The proposition that a likely consequence of frustration is aggression[54] induces an intervener to search for the frustrating cause of principals' hostility before or during an intervention. As ever, there is no infallible guide here, for in many situations it may be sufficient to recognize a problem without postulating its cause; yet in the course of the intervention it is helpful to learn the cause and then to adapt procedures to it. Likewise principles from the social sciences, even including the present volume and its guides, may be utilized in planning or comprehending an intervention, but this guidance must be cautiously and hence perilously followed.

It may be perilous to ignore knowledge, backed or not backed by theory, even when it is not completely adequate. According to the writer of the foreword to an impressive handbook, there is "consensus" now "among behavioral scientists, policymakers, and even taxpayers that early intervention is a cost-effective method for combatting the effects of poverty experienced early in life" by "economically disadvantaged children"[55]—the reference is to principals in Canada and the United States. Even if such a sweeping guide is valid, however, it is painfully clear that many children continue to suffer and do not benefit from interventions that fail to occur for a variety of reasons ranging from the indifference of responsible officials to inadequate funding. Available knowledge of some sort, therefore, is not being utilized.

Before participating in interventions, some principals possess sufficient knowledge concerning the role they will perform, the nature of the interaction, and possible outcomes; others are so informed by interveners or, being dominated, they are taken by surprise and participate. Their initial interactions may well be affected by such preconceptions, especially in multiple interventions. They anticipate that they will or will not be compelled to follow parliamentary procedure. They know or do not know who will represent their opponent. They wonder, and then are disturbed or pleased, by a busybody who interrupts what they have been doing and suggests a change in their behavior. When interveners plan interventions and especially when they select the principals or call for volunteers, their effort to provide advance knowledge may be invalidated by the surprises that occur during the actual interaction. Principals then may accept the surprises or feel that they have been misled by the preliminary briefing.

Trust

When principals have the option of agreeing to participate in an intervention, their decision is likely to be affected by whether they trust the potential intervener. What is the intervener's reputation in this respect? Quakers, whose philosophy as the Religious Society of Friends favors the peaceful and—as indicated a few pages back—carefully planned settlement of disputes, are widely known as interveners who can be trusted. For more than two centuries they have tried to intervene as unofficial diplomats in many international and other disputes so that their impartiality has been well and widely established. In addition they evoke favorable attitudes as a result of their other activities, such as defending human rights, assisting political refugees, bringing essential provisions to stricken peoples, and organizing meetings, seminars, and camps, thus enabling persons from different societies to become acquainted with one another. In contrast for many Americans and others is almost any association with the Central Intelligence Agency (CIA): being dubbed one of its agents can be a serious handicap and diminish trust since that organization, justifiably or not, has been reputed to intervene too ruthlessly or deceptively in the affairs of the individuals and groups it has investigated or influenced.

The trust fostered within each society assumes different forms. An American Indian once recalled that "there was not a doctor in the Choctaw-Chickasaw Nation until 1868 when a doctor came, but the medicine men were not such bad doctors." He added: "If I had just chills and fever or rheumatism or something of that kind I would just as soon have an old medicine man now as a doctor of medicine," although "of course it was the herbs and teas of the medicine men that did the good, not their rites."[56] Similarly, modern but somewhat traditional Africans have also indicated to this writer that they prefer to consult the medicine men of their own ethnic group rather than modern doctors when they believe the former are competent. Leaders generally are supposed to be trusted ex officio by their followers, or else they lose prestige and are less effective. According to some legal scholars, by and large American courts merit more trust than unofficial mediating organizations, which they claim adjudicate "second-class justice" when they exploit principals, extend "state control into private lives," and pay less attention to resolving "collective grievances."[57]

Trust may not preexist but can be established immediately prior to and during an intervention.[58] Again when the interventions are not dominated by the interveners, principals must believe that the interveners will behave appropriately and that in multiple interventions they will be impartial, sincere, and objective. Bonds can be established among participants who share similar friendly or unfriendly feelings toward bystanders. Principals are probably more cooperative when they believe that their views have or will have an opportunity to be fully or at least adequately expressed. Patients wish to be able to describe their problems and not be hurried. Interveners may unwittingly or deliberately favor one group rather than the other or they may be unable to spare the time to listen fully to a tale of woe. In the West mediators and arbitrators are expected to function as the chairperson of a meeting; yet they may intrude with ideas or suggestions they consider useful in the situation at hand. Third parties generally are supposed to be neutral; but whether they can discharge that role if they have other responsibilities outside the intervention—as when Henry Kissinger functioned in the Middle East in 1973 as a mediator while back in Washington he was secretary of state[59]—is perhaps doubtful. From another standpoint, it may possibly be true, as was once stated with restrained confidence on the basis of six studies and various opinions, that interveners "have been found to have the capability to strongly influence community programs" in the United States.[60] But has not the same platitude been "found" to be true of those who smuggle drugs or run for public office?

Trust emerges in interactions during dual interventions as leaders give orders or function as models for their followers; hence they are trained or train themselves to evoke responses that facilitate or create obedience. Interviews with submariners who had been on war patrols revealed that the men wished their officers to be concerned with their "safety, well-being and comfort" both generally and specifically and to be strict, consistent, and fair; in effect, they were saying, "If you will protect and take care of me, I will do whatever you ask."[61] In other situations, the actual behavior of interveners can create future trust, such as having followers participate in decision-making or sharing the rewards of an enterprise. Perilous twists, however, suggest caution for these guides. In multiple interventions, interveners unwittingly may favor one group rather than the other, perhaps because the former and not the latter has initiated the intervention.[62] Partiality rather than impartiality, however, can facilitate a resolution if the weaker of one group is favored and the more powerful group is thus persuaded to cease employing coercion and instead to employ other means.[63] Interveners who express sympathy or empathize with one set of principals may facilitate their cooperation and then elicit relevant information. Distrusting interventions can be useful when competing groups come to share an antipathy toward the intervener and then strive more strenuously to resolve their differences.

Availability

Participants may crave or have dreams concerning an intervention or the need for one, but first or eventually they must determine its feasibility. Or are interveners or principals available to interact? The child in the lake cries for help and no one hears him. Or consider an extreme, realistic illustration: the determination of a private person to intervene in order to lessen international tensions and perhaps thereby to contribute, however minutely, to resolving the conflict. The author in effect is relating his own personal, frustrating experiences.[64] The intervener in a multiple intervention may require a sponsor, such as a university or a private organization, that is respected or at least not considered biased or self-seeking by both groups. Perhaps it is necessary to document the private nature of the proposed intervention lest it be thought the intervener is "really" functioning as a secret or semisecret agent of a covert organization. Permission from governments of the potential principals may have to be secured or else they may be unable or afraid to attend. There is the mundane problem of costs: participants often must be compensated for the time they spend during the interaction; may have to travel to reach the site; may take an uncompensated leave of absence from their normal occupation, or may hire babysitters to care for children during their absence. Similar practical challenges face participants in most interventions. Can the do-gooder afford to assist yet another principal in need, can the ill person pay the fee certain to be charged by a competent physician?

Availability thus means either close at hand or at a considerable distance in space, time, or practice. Professionals cannot function unless they find principals or until principals come to them. In multiple situations, do principals seek a compromise, domination, a resolution satisfactory to everyone, or do they wish to avoid an intervention completely?[65] A mother cannot intervene in behalf of a child who finds and begins to play with matches if she herself is out of the room. Among the reasons for establishing the League of Nations after World War I and the United Nations after World War II, and other international organizations at regional levels, has been the desire to have available officials who can intervene at least to organize a ceasefire when there is armed conflict or to find solutions to disputes between nations and thus to diminish the probability of armed conflict. A Swiss jurist has made the flat statement that "peaceful settlement of conflicts, whether between individuals or nations, requires machinery, not merely declarations of willingness to keep the peace."[66] Ah yes, interveners must be available to operate the machinery, and they must have the willingness to do so.

Similarly a philosopher may be correct if somewhat banal when he indicates that justice is "the first virtue of social institutions" and that a "legal system is a coercive order of public rules addressed to rational persons for the purpose of regulating their conduct and providing the framework for social cooperation,"[67] yet in practice the legal administrators may be mistrusted or be unavailable to adjudicate. In the United States, therefore, 180 "justice mediation centers" have been established to which individuals may refer their problems and anticipate that those problems will be more fully discussed.[68] They may believe too, that "law and litigation have their darker side" and hence that legal processes "can be threatening, inaccessible, and exorbitant—usually it is all of these for the least powerful people in society."[69] Or court calendars may be crowded and consequent delays seem intolerable. In practice, however, in addition to previously mentioned disadvantages, it has also been suggested that mediation and arbitration boards may be slower and cost more;[70] and, according to a legal scholar, their judgments may be wrong and conflicts may continue after they render decisions that cannot be enforced.[71]

Interveners may make themselves available when they perceive or anticipate unresolved problems among principals. That child in the lake cries for help and his scream is heard by a passerby who then tries to save him. "Good offices" are offered and hence available to those in trouble. To reach persons contemplating suicide, the mass media have been used: radio and television spot announcements, advertisements and feature stories in newspapers, the yellow pages of telephone directories, and even billboards.[72] Individuals undergo formal training in graduate and technical schools so that as professionals they can be prepared to intervene; their availability is then symbolized by the academic degree or certificate they possess. Knowing that an intervening agency or persons are available, however, is no guarantee that potential principals will use it or them; thus all members of a community realize that police and courts are available to intervene when the occasion demands, but they may feel that it is troublesome, expensive, or embarrassing to avail themselves of those agencies.

It is too easy to locate events in which principals reject available interveners. Arbitrarily let Germans and Japanese during World War II serve as the illustration since you, the reader, can quickly find other examples from your own existence. Shortly after the end of the war, an agency of the United States government sought to ascertain the effects of "strategic bombing" on the morale of ordinary citizens. In addition to interviews and examining available records, teams of competent researchers conducted systematic public-opinion surveys in the two countries. In Germany 51 percent claimed they listened at some time to "Allied broadcasts," though it was illegal to do so and severe punishments ensued for those who disobeyed and were apprehended by authorities (38 percent never listened, 11 percent had no radio). In Japan 91 percent claimed they had never even heard of "American radio propaganda." This mode of intervention, therefore, seems to have been much more successful in Germany than in Japan, although the broadcasts were available to both potential audiences. Also in Germany 21 percent believed they had received reliable information from their own press and radio about "the general state of mind" after an air raid in their community, 16 percent believed the reports to be "sometimes reliable, sometimes not"; 54 percent considered them completely unreliable; and replies were not obtained from the remaining 9 percent. In Japan 27 percent believed their own press and radio reports about air raids to be true; 40 percent did not believe them; 9 percent believed them at first but later disbelieved them; and the remainder claimed not to know, did not read newspapers, or did not reply.[73] Perforce the local interveners in both countries were thus more successful than foreign interveners in reaching principals; having achieved that objective through the available mass media, their communications then evoked mixed reactions, no doubt because the principals had other sources of information available.

Principals may be unable to locate interveners available to function in their behalf. Homeless persons in modern Western cities search often vainly for agencies or individuals who can assist them. The lonely may not seek companions or others to make them feel more secure or less rejected. Individual citizens may have no interveners other than officials in their own government, who may or may not be receptive, to protest against the violation of human rights in other countries and then to take appropriate action to rectify the situation. A Dutch writer once proposed the creation of a "Court of International Delinquency" to which complaints concerning the violations of rights and peace in general by national leaders could be referred and which, though without the authority to take appropriate action, at least could expose those found guilty to "the world community" and recommend that they be granted no visa or permission to enter other countries.[74]

A writer on the use of psychiatry in family situations has suggested that a "relatively minor intervention" by almost any outsider "from those around" may help resolve a family conflict.[75] Here dual interveners are not necessarily professionals; their availability at the right moment is the critical factor. In international affairs diplomats and United Nations officials indicate their availability to function as mediators or they nudge political principals to request them to intervene.

Even when interveners are selected by potential principals, they may not be available for various reasons. There are mundane obstacles: they are busy with other matters, their schedule is full, their fee is too high, they dislike the person approaching them. Or they believe that the intervention will be upsetting to themselves, that it may involve issues they prefer to avoid. An attorney refuses to assume responsibility for potential clients if he or she believes they are guilty of the crime for which they have been arrested, that they have only tenuous grounds for instituting a civil suit, or that they will draw an unfavorable verdict from a judge or jury. A country's leaders decide not to intervene in the actions within another country because of moral scruples or because their armed forces are too weak or not sufficiently well organized to do so.

At the moment or in retrospect there is a human tendency to try to discover whether another person or persons are or have been responsible for an event; hence a search for present and past events that can be ascribed to one or more interveners. Again and again, however, interveners cannot be located. Anonymous donors to good causes in modern society do not wish for personal reasons to be identified. In the West private foundations subsidize projects that affect principals who remain unaware of the identity of their benefactors; victims of guerrilla warfare and of other forms of terrorism may not know who the culprits have been. In some instances, however, modern terrorists take credit as a group for a bombing or an assassination while concealing their personal identities, in order to publicize their power and the effectiveness of their cause. Historians may relate not only what has taken place in the past but also, deliberately or not, assign credit or blame to the participants; often, however, the responsible interveners cannot be located and in this sense they are not available. The persons who contribute to changes in a language frequently cannot be identified, and possibly they have not considered themselves to be interveners. Words drift from one language to another—in English, during modern times, *Zeitgeist* from German, *R.S.V.P.* from French —in the absence of specifiable interveners. Until recently feminists in English-speaking countries did not appreciate, according to their view, that the pronoun "he" or words like "mankind" can be considered sexist when they really include both genders; in their own communications and in criticizing the verbal usage of others, they then intentionally intervene and propose that "he" be changed to "they" when possible or to "he or she" (also the barbaric "s/he"!), and the poor dears likewise insist that the leader of a meeting be called "chairperson" or simply "chair."

Interveners can delegate responsibility to intermediaries when they themselves are unable to participate. Personnel managers intervene in behalf of their employers who seek qualified persons for vacant positions; they are not likely to be interested in the mental health of the applicants unless they think that such instability interferes with performance on the job.[76] Psychiatrists, even though they have their own professional codes, in a practical sense intervene as intermediaries when they are called upon by the prosecution or the defense in a criminal trial to indicate, respectively, that the individual was or was not "responsible" for the criminal action. Social workers function as dual intermediaries when they take the initiative to recommend help for the children of hospitalized psychiatric patients whose "sudden void" makes them feel anxious and perhaps burdened with more than a touch of guilt.[77] In the Cuban missile crisis of 1962, Soviet leaders employed an American reporter as an intermediary to communicate to their American counterparts;[78] both nations were intervening in Cuba in pursuit of their own interests.

This chapter on attributes of participants tries to reach a dramatic conclusion by considering a narrow but relevant conception of intervention; "the ability to get someone to do one's bidding."[79] In a sense that definition embraces all interventions, other than mediation and arbitration where the primary emphasis is upon resolving the problem for the sake of the principals, or consultation when only advice is sought and the consultant cares not whether it is followed. Some of the concepts considered by the author of that simple definition include, here arranged in alphabetical order, assault, contraception, drugs, hypnosis, information control, psychotherapy, slogans and oaths, and surgery. It is immediately obvious that each of these techniques requires that the intervener be available and hence be qualified in some respect. A timid, petite, unneurotic person is not going to assault a tall, muscular principal. A normal nonprofessional does not seek to control the pain of a good friend by means of surgery. For moral reasons a potential intervener who believes in freedom of expression will not influence others by controlling the flow of information to them. Each effort "to get someone to do one's bidding" is affected by the intervener's own attributes as well as by his oral scruples. Some of the interventions, moreover, such as the use of drugs or contraceptive devices, involve only interveners who thereby also function as their own principals. The ultimate double role is suicide; and here one quivers when trying to comprehend that action and is tempted to invoke a doctrine concerned with free will.

RATIONALE

Chapter Three

A degree of stability is always sought, achieved, or demonstrated by all persons; they have characteristic ways of adjusting to their society. Then suddenly an event occurs that produces for them a problem, and that stability is threatened. The threat may be trivial, as when an individual feels slighted or insulted; or it may be serious, like illness, unemployment, old age, death, or especially conflict in most forms. At this juncture the possibility of intervention looms, and a decision is made concerning a possible intervention, whether as intervener or principal. One or more persons recognize or anticipate the problem that must be, could be, or should be resolved. The problem provides the rationale for participants to contemplate an intervention: why is there a need for an intervention and then how do or should principals and interveners select, respectively, interveners and principals? "Suffering," a psychiatrist states as he provides an extensive survey of the events giving rise to the problem, "is the core of the human condition in a world of imperfections, contrasts, conflicts, dichotomies, and fractures." His solutions emphasize only interventionism in the sense that the principals find peace for themselves either alone, with the help of others, or with the comfort provided by religion, philosophy, literature, the arts, and work.[1]

Whether or not the reaction to an event becomes a problem depends in large part upon the motivation or "felt needs" of potential participants. Such needs may not be recognized and hence decisions, or the avoidance of decisions, can seldom be considered completely rational: people "rarely come close to understanding all the complexities of the choices they are asked to make," and their interpretations are likely to occur "after only a limited search" for alternative advantages and disadvantages.[2] Efforts to measure needs by chatting with the principal, administering a questionnaire, or securing data from public opinion surveys can crystallize or transform them somehow; thus the act of measurement may affect what is being measured, the so-called Heisenberg effect. When slavery or any phenomenon that subsequently is considered evil is believed to be part of the "natural" scheme of existence, then neither the victims nor the beneficiaries contemplate intervention in behalf of themselves or others. Interveners and principals contemplate an intervention if on some level—however abstract or concrete, conscious or unconscious, hesitant or impulsive—they agree upon the goal to be achieved, even as their motivations differ. Physicians and patients know that good or improved health is their objective; but obviously physicians would obtain satisfaction from being of assistance in their professional capacity or from earning a fee, patients hope the consultation will enable them to overcome the illness, disability, or pain. Both labor and management may wish to have a dispute settled and to avoid a strike on their own terms; the mediator or arbitrator obtains his own spiritual or material reward by intervening. Eventually, however, the needs of both participants interact either while contemplating the intervention or during the intervention itself.

The next two sections of this chapter concern the rationale employed by principals to select interveners after perceiving a problem or vice versa, and when they actually have or believe they have the power to make the selection.

Selection of Interveners by Principals

Of course principals may play no role in the selection of interveners. The child in the lake does not cry out for assistance: he is too young to do so or too preoccupied with saving himself. Two disputants are either really enjoying themselves or cannot imagine that anyone will or should settle their problem. After relevant officials have intervened by reaching their own decisions, principals who have not been consulted must punch time clocks or pay taxes. The International Red Cross reaches people in distress who have never heard of the organization or who have not cried out to it for food or medical supplies.

Principals may select themselves as participants when they believe they cannot resolve a problem at hand or when preactively they anticipate that a difficult problem will arise in the future. They seek assistance, they are in trouble: in dual interventions they summon a plumber when a pipe leaks; they consult a friend or a therapist when they are depressed. All of us, even you, are constantly disturbed by conflicts within ourselves, by passing or lasting physical ailments, by disagreements with other persons, by disappointments and other frustrations, and even by the weather[3]; therefore we may be ready, even eager to seek assistance from interveners. The drowning child cries and hopes, believes, or intuits that the cry will move someone to intervene and save him. American couples seeking or contemplating divorce who consult one of the many private mediation centers may be convinced that they can express themselves there more freely and achieve an amicable settlement more speedily than in civil courts whose adjudicating calendars are already too crowded; mediation for them is an "overdue alternative" to the legal process.[4]

The stated objectives of principals may or may not be the "real" objectives they seek. Whether it is "an established tactic for adversaries to announce that a particular issue is non-negotiable"[5] is doubtful in all instances, but issuing such a claim may affect the principal's decision to participate in an intervention, at least at the outset. The stated objective, however, may determine whether principals agree to participate as well as whether to accept the intervening the individual or organization in that role.

Potential principals of course, may reject interventions. A depressed person believes that she can take care of herself and surmount her difficulty; she has no faith in therapists. Officials in a foreign office believe so firmly in their policies that they decline the opportunity to have a third party arbitrate a dispute with another country; if challenged, they refer to their country's "sovereignty" that they assert may not be infringed. Such a policy of nonintervention has often been true of nations, large or small, that have recently gained their independence.[6] Reasons for selecting nonintervention are as numerous and perilous as all other human motives. An adolescent prefers to consult her peers rather than to heed her parents: persons of her own age know her better, she thinks, and besides it is agreeable to be en rapport with them. Citizens do not vote on election day because they claim to have no interest in politics or are indifferent to the outcome. Indeed, nonintervention may be unintentional when participants are convinced, consciously or not, that no other options are available.[7]

Principals also refuse intervention for practical reasons. Personally they may be afraid or ashamed to reach out for help. Impoverished individuals without insurance cannot afford the fee charged by medical specialists. Some loggers continue to damage forests and oppose groups lobbying in behalf of the good earth. But when individuals lack the time, the skill, or both to participate in an intervention, they can participate nevertheless by delegating responsibility to an intermediary such as an attorney or a negotiator who then safeguards their interests.

Principals may design their own intervening devices to resolve present or possible problems. Married couples seek advice from each other. In addition to the International World Court, the League of Nations after World War I, and the United Nations after World War II, a host of regional organizations, such as the North Atlantic Treaty Organization (NATO), the Warsaw Pact, the Arab League, the Organization of African Unity, the Association of Southeast Asia Nations, and the Organization of American States, have been established as interveners to resolve international conflict and hence to diminish the possibility of war. Diplomats and foreign officers either as interveners or intervening principals thus have an option or at least a tempting opportunity to employ peaceful interventions. Of the international disputes between 1940 and 1970 that involved fatalities, sixty-nine were referred and thirty-five were not referred to major international organizations for resolution and settlement; the significant finding in the present context is that those which were referred tended to be more "intense" than those not referred.[8]

Subscribers to many health plans in the West who are permitted to choose their own physician may have inadequate information or be dependent upon hearsay concerning the person of their choice. They then may seek advice from friends and follow their recommendation concerning the value of a conventional physician or a chiropractor. In the delicate language of one analyst, interveners in multiple interventions are "invited to enter the fray, perhaps to assist in identifying the issues in dispute, and to recommend or impose a settlement."[9] Undoubtedly, many, maybe almost all Palestinians and Israelis for decades have been eager to settle their conflict—at least on their own terms—but they frequently have disagreed concerning the persons or organizations that could function as interveners and be instrumental in upholding their objectives. In the Persian Gulf dispute and war of 1990 to 1991, the nations threatening and then seeking to subdue Iraq, especially the United States, selected the Security Council of the United Nations to intervene and then nominally to enforce their viewpoint.

Whenever principals deliberately play a role in designating interveners as mediators, arbitrators, or leaders, they know that eventually they will be confronted with a decision or a series of decisions: hence they seek, systematically or not, interveners favorably disposed toward their objective. Skillful attorneys try to have their cases argued before judges likely to adjudicate in favor of their clients. In a completely or partially democratic society qualified citizens ostensibly select significant leaders whose past record or promises suggest that they will foster or promote "satisfactory" legislation or political action. Interviews with a probability sample of American adults revealed, by and large, that in 1979 they considered the "ideal president" to be a person who is "honest, knowledgeable, open-minded, but neither power-hungry nor unstable"; such an individual "provides strong leadership, appoints good advisors, solves economic problems, avoids unnecessary wars, and never uses power for personal gain."[10] Around the same time another group, American undergraduates, expressed the belief that "a typical politician" has—not *should have*—attributes like the following:

> [He] smiles all the time, as if he's in a good mood even when he is not, so people never know when he means it. He tends to pose, being concerned with appearances, and putting on a front. . . . His life revolves around his career. . . . He is vain and very ambitious, and basically concerned only for himself. He rather thinks he has all the answers. He enjoys going out to social functions, mingling and greeting people; he is very outgoing. He dislikes arguing with people and he avoids controversy.[11]

Here we have wishful thinking detached from reality but not from the hopes of voters who believe that such angels will foster the good life for most of the entire community.

In yet another American study, based upon survey data concerning President Reagan and two of his prominent opponents in 1983, representative samples found it sensible to rate these three persons with respect to attributes supplied by the investigators. Their judgments centered around "a small number of central traits," so that they distinguished between competence and leadership on the one hand and integrity ("decent," "good example") and empathy ("kind," "really cares") on the other.[12] Although details doubtless vary in other American elections and surely in other societies, probably everywhere anticipations and stereotypes influence the selection of leaders by voting principals. Whether citizens then also believe (or unrealistically hope?) that they as interveners can influence their national or local governments generally or in behalf of justice and whether they are active in their communities clearly varies from nation to nation and probably also depends upon their education, occupation, and even gender.[13]

Principals learn to respond appropriately to interveners' symbols even when they themselves have not selected them in that role. The driver of a car who is hailed by a police officer for speeding has not decided to have a particular legal authority intervene in behalf of safe driving; yet, though vexed, he or she immediately has complied by stopping and agrees at least that the officer has the authority to intervene when the motorist perceives the official uniform or car. Having selected an intervener, principals anticipate roughly what will take place; patients know they are not visiting an amusement park when they enter a dentist's office.

The intervener's reputation may also depend upon the actual experience principals have had with him or her in the past or upon the experiences of others whose opinion they value. Management and union members, when the choice is theirs, submit a dispute to the intervening organization that has enabled them previously to reach a solution they now consider satisfactory. During the interaction if the intervener deviates from what the principals had perceived to be his or her objective or means of attaining it, they themselves may intervene by attempting to induce the intervener to conform to that expectation. Or they may avoid the person on another occasion in the future.

Selection of Principals by Interveners

Even as some principals do not or cannot select interveners, so some interveners are similarly powerless with reference to the selection of principals. The previous discussion of artists as interventionists suggests an inescapable observation: creative persons like Johann Goethe or Sergey Prokofiev could not possibly have anticipated the principals in succeeding generations who would be affected by their creations. And without again stretching the conception of intervention too far, it may be said that the valiant person who rescues the pathetic drowning child selects him as principal at the crucial moment and that someone else, who receives herewith hypothetical scorn, has been responsible for allowing the youngster to be in the lake without adequate protection or supervision.

Even as the susceptibility to be hypnotized, whether voluntarily or not, and hence to submit to a dual, not necessarily dominant intervention, varies from person to person,[14] so in other interventions the suitability to function as principals depends upon background, previous experience, and present motivation. Although individuals are never completely passive, in some situations they may be selected by interveners and have little or no choice as to whether they become principals. Never completely passive? Adult hospital patients accept the drug administered by the physician or nurse; yet they can refuse medication. If they are comatose or unable ever to be independent of life-sustaining equipment, the consent of relatives or legal authorities may have to be obtained before a lethal dose of medication is administered or before the equipment is removed or shut down. The inhabitants of a small country that is overrun by the forces of a major power have not consented to be dominated principals. But they can display token resistance thereafter or be shyly uncooperative. Persons accused of a crime by government officials or named in a civil suit have no alternative except to appear in court unless they can find an intervener who enables them to cancel the charges or unless their motive to avoid the legal procedure is so strong that they somehow are able to exile themselves from the authority.

In dual interventions interveners perceive one or more persons as potential principals either because they believe the latter would appear to benefit from assistance or because, by demonstrating their own ability, the interveners themselves will benefit from success or from whatever spiritual or material compensation they receive. Missionaries seize upon heathens to enable them to qualify for everlasting lives. The conviction of interveners is conveyed through an appropriate communication. The challenge here is identical to that confronting any advertiser or public figure who would attract customers or followers.

Complicated are interventions in which the interveners seek to attract or select principals likely to interact productively and creatively, however productivity and creativity are defined. Considerable experimental investigation has been devoted to isolating the personality traits inclining subjects, chiefly American students, to engage in "negotiating behavior." Positive if slight statistical relations have been found between such an inclination and general tendencies to be "cognitively complex," to favor conciliation in principle, and to be dogmatic. Why "dogmatic"? Dogmatic persons seek support! Negative statistical relations to the same inclination have included tendencies to be anxious, authoritarian, suspicious, and high in self-esteem.[15] Here, however, you and I must recall from the two previous chapters all the perils associated with such a guide: the contrived situations, the limited cultural backgrounds of almost all the subjects, the usual nature of the measuring instruments (questionnaires), and the exceptions to the central tendencies.

In contrast, *interveners in "real" life are not likely to have such intimate information available; they do not possess psychic rays enabling them to penetrate principals' personalities.* It is not a simple task for them either to discover the "true" self of principals (as distinguished from the ways in which they present themselves to others or even to themselves as they evaluate their own behavior or feelings), in the present or future or to probe validly into explanations the principals usually and easily offer concerning their precious selves.[16] Do they feel helpless or hopeful regarding the problem that has given rise to the possibility of an intervention? Selecting persons who are competent in the sense that they have "a sufficiently broad range of capacities under a variety of circumstances"[17] is extremely perilous. One group of principals in contact with another group may shift their feelings of identity and hence their mode of expression in order to demonstrate loyalty to their own or yet another group or to a viewpoint with which they feel fully or partially identified. In addition, when multiple interventions require prolonged interaction over time, the actions of a single individual—one who is domineering or who turns out to be too devoted to alcoholic beverages—may adversely affect the intervention or create additional problems. But can such a person be identified as principals are recruited and then accepted or rejected for the pending intervention? This question is not a bit of rhetoric but a serious challenge to the organizers of interventions.

Interveners are never completely ignorant concerning potential principals. They know they are evaluating human beings who come from a particular society and stratum therein; and they may also be acquainted with their culture. Especially in multiple interventions, they may anticipate certain attributes, such as the principals' mode of expression or their preferences and antipathies. A Belgian writer suggests that the "diplomat's conceptualization of the world" must be considered "an intervening variable in the international relations system,"[18] an academic if clumsy tribute to the importance of that cognitive factor. Knowledge of this sort performs two functions: it enables interveners to estimate at the outset whether individuals are likely to agree to participate as principals and whether they will function effectively in the course of the intervention.

Although no checklist is available to select persons by noting their traits, interveners seek such information and so gain valuable knowledge related to recruiting principals, particularly for a multiple intervention. They discover whether those individuals consider an intervention feasible. Insight may be obtained into their attitudes and feelings toward the problem in question. Rapport can then be established among those expected to participate.

Interveners who believe they possess adequate knowledge to resolve specific unresolved problems may try to locate persons who in their view will benefit from becoming principals. Indeed, "certain populations clearly at greater risk than others for poor cognitive, social, or emotional development (e.g., teenage mothers, low-income families, infants with low birth weight, and chronic physical illness)" in the United States[19] are promising if discouraging candidates to assist. For young children at risk—undoubtedly also for adults—"the serious problem in health care is to get the people who most need preventive health services to use the services that are already available"[20]—yes, but provided the services are really available.

Furthermore, persons considered to be appropriate as potential principals must be persuaded to participate when they are unable to spare the time or expense required by the intervention. They may also have no confidence in the intervener or believe that intervention is useless. Management or union officials may be disinclined to submit a dispute to an established arbitration board, even when invited to do so, perhaps because they anticipate gains from having the dispute continue or because they believe they can eventually reach a superior settlement in some other way. Officials may complain to the International Court at The Hague, but neither they nor the court itself can compel the opposing side to appear. A disturbed man refuses to consult a therapist because he does not recognize therapy of this sort as a desirable intervention or because he believes that only weak persons consult and compensate others to resolve their own personal problems.

With a realistic freedom of choice, interveners can be confronted with additional perilous challenges as they recruit suitable persons, especially for a multiple intervention. How many persons should be invited to participate in a workshop when the opposing groups have a serious conflict? No lengthy digression is needed to document the guide that *the presence or absence of other persons is likely to have some effect upon individuals' internal reactions or external behavior.*[21] Principals react quite differently when confronted directly with an intervener in a face-to-face intervention than when contact is established in writing or by telephone; similarly, their reactions are different in shuttle diplomacy when the groups in conflict are kept separate and the intervener functions as the intermediary between them. Small groups of principals may possibly be able to intervene creatively and to establish trust and rapport more easily than large groups. Whether groups reach a decision by focusing upon personal, interpersonal, or moral values[22] may depend upon the number of participating principals: perhaps the greater the number, the more diverse the viewpoints that are expressed. Diversity, however, may or may not provoke more innovative proposals. In multiple interventions principals may hesitate to speak out: although they share views similar to those of friends and other bystanders concerning a desirable resolution to the problem at hand, they may fear that what they say will be reported later to powerful authorities who will punish them for being deviant.

There is, in short, no eternally valid guide to the optimal size of interventions. Unofficial and official interveners who select principals may utilize previous experience, but at their peril and with guesswork. Two Norwegian political scientists argue, on the basis of existing literature and theorizing which they consider to be inadequate but at least "a starting point" for analyzing multiple negotiations, that larger numbers attending a conference increase the likelihood of a "less lucid, more complex, and . . . more demanding" interaction, but also provide "ample room" for creative suggestions; the agreements reached by larger conferences, moreover, are likely to cover only some of the agenda, and latent disagreements will remain.[23]

Next there is the problem of the principals' status in multiple interventions. On the one hand, it may be highly desirable to have that status as high as possible. Since government officials and company leaders make the decisions for their organizations, they eventually must approve or support whatever agreements are reached during an intervention. If they themselves have participated in the interaction and subscribe to the emerging resolution, they are then in a position to carry out their part in the agreement. High status in the society is likely to be related to subsequent influence. Middle-aged and elderly persons may now possess prestige and power in their society or organization, but eventually they will be replaced or die. At a given moment interveners must deal with existing age groups; hence the selection of principals may determine whether an intervention is to be effective in the short or long run. Older and established principals may stubbornly defend their viewpoint during the intervention and hence resist being innovative or creative.

On the other hand less important principals without authority— sometimes called "preinfluentials"—can possess the very desirable attributes lacking in their superiors. They have the time to attend a workshop. They participate with less of a rigid agenda and hence may be open to create new ideas. But then, even though during the actual intervention they arrive at a promising resolution or at least the possibility of improving relations between opposing groups, subsequently they are confronted with the problem of persuading their superiors or the rank and file who do not or cannot accept the new proposals. Reentry from workshops is thus difficult; the seemingly magnificent ideas in the give-and-take with opponents may be rejected by bystanders.

The relation of potential principals not only to each other in their own organization or society but also to powerful persons, the bystanders, may need to be considered a highly relevant factor if the contemplated intervention is to be prolonged. For these other persons may influence the participants during the confrontation, and the influence can be either detrimental or useful. If detrimental, the principals feel constrained and may be unable to be creative. If useful, the principals remain aware of the problems they will have at reentry, and when possible they can consult their superiors and others as the interaction proceeds so that their proposal can be well received.

In any case, no matter how they are recruited or no matter why they consent to participate in an intervention, *principals possess beforehand or quickly acquire expectations concerning what they believe the intervention can or will accomplish.* A mediator sets the stage for them by indicating the issues to be discussed and even some of the possible resolutions that can be achieved.[24] Lay interveners who organize workshops may not reveal the "real" purpose of their intervention as they recruit principals lest the revelation discourage them from attending. Such concealment, however, can be branded as unethical or lead to disillusionment during the interaction when its purpose becomes known. The true or ascribed objective of interveners is interpreted by principals as they wish and plays a role in their willingness to participate. Two persons whose conversation is interrupted by a busybody agree or disagree to listen. If they do agree, they may immediately appraise his motives and his competence. Expectations are inevitable.

Politically and morally the number of participants influences the assignment of responsibility for the outcome of an intervention. A single intervener or principal perforce is the responsible party, provided pressure by or influence from bystanders is absent. In multiple interventions principals may formally or informally vote to accept or reject an emerging resolution and avoid being praised or blamed if they have cast secret ballots. In an epistemological or realistic sense, however, it is polite to raise, at least in passing, the problem of who has been ultimately responsible for decisions during interactions. Regardless of the number of participants, moreover, there is always the peril of oversimplifying either the causes of an event or the intervention itself; thus clichés such as capitalism, communism selfishness, or benevolence may be invoked and considered to be the responsible factor—perhaps evasive, verbal nonsense?

Alacrity

The decision of interveners to intervene depends not only upon their individual attributes—their confidence, adaptability, knowledge, and the trust they engender in potential principals—but also upon the recognition that a problem is unresolved and that they possess tacit or explicit permission to resolve it. Often they simply must be alert. Consider again the overwhelming importance of early, dominating, dual intervention by parents. Mothers know they must constantly intervene if their infants are to survive; and gradually children crave the intervention when they are thirsty, hungry, or otherwise uncomfortable. Precise details, however, vary with the mothers' alacrity that reflects both customs in the society and their own personalities. Should an infant be fed on demand or should a feeding schedule be followed as quickly and regularly as possible? Should both parents always or almost always try to discover why a child is crying, or should they ignore the cries unless there is a real crisis? Eventually all children are weaned figuratively or literally, and thus the degree of independence they achieve as children and adults depends at least slightly upon the parents' readiness to intervene less frequently and also upon their own experiences. When and how are children taught explicitly or by example that they too must learn to intervene in their own behalf?

Institutions are available that encourage interventions and hence alacrity. In Western societies individuals who believe they have been wronged by identifiable persons can seek compensation through civil action in court or through mediation with or without assistance from attorneys—provided of course they can afford the costs and time to do so. As a contrast, in some oriental societies such formal litigation has been considered "a shameful resort."[25] Other forms of formal litigation may be at hand. The role of a class of intellectuals, the so-called intelligentsia, in producing or helping to produce change within their own society is a topic that has been raised again and again, especially by Russian scholars and Marxists as well as by those they have influenced.[26] Here let it be noted only that such persons, whatever their social-class origin, may be sensitive to events which they believe fit into their broad philosophy; they are eager not only to advocate their own viewpoint but also to seek in diverse ways to bring about what they consider to be significant changes.

The catalog of perils confronting academic intellectuals and especially official interveners in high positions is long, ranging from their own personal fears to wishful thinking, either of which can provide a distorted view of opponents or principals. They include the fallacious assumption that a government, corporation, or union is functioning like a single individual and hence is engaging in rational calculations.[27] Participants generally may have confidence in an untrustworthy source that provides them with information strengthening their own prejudice. They may commit similar errors in selecting or appraising leaders who influence communication media to achieve popularity, support, and consent.

In arriving at decisions concerning interventions, individuals may be alerted by bystanders: relatives, friends, peers, and officials of any kind. Whether they esteem, modify, or reject these contributed views is related to their evaluation of the source and its importance to them. The wives of leaders may or may not play a role in their husbands' decisions to intervene. Article 62 of the International Court of Justice permits an outside state to "intervene" in its proceedings when it has "an interest of a legal nature which may be affected by the decision in

the case"; after reviewing the actual role of third parties in the proceedings of that court, a German scholar suggests that its jurisdiction
be extended so that states with such an interest routinely be included
as intervening amici curiae, friends of the court who are not directly
principals in a dispute.[28] The citizens of a country in the role of
bystanders are affected by and affect the decisions of their leaders
without being fully aware, in advance or later, of themselves as interveners or of the implications of their interventions. Pressure groups
intervene directly and seek to influence political decisions.

Public opinion surveys have become important in the twentieth
century as alerting signals to interveners concerning the attitudes and
judgments of their actual or potential principals. Instead of guessing
or relying upon casual conversations or not necessarily typical informants, interveners can consult polls or use their own resources to
survey their constituents. Even in some developing countries this research tool possesses prestige and respectability, although one still
hears "but I myself have never been interviewed by a pollster." Few
significant events occur without some organization locating a sample
of respondents and asking them relevant questions. Polling results are
of general interest and hence are publicized in the mass media of many
countries, unless they have been privately commissioned and sub-
sidized by political or commercial interests. Their findings merit
respect and credibility. Pollsters employ systematic ways to obtain
representative samples. They usually are aware of the misleading impressions that can be given by biased wording and the order of questions. In spite of blunders now and again, they successfully forecast
the results of elections in democratic countries some time in advance
or before voting has ceased and all the ballots have been counted.
Interveners are able to obtain measures of their popularity and can
determine, often covertly, how the so-called public will react to contemplated interventions.

Both methodically and morally, however, polls as alacrity guides
merit considerable skepticism. They may be misleading in the short or
long run. Those in a pollster's sample may register their opinions
falsely when suddenly confronted by a stranger who asks them to

answer questions or to rate a policy. Even if the opinions are truthful, moreover, they may be superficial and not represent the more mature or more qualified judgments that individuals would and could make if they considered all the relevant issues or if those issues were to be made salient to them. Equally challenging, perhaps more so, is the role "public opinion" should or must play in the formulation of national policy. Should interveners simply satisfy principals as their reactions are ascertained on the polls, or should they assume the initiative, ignore those expressions, and hence lead them toward innovative goals not ascertainable in surveys? Or to be successful as interveners, must they pay attention to polling data?

The concept of alacrity in this section has referred to the readiness of participants to respond to events and problems. Involved also are their alertness, their eagerness, and their readiness to respond. Alacrity, consequently, has a temporal dimension, to which topic the next chapter is devoted.

TIMING

Chapter Four

In a perfectly rational world, which sometimes almost exists, the preparation for an intervention would follow the order in which the previous chapters have been presented. An event has given rise to a problem for somebody who then becomes the potential intervener or principal for a particular reason. One or both decide whether or when the intervention should occur. The world, however, is seldom orderly and hence the temporal factor may precede one or more of the other decisions. Do you seek advice right now, and will you therefore consult not the best but the most readily available intervener?

In chapter 1 a distinction has been drawn between interventions that are initiated either when a problem looms or shortly thereafter (preactive) and those initiated after the problem has arisen (reactive). Parents intervene preactively as they rear their children by seeking to keep them healthy and by providing what they believe to be an adequate diet; when the children become ill, they reactively intervene by modifying the diet and the daily regimen, by giving them medicine, or by consulting a physician. In Latin American countries breast-feeding of infants was once declared to be "deeply ingrained"; hence it was proposed to identify "risk pregnancies" at an early stage so that guidance could be given concerning problems that might raise a "mother's anxieties and, as a result, disturb her lactation."[1] Although the temporal distinction between preactive and reactive interventions perforce is somewhat fuzzy, still it suggests a continuum ranging from before to after the existence of a problem. From a social, political, or moral viewpoint, however, there may be a critical point on this continuum. An international organization whose officials believe that a serious conflict between two nations may lead to armed conflict must decide to intervene before or after actual hostilities have begun. The present chapter seeks guides for determining the factors affecting the point on this temporal continuum when the decision to intervene occurs or has occurred: when and why is the decision to intervene preactive rather than reactive and, if reactive, immediate or delayed?

Temporal needs vary with the potential participants. Principals may believe the unresolved problem is more pressing than do potential interveners or vice versa. Professional interveners in particular may be convinced that disaster will be the consequence if there is a delay; even then it may be difficult for them to recruit potential principals and to persuade them to participate. Temporal agreement is not reached in dominating interventions, yet a principal must be available at the time specified by the intervener.

Like any other decision, interventional decisions, whether preactive or reactive, are thus made immediately, after a delay, or not at all. That passerby knows he must rescue the child in the lake as quickly as possible. An ill person consults a physician after his illness becomes distressing but not severe; at the outset he may have believed that medical assistance was not needed. An individual listens to two acquaintances carry on a heated discussion but does not intervene until she feels that their relationship will be damaged or that they will come to blows. A specialist in international relations, after observing the course of relevant disputes during this century, concludes that mediation is "more effective when it follows, rather than precedes, some of the disputants' own efforts at deescalation:; "the passage of time, a stalemate or a painful impasse" can eventually initiate such interventions.[2]

The timing of an intervention can depend upon the advance preparation considered necessary before reaching a decision to intervene or not to intervene. An emergency of any kind means that such preparation is or must be reduced to almost zero. On the other hand, delays occur if interveners or principals must be located and induced to participate. Data concerning a possible or actual problem may also have to be at hand or gathered. No magic guide prescribes whether the ensuing intervention, if there be one, is thereby hindered or improved.

It seems clear, if perilous, to assume that *after an event the timeliness of intervening or not is appraised by one or both of the participants*. Psychiatrists seldom select their patients, rather they intervene after principals come to them. On occasion, however, a psychiatrist may modify this procedure when he notes preactively that someone is suffering and could benefit from psychiatric assistance; then he suggests to that person or to his family that psychiatric assistance is desirable. Such assistance is essential reactively, however, when a disturbance is so severe, as in psychoses, that the individual himself is unable to perceive the difficulty, much less recognize that a psychiatrist is needed; hence an intermediary for the potential patient may ask a psychiatrist to intervene relatively soon. In contrast are standing arrangements requiring interventions to settle disputes between groups of principals. Management and labor in an industry agree to submit their opposing views to mandatory or advisory arbitration, within a specified period of time, when unresolvable differences between them arise.

Bystanders whose consent is required before starting an intervention can influence its timing. Neighbors intervene by reporting that a child is being abused; and then parental permission may be necessary for social workers or officials to intervene directly by investigating the initial report. Months or years often pass before lay, unofficial mediators obtain permission from governments to be allowed to invite principals to a workshop, a frustrating procedure that is costly in time, energy, and expense. When and if consent is then obtained, the most propitious moment to have launched the intervention may have gone by; yet the problem remains. Intervention may still occur, if less auspiciously, at a later date. The timing of an intervention can be affected by the nature of the problem at hand. That struggling child will certainly drown unless rescued immediately. In American society homeless people may be granted shelter for the night, but dominating interventions to decrease appreciably the economic and other factors responsible for their sorry state have been and are being long delayed. Again, it is not stretching the concept of intervention too far to insist that professional or amateur critics of all kinds are interveners. Any creator whose book, play, musical composition, or art has drawn a larger or smaller audience after favorable or unfavorable reviews will not dispute the fact that critics have been consulted and then have intervened. By tradition such intervention occurs reactively after the product has been exhibited and hence is subject to evaluation. The publishers, producers, orchestra leaders, and administrators of art galleries have previously intervened preactively by agreeing to submit the composition to public scrutiny or patronage. There are also revivals of artistic work resulting from changing tastes or moods, the demands of potential audiences, and also from the intervention of other critics at a later date. The original creators, the principals, play a creative role. For intricate reasons both numerous and idiosyncratic they record their inspiration; and to the extent that they communicate what they have felt and pondered they submit their wares for judgment concerning which they may or—if you can imagine they lack a sensitive ego—may not attach great significance.

The decision regarding the timing of some multiple interventions can be spontaneous or planned. The usual posture or "formalized stance" that is taught to soldiers influences their own morale and hence enables them perhaps to perform better and to protect themselves;[3] simultaneously it conveys to bystanders their capability and possibly their inclination to intervene militarily. In 1991 "two-thirds of 1,023 graduating seniors" in an American black college remained seated instead of standing and were silent instead of applauding when President Bush was receiving an honorary degree; they were seizing the opportunity, as planned, to express their disapproval of his civil rights policies[4] and were thus harmlessly if impolitely intervening against those policies. Often, too, general personality tendencies affect the momentary decision to intervene; whether you respond aggressively or yield when another person pushes ahead of you in a long line may be another example of how you usually react in situations of this sort.[5] Previous experience thus determines how rapidly interveners react to problems similar to the one at hand. Parents can function more effectively and quickly as guardians of a child's health after rearing one or more older siblings.

According to an Armenian folktale, a cello player, when asked why he used only one string on his instrument and kept his finger on the same spot, explained: "Of course others move fingers constantly; they are looking for the place. I have found it." Someone who hears this sad joke enjoys it so much that he wishes to repeat it and thus intervene before an audience of other persons. He knows he cannot stop a stranger on the street and tell the tale: he would be invading that person's privacy and run the risk of being declared a trifle insane. He meets a friend who immediately tells him about a misfortune he has just experienced; is such a person in the mood to be his immediate audience? He sees another acquaintance who appears to be in good spirits; then he springs the joke. Timing here has depended upon the principal's mood and its perception by the intervener: the friend might have enjoyed the story after recovering from a misfortune; the stranger, being in a gloomy mood, might have been loath to listen. Or should the intervener use the joke to help a person dispel his gloom? A real intervener, experienced in diplomacy and perhaps also with cellos, once suggested that the atmosphere was favorable for an informal workshop between two Cypriot leaders because in previous negotiations "they were at a stage of their discussions at which some outside nongovernmental comment might be pertinent and helpful."[6] "A good sense of timing in a comedian or a politician," therefore, is a desirable but elusive attribute.[7]

Moods are a tricky variable either to attempt to control or understand.[8] Interveners planning interventions of any kind may be able to affect such potential mood-related factors as the official time of the intervention: the hour of the day, the day or days themselves, the month, the season, even the year. Other factors, like the prevailing weather or the health of the participants, obviously cannot be arranged, but instead may require changes in scheduling. Participants' attitudes towards time may help determine the duration of an intervention, which may be too long for those who are impatient or have other interests or responsibilities; it may be too brief for those demanding adequate coverage of the issues at stake. At a given moment during the intervention temporal plans can be facilitated or disrupted by the words or behavior of one or more participants. The perilous aspect of moods also arises when they are difficult or impossible to anticipate or assess; thus the pleasantness or unpleasantness of the seasonal weather in two African cities as designated by common usage was once found to be unrelated to the expression of attitudes, at least on a public-opinion survey.[9]

At any time—before, during, or after an intervention—it may be necessary to decide whether an intervention should be made public or kept secret. A so-called code of ethics, as in medical and legal professions, would solve this problem by decreeing that contacts between interveners and principals must remain confidential. The information obtained by secret or diplomatic agents that affects international decisions is usually not revealed until the problem no longer exists or is of only historical interest; premature revelation may jeopardize the ways in which the data have been obtained or reveal unpropitiously the plans or goals of the participant. On the other hand, publicizing the intervention at a given moment, in the 1990s increasingly common as a result of pressure from the mass media or the egos of the participants, may influence the intervention itself; bystanders can exert pressure and additional information is obtained. Unless proceedings of an intervention re available immediately or eventually, future participants cannot evaluate the experience and thus perhaps—perhaps, perhaps—profit from what may have been learned.

Temporal Perspective

Both by definition and through a reference to common sense and systematic research it is clear that all interventions require some temporal renunciation, and hence a temporal stage is evident.[10] One cannot intervene to affect someone else without relinquishing what one has been doing; and principals cease their present activity or are compelled to do so as recipients of an intervention. Even an intervention at the spur of the moment requires some change, especially when an effect in the future is anticipated. The rescuer of the child no longer strolls or cogitates or carries on a conversation as he plunges into the water; only figuratively does the child who cries out to be rescued devote an appreciable amount of energy to seeking intervening help.

Potential participants have a somewhat characteristic way of responding to many, yet obviously not all, events: they tend to be impulsive or reflective, with numerous degrees of hesitation between the two extremes.[11] *Carpe diem*—the Latin platitude urging you to seize the day or the moment is a bit of folk wisdom that is not an infallible guide to intervention or any other decision or action. Perhaps the overwhelming impulse is to seek an objective without delay and hence to be an intervener or a principal when the problem arises—other things being equal of course, and there's the rub. Your reactive impulse is to rebuke, insult, or possibly murder that person who humiliates or contradicts you; but you quickly repress and modify that mode of intervening in behalf of righteousness or your tender ego because— and you know very well why you do just that. "A frequent social science error," according to a thoughtful political scientist, "holds that when the volitions of various people or groups of people conflict with each other a reconciliation must be imposed"; instead of calling upon the government or the state to resolve a conflict right now, he maintains, people should patiently probe and acquire more information before trying to resolve conflicts.[12] And so let it be gently asked: is it now or never, or would it be better to procrastinate?

The "now," however, refers both to the problem at hand and to the attributes and goals of principals. Only gradually do children acquire a conception of their country toward which they are supposed to feel patriotic,[13] and therefore it is necessary for any intervention that would instill or strengthen such sentiments to be adapted to their age or mental development. Timing is an especially challenging problem for long-range multiple interventions. When there has been overt trouble between different groups, as between blacks and Koreans or Orthodox Jews in parts of New York City during the late 1980s and early 1990s, officials and the police have intervened to curb the violence and to restore order. In the long run, however, the time to intervene is preactively at an early age when children acquire attitudes regarding other groups; later these attitudes serve so many functions that they cannot easily be modified.[14]

Interventions are likely to occur immediately when participants are convinced that delays will bring disaster, increase monetary or other costs, or preclude the possibility of successfully intervening at a future time.[15] An American worker who in his opinion has been unfairly discharged from the job and who has no other way to earn his living may immediately protest to his union or governmental authorities. A Canadian family that observes land next to their property being surveyed and learns that a road, building, or waste disposal site is in the offing protests to a zoning or other authority. A parent suddenly grabs a child who appears to be about to fall from a high place. Propaganda Minister Joseph Goebbels killed himself in a Berlin shelter only after a succession of events had occurred: the Soviet army was advancing and bombs were falling in the area; he had observed the burning bodies of Hitler and his bride of two days (both suicides); and his own wife had apparently agreed to poison herself after poisoning and thus murdering their six children. It was then and only then that he knew it was necessary to carry out his preconceived plan, as he had written in his diary, to perform "the best service I can to the future of the German people" and thus to imagine and anticipate how this honorable death of himself would appear to posterity, at least among Germans.[16]

Professional interveners likewise intervene without delay when events create situations in which they know they are supposed to intervene: police seize and arrest a burglar caught in the act. The need for immediate intervention, however, is subject to interpretation by the participant. A friend who hears that the disagreements between a married couple are increasing may believe that a breaking point has been reached and decides to intervene; in this instance the decision is his or hers and not that of the wife or husband. In 1983 the Reagan administration sent an invasion force to Grenada undoubtedly preactively to protect the Panama Canal and American trade with other Caribbean countries, but he justified the intervention reactively by claiming it was necessary at that very moment for the sake of the United States citizens stationed or studying there.[17] "It is later than you think"—just as the intent of this slogan is communicated subtly and unsubtly by advertisers who would market their products and by propagandists during war who spread rumors to the enemy in order to create panic,[18] so interveners may seek preactively to create or principals to claim a sense of urgency which, they hope, will prevent nonintervention.

Potential interveners may be convinced that an intervention must occur immediately if disaster is to be averted, but they will not intervene when they lack the budgetary means to do so or when no feasible method is within their grasp. Unofficial or lay third parties can envision a workshop that could contribute to the solution of a knotty problem between groups, but they usually lack the financial means to proceed or, in countries like the United States, fail to obtain support from grant-giving foundations.[19] In the 1980s the Human Sciences Research Council, the competent semigovernmental, largely Afrikaner-dominated organization in South Africa, reached the conclusion that "the political ordering of intergroup relations" in that country had "reached an impasse" and that "constructive relations" among the ethnic and political groups could no longer be "developed."[20] Although "millions" then were being "spent annually on research devoted to find solutions," only "contradictory" advice seemed available[21] and hence temporal urgency at that time inspired no even remotely acceptable solution.

The editors of an impressive book, *Preventing World War III,* began their preface with these two sentences: "Nuclear war is not inevitable. The belief that it is inevitable can help make it so."[22] They and their collaborators presented convincing preactive proposals to avert such a war, only some of which have since been adopted, even though the danger of such a war, though perhaps diminished, certainly has not been averted. A skeptic must conclude the present discussion with a perilous guide: many interventions appear eternally impossible now or ever unless force is employed, and even then the outcome may be both tenuous and temporary. Can one intervene to abolish or even temper patriotism, "the last refuge of a scoundrel" (Samuel Johnson) and a recurrent theme during presidential elections in the United States?

To delay, postpone, or renounce almost any impulse of the moment is likely to be very difficult.[23] Children only gradually learn to be patient and to wait during some specified or unspecified period of time. A highly valued if often neglected attribute of people in Western societies is the capability of sacrificing the present for the sake of the future in order to save, make capital investments, and plan housing and transportation. A difficult change for those in non-Western societies, as they westernize themselves or are westernized, is to learn to curb present desires and to plan.[24] For the same reason, potential principals everywhere often find it unpleasant to postpone interventions when it seems evident that they must do so. The reluctance to renounce, however, though highly significant, is not an infallible guide since every normal or almost normal individual on occasion wishes or is compelled to expend efforts in the present for the sake of the future: training or schooling, spending time hunting or cultivating crops, or adhering to the rituals of one's faith to avoid punishment is essential.

Interveners may decide that the time is ripe for them to intervene without consulting potential principals directly. Recently, crime in large American cities has reached a point at which the authorities have believed it necessary to strengthen the police force. When unemployment in an area or a community is high, academic researchers, like sociologists decades ago in Austria,[25] appraise its effects upon indi-

viduals who unwittingly function as informants and potential beneficiaries resulting from the publicity given the findings.

Clearly there can be bad timing, bad especially from the intervener's standpoint. Assistance is sought when the patient's disease is
already too far advanced for medication or therapy to be effective.
The United States and Canada in the mid-1980s began reactively to
intervene—or to consider intervening—after the emissions of sulfur
dioxide had already begun to damage lakes, forests, and wildlife; and
volunteers protested the construction of a nuclear power plant in
California after that plant had been almost completed.[26] But can it be
said that great prophets like Confucius, Jesus, and Muhammad badly
timed their interventions in behalf of all mankind because then and
now all peoples have not responded to their dicta that favor the good
and oppose evil? Part of the reply here is reassuring: they have inspired
converts and followers, their words and deeds have been remembered
for centuries. And what would have happened if they had never existed or if they had delivered their messages at another time?

Is it ever too late to intervene reactively? It may be impossible to do
so: the child has drowned before he could be rescued, the disease is
incurable, the strike has crippled the industry beyond repair, the war
is over and the ensuing hatreds last for generations. The question
often must be refined: although the optimum time has passed, cannot
a later intervention at least achieve some goal if with greater difficulty? As previously indicated, "early intervention" to assist children
and their families who live under unfavorable conditions is highly
desirable and frequently practical; yet in medical terms what is called
secondary prevention ("after the disease has been identified but before it has caused disability") or even tertiary prevention ("after
disability has been experienced, with the goal of reducing further
deterioration") may be necessary and helpful.[27] It would have been
better preactively to have prevented pollution, to have preserved forests and endangered species, and to protect the rights of minorities
and ethnic groups; yet now at least additional damage can be prevented.

Another possible conclusion: some interventions in fact may be too late to be effective. When the disturbed child becomes an adult, his mode of living may have become so strongly reinforced that for practical purposes (in terms of contemporary knowledge or the availability of trained experts or adequate funding) nothing can be accomplished to prevent him reactively from being addicted to drugs or engaging in antisocial actions. Or that grand person you were too shy to court has married someone else. Ever since Americans exploded two atomic bombs over Japan, efforts have been made to prevent more of these weapons from being manufactured and to destroy those already in existence; perhaps the best and only time to have intervened, as proposed by Albert Einstein, J. Robert Oppenheimer, and some of the physicists who originally helped design the weapons, would have been before they were manufactured or before their lethal effectiveness was demonstrated by being dropped on two Japanese cities.

In international affairs interventions are frequently reactive and not preactive. At the Nuremberg trials in 1945 to 1946, however, Nazi officials were punished on the basis of "planning, preparation, initiation, and waging of a war of aggression, a war in violation of international treaties,"[28] thus clearly indicating both past reactive and future preactive temporal factors. Similarly, aggressors are usually also punished after they have been militarily defeated.

Preactive international measures to date have usually been less frequent or effective. The Security Council, according to the original charter of the United Nations, is supposed to intervene preactively by investigating any situation or dispute that "might lead to international friction or give rise to a dispute"; it "shall determine the existence of any threat to the peace, breach of the peace, or act of aggression" and then decide on measures to be taken. The request to investigate may come from a Member or even a nonMember.[29] In 1992, in view of dramatic and far-reaching political changes in Europe and elsewhere, the Secretary-General called upon all nations to engage in "peace-building" or "action to identify and support structures which will tend to strengthen and solidify peace in order to avoid a relapse into conflict."[30] After Iraq invaded Kuwait in 1990, the council reacted presumably not only to restore Kuwait's independence but also to prevent Iraq from invading or dominating other countries.

The council's problems have been evident in the reaction of many nations to South Africa's policy of apartheid. Beginning in 1948 and lasting almost half a century the Security Council, the General Assembly, and a Special Committee of the United Nations debated and passed resolutions concerning the evils of apartheid and ways to combat that policy and its consequences. Thus the section of the UN Charter concerning nonintervention in the internal affairs of a nation was ignored and one advocating human rights was invoked. The retroactive interventions that were considered then included an arms embargo which at first was phrased as "advisory" and later as "mandatory" and also the never-implemented decision to expel South Africa from the United Nations. Funds were provided for South Africans to study abroad and for two leading antiapartheid political organizations to rent offices in New York City close to UN headquarters. Members of both the council and the General Assembly had different interests in these maneuvers that reflected their judgments concerning the effectiveness of the proposals as well as their own political alliances, particularly whether they were representing other African states or one of the Western powers. Except for the mandatory arms embargo against South Africa—which stimulated that country to develop its own armament industry—the council did not reach an agreement concerning other mandatory economic sanctions. By and large, "an image of the Security Council" as a body "essentially *stymied* on the issue of what to do about apartheid emerged."[31] Its bickerings, however, as well as the sentiment against apartheid among most of its members, were well publicized and may have contributed to the sanctions and the policy of divestment by individual nations. In addition, South Africans themselves were thus provided with evidence of worldwide hostility toward their country's racist policy not only by other African states but also by many—if not all—nations whose respect and economic ties remained important to them. In short, for decades the time had been ripe to intervene against apartheid, but with few but notable exceptions, action was delayed in favor of symbolic resolutions that in turn may possibly have contributed a mite to the dismantling of that racist policy. The council's procrastination in general can be traced in part to other, contradictory provisions of its charter which mandate nonintervention regarding "matters which are essentially within the domestic jurisdiction of any state," while also calling upon the United Nations to "promote . . . universal respect for and observance of human rights and fundamental freedom for all without distinction as to race, sex, language, or religion."[32]

Hesitancy regarding intervention may be overcome when principals' beliefs or attitudes change. Before the United States entered World War II, perhaps one-third of Americans were "isolationists" and tended to suppose that Germany would win the war, that a German victory would disturb neither themselves nor their country, and that therefore they should not intervene in that European war; but after the Japanese attack on Pearl Harbor, "the nation was welded together in one solid group"—well, somewhat or almost—and the feelings that had led to supporting nonintervention virtually or allegedly disappeared. In this situation and in other situations, hesitancy may be replaced by impulsivity when other persons favor intervention.[33] The ill principal suddenly decides to consult a physician recommended by a friend as the person who has brought relief to sufferers from an apparently similar ailment. In international affairs, interveners "endeavour to gain international approval" for the policy they would pursue;[34] hence the leaders of friendly powers in modern times have usually consulted one another before taking far-reaching diplomatic or limited military action.

Bystanders can affect the decision to intervene at a given moment. In New York City thirty-eight persons once witnessed, from their windows that overlooked the ghastly scene, the slow, brutal killing of a young woman being beaten by a maniac. They only stared at what was happening; they seemed fascinated or distressed, but they did not intervene to rescue Kitty Genovese. Perhaps if one or more of them had attempted to intervene, others would have joined them. Or even one person could have intervened without personal risk by simply telephoning the police, an action to be "expected by any [*sic*] ordinary members of this society."[35] This incident has inspired academic experiments with American students in which it has been found that intervention in behalf of a laudable cause—reporting that smoke was seeping into a room through a small vent or quickly helping a woman who had allegedly fallen in another room and was crying for help—occurred more readily when the experimental subject was alone than in a group. "If others are present," the investigators conclude, "the onus of responsibility is diffused, and the individual may be more likely to resolve his conflict between intervening and not intervening in favor of the latter alternative."[36]

On the other hand, when crowds become mobs and engage in destructive activity, bystanders may quickly join the intervention. Alone they might have been afraid to be destructive, but the sheer number of principals may induce them to believe that their opportunity has arrived and that they simultaneously can avoid being held responsible for their actions. American subjects in a realistic study—chillingly realistic in this instance—administered, as assistants in an alleged scientific experiment, what appeared to be strong and painful electric shocks to another man (actually a confederate who cried out and asked them to desist). They generally ceased "shocking" and withdrew from the "experiment" when bystanders (also confederates) intervened by refusing to continue to witness the simulated agony of that individual. In a variation of the same experiment, however, other bystanding subjects generally did not intervene; they withdrew from witnessing the "shocking' when not they themselves but someone else (again a confederate) was apparently the torturer.[37] Thus the bystanders either did or did not intervene, depending upon their assigned role in the situation.

Strength of Motivation

It is platitudinous if somewhat misleading to be reminded that *strongly motivated persons are likely to seek a more or less immediate outlet to attain relevant goals.* Principals would consult a therapist or a friend when a disturbance appears intolerable or when they realize that its intensity is almost certain to increase; here the appropriate interveners are standing by to offer assistance. President John F. Kennedy, in the words of his brother, praised a metaphor from Dante to the effect that "the hottest corner of hell was reserved for those who preserved their neutrality in times of moral crisis,"[38] by which he presumably meant that intense moral indignation should give way immediately to appropriate action. Persons genuinely civic-minded who link their own welfare to significant groups[39] are likely and perhaps eager to consent to become principals in projects involving community development and welfare when interveners enlist their cooperation. Educators and reformers who believe that minorities, various ethnic groups, and the disadvantaged in general suffer from discrimination would intervene preactively and domineeringly in early childhood and try to stimulate or inspire young persons in school and eventually as adults; they have faith in such interventions in contrast with those subscribing to genetic rather than environmental explanations. Supporters of a genetic guide, however, do not necessarily advocate nonintervention for children: they also admit that at least "vanishingly small increments" are added by "environmental measures that interact with genetic differences."[40]

A guide concerning the relation between motivational strength and a need for immediate intervention is valid only under certain conditions. Strongly motivated principals who cannot intervene at the moment to obtain their objectives may persist in their quest until they find a suitable opportunity at a later date: then a strong motive lengthens rather than shortens the period of time before intervening. An intervener must also be available. Millions and millions of persons would abolish war right now, but no matter how strongly they feel—because they have been soldiers, because they have lost precious persons in combat, because they are pacifists, or because they belong to an antiwar organization—they cannot discover an effective way to achieve their objective immediately. In contrast but in another sphere of social existence, mandatory arbitration between principals in conflict can set time limits during which interveners are permitted or required to impose resolutions. These and other interveners await the moment when the potential participants themselves come to recognize the need for interventions, or they do not take the initiative until they themselves believe "the time is ripe." Strongly motivated principals, however, may also resist interventions: the solution to the problem at hand must be the one they advocate, hence they oppose interference by a third party; they would defeat the enemy in the manner they contemplate; any other action is appeasement or compromise.

The time for an intervention is propitious when potential participants are motivated to change the status quo. In so-called capitalist societies manufacturers seek to discover, invent, or improve products and thus strengthen their appeal to potential consumers and increase their own profits. If uncertainty is "one of the reasons organizations are static,"[41] then it can be said that interventionists are active to restore stability for themselves or to prevent a pending change. Clergymen in many religious denominations, eager to intervene in behalf of their own theological and metaphysical principals, would convert the momentarily as well as the ceaselessly depressed and uncertain.

When the need to change is pressing but when potential principals themselves are unable or unwilling to participate in an intervention, interveners may utilize intermediaries to function in their behalf. Parents can have so many other responsibilities that they may ignore or be unaware of some of the problems their sons and daughters experience; then school-teachers or clergy may gently and effectively intervene and try to assist the children. American lawyers sometimes propose that crowded court calendars make it advisable to seek a decision through private mediation or arbitration; a settlement can perhaps be reached long before the case could be adjudicated in a formal trial.[42] On occasion an officer in a court may suggest that a complaint or a case can be resolved more informally through negotiation, perhaps with the assistance of another government agency (such as the Federal Trade Commission in the United States) or a private professional organization devoted to arbitration.[43] On the other hand, neutral interveners may delay interventions even for principals strongly motivated to resolve their conflicts: they are otherwise occupied or believe that a delay will make those principals more amenable to resolve their differences.

Partial intervention or nonintervention may be employed when motivation is strong, so that a definitive resolution is delayed. A bartender tells a joke and thus prevents two of his slightly inebriated customers from settling their argument in a brawl. After the Cuban missile crisis of 1962, leaders in Moscow and Washington established a so-called hotline between themselves so that the two countries would not initiate reactively an attack as a result of a misunderstanding which might induce one of them to intervene militarily in the affairs of the other; that line, moreover, transmits not voices, which can be misunderstood, but employs a teletype machine (for the United States located in the Pentagon with a telephone connection to the White House) so that an accurate record of the conversation is immediately available.[44] Slower diplomatic contacts to achieve the same objective employ the usual channels of communication.

A delay may occur in multiple interventions when each set of principals is strongly motivated to achieve incompatible goals. Recently concern has been shown for what is called sustainability, a term that refers to the planet and its ozone layer, to endangered species of plants and animals, to pollution that damages forests and affects the health of all living matter including human beings, and the traditions and values of developing societies and of minorities everywhere. Intervention on a broad scale is called for, and the need for it is recognized by some potential interveners.[45] An overall intervention that could encompass those areas, however, is not apparent at the moment. Conservationists in the United States believe that legislation to protect the wetlands or to preserve forests, rural areas, or historic sites is needed immediately or otherwise the areas will be forever destroyed. Other persons and groups do not wish to diminish their profits from logging so extensively that large forests cannot reproduce themselves and some animal species therein cannot survive; they argue that employment for the loggers and others attached to this industrial sector is more socially compelling than saving the endangered owls. Each group in this significant conflict seeks to enlist cooperation from political leaders and the general public. In the meantime, both sides win and lose as actions are taken concerning specific issues such as the use of certain pesticides and prospecting for oil offshore. Generally, a guide suggests, when potential participants would eagerly participate but are uncertain or insecure—often prior to the outbreak of a war—interventions are delayed until allies or supporters have been secured; and these others then function not as bystanders but as cooperating interveners or principals.

Knowledge Concerning Resolvability

Frequently individuals feel powerless to intervene when confronted with events over which they believe, perhaps correctly, they have no control. Illustrations are too numerous, but let both the plight of the Kurds in the first half of 1991 after the defeat of Iraq and the 1991 cyclone in Bangladesh be quickly recalled. Many Kurds fled over difficult terrain to neighboring countries because they feared they would be attacked by the Iraqis or because their leaders sought independence and had begun a civil war; people in Bangladesh were drowned or stranded on isolated islands without food or water. Such suffering was vividly and frequently displayed on American television and in the printed media: one could see the dead bodies and the pathetic people. An American housewife with four children is reported to have complained, "I want to do something, but I don't do anything, And I feel guilty. . . . I get upset watching the babies dying. Who the hell wants to see that? I switch the channel. There's so much going on at once." This woman wished she could intervene, and nonintervening drew her away from the painful scenes of the disasters. Some persons, the same report suggest, gave money to organizations attempting to help the survivors, musicians staged fund-raising concerts, but "many other Americans, feeling the squeeze of recession and seeing the outstretched palms of the homeless on their own streets, have let the tragedy hit them in the gut, but not in the pocketbook."[46]

Do participants believe that adequate knowledge can be made available to resolve a problem through a preactive or reactive intervention? Planned interventions by definition are based on the preactive assumption that, at least in general terms or at a particular time, resolutions can be realized; hence they may specify the temporal interval that is expected or considered desirable to elapse before the start of an intervention. It has been argued that "as a prelude to a period of extreme 'interventionism,'" Russian and other former Soviet authorities had to free themselves from the nonintervention inherent in the "doctrinal shackles of determinism," as implied in one not completely accurate interpretation of Marxism, before they could launch their "long-range industrialization and collectivisation campaigns."[47]

If no way to resolve a problem is practical or available, no matter how pressing that problem is, nonintervention is likely to be the consequence. Our hypothetical person does not dive into the pond to rescue the child when he himself is confined to a wheelchair. A mediator learns from what he considers to be a reliable source that workers are determined to strike and that their leaders will not submit the disagreement to mediation or negotiation under any conceivable circumstances; he does not attempt to intervene. On the other hand, interveners who deeply believe they can resolve a problem at the moment may intervene even when principals believe the problem unresolvable. Diplomats come up with magic formulas—or try to. In multiple interventions preliminary considerations may suggest that the groups wish to have the conflict resolved, that both sides are willing to participate in some kind of interaction, and that one or both are prepared eventually to accept some person or organization as the intervener.[48] Or other things being equal—ever that perilous qualification—when traditional or legal procedures are not prescribed and when therefore participants quickly select the mode of intervention, are only less serious and less complicated problems likely to be involved and eventually resolved?[49]

In international relations interveners may have various theories that require them to intervene at a given moment. In the last decades of the twentieth century, it was conjectured that foreign offices were being influenced by a so-called domino theory: the collapse of one country sets in motion forces that cause several others to fall likewise. Intervention, it was thought, would be required to prevent the first domino from tumbling. When the leaders of a nation feel that it is necessary to intervene in the affairs of another country or to exert influence upon its leaders without declaring war, they have various means at their disposal, such as recalling their own diplomats, or applying economic pressure.[50] At any given moment, one of these techniques may or may not appear appropriate and obligatory as the actions or ascribed machinations of other nations or the state of their economies is surveyed.

Information concerning principals may be difficult to obtain and hence a delay results before it can be secured or inferred. Interveners then depend not on facts but on their general knowledge or upon their own inferences concerning those principals. "How far the *intention* of the putative aggressor is a constituent element of what is stigmatised as aggression," according to an Australian scholar in 1977, "has been perhaps the most continuously central issue throughout the fifty-year debate about the definition of aggression" in the United Nations.[51] With respect to present and future "security" in international affairs, "intelligence" is gathered, whether by the usual open methods of research or through covert or clandestine means, in order to determine whether and how a hostile country will respond to a diplomatic maneuver or an attack;[52] the gathering is time-consuming and probably delays the intervention. One basic question, however, can never be completely or adequately answered: exactly how much information is absolutely essential to decide that the moment is propitious to intervene in situations involving many principals? After an intervention is contemplated details concerning the problem at hand may have to be ascertained. By devoting an entire book to one incident, a writer has demonstrated the length to which it may be necessary to go to comprehend a single international intervention: his analysis concerns the Soviet decision to invade Czechoslovakia in 1968, which, he demonstrates, required an appreciation of innumerable factors including not only the Czechs and their rebellious leaders but also Soviet relations with China at that time.[53] The owner of a new product must often delay its production in order to conduct market tests to determine people's responses to it, the most effective appeals to be employed in advertising copy, or even the desirability of changing features of the product itself.

The absence of completely adequate information to realize an intervention does not mean that nonintervention becomes the decision, however great the uncertainty and perils; but some hesitation and delay may then be essential. In this century two problems have arisen dramatically for interveners. The first has been the avoidance of nuclear war. Decades passed, nevertheless, until American and the former Soviet and then Russian leaders began to decrease gradually and then later relatively drastically their stockpiles of those weapons. Intervention had been consisting of increasing one's own arsenal in order to frighten opponents and thus to weaken their decision to resort to war as the mode of intervention. But the danger persists, and intervention to produce disarmament has remained unfulfilled. The second challenge has been AIDS, for which a cure has been sought but found to be agonizingly elusive. Interveners have tried to decrease its incidence by warning to principals who they believed were especially vulnerable: homosexuals, adolescents and others failing to use condoms, drug addicts, those using unsterilized needles. Sterile needles and condoms have also been distributed as a form of action.

Another source of delay in realizing an objective is the inability to locate relevant principals even when interveners possess adequate or nearly adequate knowledge concerning desirable interventions. Professional interveners may have to await a call from principals or their own organizations before beginning to function. Then, even when potential principals are clearly available, official and unofficial interveners in American society fail to realize their objective: they cannot easily weed out persons who actually or potentially display violence toward their spouses, young children, and the elderly or those who are prone to commit incest *before* they do so. The interveners are dependent, therefore, upon "a combination of factors" that suggest higher risk potential.[54] Two pediatric physicians and a third physician concerned with social services list under three headings factors related to child victimization: the child's own vulnerability (twenty-six factors such as hyperactivity, low birth weight, low IQ); parental vulnerability (forty such as aggressiveness, marital strife, economic hardship); and environmental vulnerability (sixteen such as the sanctioned use of force in society, divorce, social isolation).[55] Lists like these provide a rich variety of instructive factors that have been associated in the past with violence, yet they function only as a general preactive guide when an intervener at a given moment would intervene to protect a child from abuse or to prevent an adult from abusing a victim—unless specific information is available concerning the past record of the particular principal.

Principals likewise may be either frustrated or annoyed when an appropriate intervener is not available. "A welfare mother has just received notice that her benefits have been terminated"; "A consumer bought an expensive automobile and every imaginable mechanical problem has occurred."[56] The quotations come from a book titled *The Sense of Justice,* under which category too many additional illustrations are self-evident in an era when the homeless, drug addicts, war victims, and citizens forced to live under authoritarian regimes require assistance that interveners, if they were both willing and available, could provide.

Duration

In planning or analyzing interventions attention is paid to their probable or, afterward, their actual duration. The drowning child may be quickly rescued, other unresolved problems require longer or indefinite periods of time. Certainly it is true, in the words of a French social scientist, that "it is practically impossible to determine a priori the duration of an intervention," which depends on "two numerous factors, the internal as well as the external."[57] Psychoanalysts and other psychiatrists, however, may limit each of their sessions to a fixed period of time like a little less than an hour, and the fees they receive may motivate their patients to cooperate quickly in order not to require too many costly hours; yet even they do not or cannot specify in advance how many sessions ideally will be required. People everywhere are addicted to regularity and hence to routines,[58] so that particular interventions, especially if they are unusual, may be resented when they interrupt the "normal" stream of activity. On the other hand, the normal may become boring or lack stimulation, so that a sudden or novel intervention can be a welcomed change. The duration of multiple interventions can affect the decision to participate: all or some of the participants may have only limited time to devote to the activity, or their superiors may grow impatient if too much time is required to find a resolution. When the existence of international interventions is publicized, the mass media grow impatient during a prolonged interaction.

There is no magic guide to determine the optimal duration of many interventions. When the objective has been attained, the intervention is complete, at least for the time being. A dual or multiple intervention is proposed to avert a strike over wages, but will there also be a discussion concerning actual conditions in the plant so that another walkout may be avoided later? A Quaker intervener who has sought to halt conflict between countries by mediating directly between their leaders reports that his efforts "have lasted up to four years and never less than two," though he was "not of course on the spot the whole time."[59] How different are "real" interventions from academic exercises in which a conflict is simulated among students in a classroom or by appointment, or over a long weekend during which the students or intermediaries of groups or countries in conflict interact in a search for common ground! Mediation in the United States to prevent a divorce or to produce an amicable settlement between a quarreling couple may require more than one session, particularly—or perhaps?—when the mediator is a private person rather than a public official appointed by a court.[60] Participants may be inspired to speed up their deliberations and to reach a resolution when they know they are working against a fixed temporal deadline. There is no guide, however, concerning whether decisions reached under such circumstances are better or worse than those achieved relatively leisurely with no temporal restriction.

A multiple intervention lasting several days or even weeks and months has advantages, provided its problems regarding site (to be discussed in the next chapter) can be settled. Principals have an opportunity to express themselves fully and, if not to fraternize with one another, at least to become better acquainted inside and outside the actual workshop. Interveners then are able to employ a variety of methods to clarify the problem at hand, to instruct the principals concerning themselves and their ways of generally viewing events, or to do both. From the opposite standpoint, however, a workshop of long, fixed duration may encourage dawdling and inefficiency; without the pressure of time, principals keep postponing a decision.

In some situations it may be unwise to intervene in one full swoop; rather, partial interventions over time may be more effective. A parent, spouse, or friend believes that a person should be less tense or compulsive. As an intervener he or she is never a pedantic lecturer, nor tempted to employ an obvious form of therapy. Instead this intervener functions continually as a model and hopes that eventually the principal will behave appropriately. Much of the news, commentary, features, and propaganda that many but not all so-called information agencies transmit to friendly, neutral, and unfriendly countries follows a similar pattern. Daily broadcasts and telecasts, magazines, books, and speakers are supposed to reach citizens and officials in the targeted areas. At a given moment the objective may be specific regarding the interpretation of an event, but in the long run the aim is to display one's own thinking, history, and institutions in the hope that the recipient's views will be changed if they are hostile or strengthened if they are friendly. American and especially British communications also transmit some items unfavorable from their own viewpoint (though usually in an explanatory context) in order to strengthen their own credibility so that they can thus intervene continually and more directly in a crisis. In addition, a modeling approach is employed when officials from other lands are invited to come for a visit or for some official reason, and also when an exchange of scholars or students between countries enables those principals to experience directly each other's way of living. In multiple interventions it is sometimes necessary or desirable to consider phases of the unresolved problem over a period of time, so that principals must push aspects of a solution into a series of interactions and be willing to proceed step by step.

Timing, it must now be evident, not only can determine the onset of interventions but may also be determined by one or more of the other variables in their calculus.

METHOD

Chapter Five

Now let it be assumed that after an event participants are confronted with an unresolved problem and that either the intervener or the principal or both are ready or almost ready to consider the possibility of an intervention. Motivation is adequate; timing has been determined or at least considered. Or let the same assumption, but in the past tense, be made for analysts and historians who would comprehend a completed intervention or a nonintervention. At this point or earlier in the decision-making process another vital question is raised: if there is to be an intervention, what should or will be the method or technique to be employed or to be experienced? Without a seemingly adequate or tolerable method nonintervention may be the consequence or the appropriate choice. To rescue that child—by now in these pages he has been in the water so long that he really must be drowning—the available intervener decides either to swim if the tot is a short distance away or to jump into a boat or helicopter if swimming is not feasible. When the two superpowers reigning in the late 1980s and very early 1990s decided to reduce their armaments and also to allay suspicions, their leaders tried to include in their pacts detailed procedures for inspecting each other's arsenal. In this chapter, then, attention is focused upon guides affecting the ways in which intervention methods have been selected.

Cultural Setting

Before plunging into the intricacies and perplexities that inevitably arise whenever participants would select a method of intervention or a decision is made ex post facto concerning why a particular method was once or twice or hundreds of times selected, however, the range of possibilities can be narrowed somewhat by considering the norms for intervening or nonintervening in particular ways within the society where a problem exists. Such a cultural approach becomes convincing by examining societies with apparently different methods. Members of a small ethnic group in the Solomon Islands believe that individuals' thoughts and actions affect not only themselves but also the community as a whole. An unresolved problem has to be "disentangled" (their word as translated by an American anthropologist): the "bad feelings" must be expressed in front of those connected with the problem as well before other onlookers. Once the intervention of a Western-style physician failed to alleviate a woman's serious physical pain; her friends and acquaintances assumed that the bad feelings between her and her husband were interfering with the cure. When a pig was lost that was to have been included in an important occasion, the loss was attributed to the bad feelings of those who had been hindering the search. To eliminate the "obstructions" in both instances the persons involved directly or indirectly met in public and expressed their feelings. Both problems, it is reported, were subsequently and consequently resolved. With this method the principals themselves or someone else became the intervener and called the "meeting" at which the conflict was disentangled.[1]

Among the Dou Donggo in eastern Sumbawa of Indonesia, the central value has concerned the emotions evoked while resolving a dispute. Principals there have tried not to summon Western-type police when a dispute arises; rather, they call upon an elder or a village headman, who holds no formal office, to adjudicate the dispute, as the anthropologist maintains, without washing their dirty linen in public. Shame and humiliation are thus avoided.[2]

China has had a long tradition against settling disputes by the intervention of the state. Mao Tse-tung himself argued that such disputes should be resolved by "democratic methods, methods of discussion, of criticism, of persuasion and education, not by coercive, oppressive methods." For Confucians legal intervention is considered "a regrettable necessity" under some circumstances. Traditional family disputes have been settled "frequently" within the family by the father or grandfather. Likewise, efforts have been made to resolve other kinds of disputes before appealing to a local or regional authority. A Communist slogan is said to have been that "mediation is the main thing, adjudication is secondary." There have been, therefore, according to one report, "more than two hundred thousand semi-official people's mediation committees" throughout the country.[3] The Chinese thus have attempted to decentralize authority, except perhaps, as in Tianamen Square, when the central government itself feels threatened.

For numerous reasons, knowledge of such cultural settings provides a valuable, though only a perilous, guide to intervention methods. Variability to cultures is somewhat limited by the human participants and the relationships they inevitably have and regulate. The following statement, though written at the beginning of this century, remains a useful guide: "An individual is placed in various sections of society, synchronically and in succession; in order to pass from one category to another and to join individuals in other sections, he must submit, from the day of his birth to that of his death, to ceremonies whose forms often vary but whose function is similar." As a result, there is "general similarity" from society to society "among ceremonies of birth, childhood, social puberty, betrothal, marriage, pregnancy, fatherhood, initiation into religious societies, and funerals."[4] The details are very important; here it is sufficient to note that through tradition certain persons intervene as the human body matures and grows older in order to symbolize the change in physical and social status and also to provide instruction concerning the next stage both to the individual and his peers. The methods of intervention range from circumcision through bodily decoration and clothing to burial rites that usually have transcendental connotations. At first glance it might appear that Indians in northwest North America had a completely unique custom, the potlatch: one person intervened to assert his superiority over another person or to make him feel impoverished him by a display of wealth and by bestowing gifts upon him; then the second person was expected to intervene with an even more lavish display and with more impressive gifts to the first person. Sensible persons like you and me don't have potlatches, do we? But surely some of us display our wealth by the clothes we wear and the houses in which we choose to live, and on designated occasions we shower gifts upon friends and other beneficiaries in order to impress them—and maybe we even secretly expect them to reciprocate or to feel humiliated. Our motives and those of the Indians may be quite similar; details in the methods of intervening differ.

Then, the validity of generalizations about intervention methods in allegedly similar societies may be difficult to establish. An examination of a modestly small number of "nonindustrial" or traditional societies reveals that mediators there are "respected, influential community members with experience and acknowledged expertise in settling disputes."[5] They also reflect and enforce the "norms and values of their communities;" they are "generally neutral," but "rarely disinterested" as they function promptly to resolve disagreements. Aside from the forthright qualifications of "generally" and "rarely," such a guide must also be applicable to some if not quite so many interveners in Western societies. Straws of evidence once suggested, when samples of Chinese in Hong Kong were compared with Americans and a sample in Nigeria with one in Canada, only slight or no differences in the preferred methods of settling disputes were evident, and there was considerable variability within each sample.[6] These studies must be cautiously evaluated: almost all the subjects were students who were simply asked to imagine—yes, imagine—the method that they would select when they themselves were in a dispute with another person and wished to emerge the victor or that they would recommend to others to settle a dispute. It is likewise perhaps not surprising that for five "pluralistic democracies" which on the surface might have been expected to resemble one another with respect to intervention methods—Australia, Italy, Japan, the United States, and West Germany—the actual details concerning industrial disputes were so diverse that "easy transplantability" of the techniques seemed impossible.[7]

There is, in addition, variability of methods within a particular society.[8] It is probably true in the West that the search for justice affects the ways in which courts of law are conducted. The aim is to determine whether the accused is guilty or whether damage has been or will be sustained by the plaintiff. Attorneys are hired or appointed to increase the probability that a "fair" hearing takes place; and judges, other officials, and juries are recognized as the interveners to administer the conventional procedures. Similar steps are supposed to be followed whether the procedure involves arbitration, mediation, or consultation: all principals must have the opportunity to present their version of the conflict. Concretely, however, the details of legal and extralegal procedures are not standardized and in practice depend upon the training, experience, and temperament of the interveners, as a glance at the tactics of attorneys and other interveners easily demonstrates. If citizens are to obey the law, they presumably must be acquainted with legal regulations and the ways in which a particular regulation has been enforced or interpreted in the past. This doctrine of following precedent, stare decisis, becomes a perilous guide in legal proceedings when it is uncertain which precedent is applicable to the situation at hand. Also, are some situations really unprecedented?

Cultural or other fairly rigid differences within a society influence the intervening method that is to be or must have been employed. Principals in the upper echelon of a society have access to and utilize different methods from those in the lower groups. The uppers, however defined, are able to employ more competent or more professional interveners than the lowers, who may possibly resort to informal yet effective methods like violent or nonviolent direct action. Within either group some persons are inclined to lead or to follow others when a crisis arises. One analysis performed in American society suggests that when individuals are very depressed and find life hopeless, they may commit suicide or become excessively dependent upon alcohol or other drugs. Suicide has tended to be more prevalent among women than among men, and the reverse tends to be true for drug abuse. Gender thus has played a role in the kind of self-intervention adopted by American adults; and cultural factors also affect these tendencies, since it may be "unmanly" to commit suicide but "manly" to be drunk. For psychiatrists and social workers to intervene successfully in order to try prevent suicide or substance abuse, the same writer indicates, those prone to suicide may require individual treatment, whereas those seeking consolation in drugs may be referred for treatment to organizations such as Alcoholics Anonymous.[9]

Finally, *the cultures of most societies are not static and hence their goals and interventions change with the passing of time.* Toward the end of the current century, increasingly larger numbers of individuals in the West have subscribed to what has been called participatory democracy—"People whose lives are affected by a decision must be part of the process of arriving at that decision"[10]—and therefore they have striven to enlist the assistance of interveners to achieve the right to control their existence or at least to improve methods enabling them to participate in the decisions affecting them. Leaders of coups against prevailing regimes or of revolutionary movements have attracted supporters who were dissatisfied with the status quo or who believed they would profit from a change. Consultation in many industries has increased over the years: "The employer seeks the advice and views of employees, but retains the final decision."[11] With this method employers have learned to intervene to prevent a strike or to improve the efficiency of their company's operation, perhaps only to convey the belief that they are interested in their worker's welfare. In the West, too, police are increasingly called upon to intervene in order to prevent disorder when hostile groups confront each other, but they have been taught and hence operate under certain rules that specify when they may use force; they know that if their efforts lead to serious damage or death, they will be subject to an inquiry or court trial which will determine whether they acted justifiably in self-defense. In days of rapid political change there are frequent interventions in behalf of what are called human rights. These are variously defined; are not expressed specifically in a so-called bill of rights or its equivalent; refer either to an overall objective like "the quality of life" or the "pursuit of happiness" or to specific objectives, such as adequate food or housing; or function symbolically or realistically or both.

The guide in summary is quite clear: *a knowledge of the cultural setting provides preliminary clues to some but not all interventions and to the method likely to be employed or to please particular principals.* It is perilous to generalize about a whole society or about a person when the choice of methods may depend upon the particular problem to be resolved. Some insight, nevertheless, is provided by personal experience, the systematic probing of the society by anthropologists, or a knowledge of the relevant history. Thus the etiquette between two persons, the required procedure in a courtroom, or the opening claims and insults of leaders in international conferences are not surprising or less so.

Site

Even after cultural factors are respected, the actual site of an intervention may be highly influential.[12] The geographic location must first be considered. A patient expresses himself differently in a physician's office than over a telephone or in a hospital. A therapist can provide advice to a desperate person who telephones him in the middle of the night, but literally or figuratively he may prefer to have the individual reclining on the proverbial couch where he is encouraged to associate freely as he recalls his dreams and the events leading to the present crisis. Treating such patients in their home rather than institutions has been found in countries like the Netherlands and the United States to have numerous advantages, such as helping those who might not otherwise become principals or who react more favorably in their normal environment.[13] The general atmosphere of a seemingly neutral site like The Hague is different from the capital of the country petitioning the International Court. The neutrality of a location is important when it provides principals with a sense of detachment from the conflict that has given rise to the intervention; on the other hand, they may feel insecure in strange or hostile surroundings. A principal unresolved problem, as representatives from Middle Eastern states and Israel agreed to meet in the fall of 1991 largely as a result of the intervening efforts of the Soviet Union and the United States, was the site of the interaction; in October of that year they finally assembled in Madrid and there decided to accept the American offer to meet a second time in Washington. A series of meetings did occur there; and once more the site was the topic "aired more than any other in a week of talks about talks."[14] In each instance a proposed site as well as the room within the meeting place had symbolic significance for these principals.

The distance participants must travel to reach the site of an intervention or the time required to do so can affect whether they agree to make themselves available as well as their mood or spirit, at least at the outset. During a prolonged workshop when principals are to live away from their homes, the site must offer suitable recreational facilities, and a hotel or its equivalent must be available. Such practical matters become difficult when the intervention, particularly when it is a multiple one, is planned to be in stages so that interactions occur over a period of time. For the first meeting the site may be both available and suitable, but later the place or the building may be needed for other purposes; will participants be more or less pleased by the change?

Actual conditions at the site can affect the intervention. If a face-to-face intervention or workshop is planned, the season of the year and the prevailing weather may determine whether participants wish to interact indoors or outdoors. A suitable and available building can evoke responses related to the intervention: it may be impressive, inhibiting, or neutral. The architecture of a church if it be the site or if it attracts participants during pauses in the interaction may influence Christians and others, who perhaps are encouraged by the relative simplicity of Romanesque buildings to function as interventionists within their own private frameworks or by the relative ornateness of Gothic buildings to lift themselves to greater spiritual heights. The building that houses the interaction undoubtedly must provide for the comfort of the participants as viewed from their cultural or individual standpoint.

In multiple interventions the literal shape of the table may be important: should it be round so that all principals face one another or should it be oblong in order somehow to signify their statuses; should the opposing groups occupy distinctive sections of the conference table or of the meeting room or should they be mixed together, should the choice be theirs or that of the intervener? Shuttle diplomacy, employed by President Jimmy Carter for representatives of Egypt and Israel in 1977 and later by the Secretary-General of the United Nations for representatives of the Greek and Turkish communities of Cyprus, occurred after the participants had assembled at one location and then were assigned to separate suites; the intervener delivered written comments back and forth to the two groups. This technique has advantages: principals are not embarrassed or aggressive as they might be in direct confrontation; after communicating through the intermediary, they have an opportunity to consult higher authorities regarding proposed resolutions; they may waste less time wrangling or in massaging their own egos. Perhaps aggressive or extreme views are expressed in the absence of the opposing group.[15] But are such views more valid, do they help promote a resolution to the conflict? Within each separated group, moreover, rapport can be established or strengthened, both sides of the dispute can be considered dispassionately, missing information can be indicated, perhaps hostility can be reduced. Later, under the supervision of the intervener, the two groups perhaps meet face-to-face; or they remain separate and the intervener continues to function as the channel of communication between them. This procedure, however, may backfire when decisions in the separate groups are made on the basis of inaccurate information or "self-enhancing" resolutions which the opposing side might have been able to correct or change in a face-to-face interaction.[16]

In workshops or generally in multiple interventions that extend over time both the site and the arrangements within the building may determine whether the principals of the opposing groups have contact with one another during pauses or after the workshop has recessed for the day. If possible, do or should they go home or remain at the site? When the workshop is conducted at some distance from the home base over a period of days, informal contacts outside the interaction may be helpful or not. Off-the-record conversations while eating— perhaps especially while drinking alcoholic beverages if they are permitted or tolerated—may possibly result in increased knowledge, perhaps trust, even the start of genuine friendships among the principals. On the other hand, security matters connected with governments, if there be such, can be endangered by semi-intimate contact of this sort and prolonged or informal contact may lead members of one group to discover that members of the other group are hostile or impossibly rigid.

Finally, practical matters again intrude. Sites at a distance from the homes or offices of the participants require adequate funds to pay for transportation, living expenses (if only for light beverages served during pauses), and compensation for the building's owner. When interventions involve strong hostility between or among the participating groups or the surrounding population, security arrangements must be made with the local police, other authorities, or the interveners' own colleagues. Participants who know that the selected site will be available for only a limited period of time may feel compelled to speed up their interaction, which may or may not be advantageous from the standpoint of resolving the problem at hand.

Peace

The uncertainties that confront participants as they select the intervention method they think is most suitable for the problem at hand are especially numerous and agonizing when war is possible. Should military action be employed unilaterally by invading another country, by supporting that country's forces against rebels or vice versa, or by aiding either side after a third country has intervened in behalf of one of the sides? In "an intervention-prone world," it was once suggested, interveners may have no basis for reaching a decision, whether they rely upon historical analogues, upon their estimate of how the opposing leaders will react,[17] or upon their own ambition to achieve immortality on the historical record. Ordinary citizens and bystanders have their views, including pacifism, a belief in the just war (just from whose or what standpoint?), and the conviction that waging war may have economic and psychological advantages.

Even morons and dictators appreciate the high costs of armed combat, whether reference is made to human lives, property, or straight costs; therefore available are substitute forms of intervention through which hostility can be expressed or similar objectives attained. Interveners can launch verbal attacks unilaterally in the mass media or more subtly by planting rumors. They can seek to isolate an opponent economically through a boycott or the withdrawal of capital investments. They can openly or secretly sabotage a country's installations. Since World War II the great and small powers have employed dangerous confrontations: whether constructing the Wall in Berlin or closing the frontier with Gibraltar, a third world war has been avoided as relevant preparations for war were displayed.[18] Within very recent times, there seems to be a tendency, with many exceptions, for political leaders not to intervene militarily in the affairs of another country until they receive the approval of a regional or international organization.[19]

As the United Nations Charter was signed in 1945, the signatories were so concerned with "the maintenance of international peace and security" that they listed a miscellany of techniques for finding "a solution" that could resolve international disputes peacefully: "negotiation, enquiry, mediation, conciliation, arbitration, judicial settlement, resort to regional agencies or arrangements, or other peaceful means of their own choice." One of these techniques, no matter which one, it was hoped would or could avoid war. Relatively infrequently— with notable exceptions that have involved Korea, Cyprus, Zaire, the Middle East, and Iraq—has the Security Council, in the words of the UN Charter, been provided with "armed forces, assistance, and the facilities, including rights of passage necessary for the purpose of maintaining international peace and security"[20]; prior agreements among the relevant nations concerning the precise method to be employed have not been attained.

As might be expected, scholars have laboriously and conscientiously counted the number of international disputes that have been submitted to mediation and hence to intervention by a third party. By and large, though the percentage varies with the mode of analysis, such interventions occurred in over half of the conflicts during the latter part of the twentieth century.[21] A careful but perilous analysis of 38 international conflicts between 1919 and 1939 and of 39 between 1945 and 1965 suggests that in the first period the League of Nations attempted to bring about a settlement in 31 percent of the situations; in the second period the United Nations and other regional organizations tried to settle 41 percent. Significantly more attempts were made during the same periods through "bilateral negotiations and *ad hoc* mediators or unilateral conferences."[22] These figures do not indicate the precise methods employed by the interveners; interventions by international bodies assumed different forms such as passing resolutions, urging the disputants to negotiate, or deploring their noncompliance with such resolutions. These organizations possessed no military means of their own to enforce a resolution. Nor do the figures reveal which type of intervention succeeded or failed to resolve the conflict: for this purpose, as the same writer also demonstrates, each conflict has its own peculiarities, so that a box score in this respect is quite useless.

Another historical analysis reports that only 31 of the 97 international conflicts between 1929 and 1986 "were handled through institutionalized procedures, ranging from bilateral negotiations between the adversaries, to international conferences, mediation, and adjudication"; but half of the outcomes were settled through "manipulation and use of armed force," that is, by conquest and successful deterrence.[23] Of the 142 wars between 1800 and 1980, 38 have been classified as being settled by negotiation after an armistice, 37 by capitulation, 26 by extermination or expulsion, 19 by negotiation before an armistice, and only 9 by an international organization (and 8 of these by the UN Security Council after it came into existence in 1945). Interventions thus played a minor peacemaking role and were "invariably preceded by considerable bargaining in the corridors" of the UN. The overall "lesson" for this time period is not very inspiring: "If the war is international but involves no major powers and has not lasted long, it may end through the action of an international organization."[24]

The rationales for intervening in the affairs of another nation vary. They include the fear that a civil war there will affect the intervener adversely; that economic relations have been or will be disrupted; that refugees from the war will become a problem; or that for ideological or other reasons one side in the war should be favored and assisted by the intervening nation. On occasion, as in Uganda during the declining years of the Idi Amin regime in 1973, an appreciable number of persons within the country itself objected to the prevailing regime and appeared to welcome outside interveners. Actual international interventions are affected, though not completely determined, by the motivating objectives.[25] As conventional diplomacy fails to achieve its objective, political leaders may alert their armed forces and thus threaten a potential enemy without actually waging war. Alerts of this sort may be perilous, as President Kennedy is reported to have muttered during the Cuban missile crisis with reference to a flight at the time by an American plane: "There is always some son of a bitch who doesn't get the word."[26] Since World War II, first the superpowers and then other countries have possessed nuclear weapons with which their objective might have been attained but which they did not employ. This form of nonintervention, arising from uncertainty about the probability of retaliation by the adversary—and possibly also for moral reasons—is brilliantly called "mutual deterrence" and is said to stand "on hallowed ground."[27] For such deterrence to be effective, leaders must be convinced that if they do intervene, they themselves will incur undesired losses similar to those they inflict upon their opponents. In this sense any legal action or taboo that prescribes an action is a form of deterrence that seeks to prevent principals from engaging in a specific action.

Persons opposed to war and its consequences and in favor of peace try to intervene by holding public meetings in which prominent and other individuals express these viewpoints. An organization known as International Alert, with headquarters in London, calls itself "a new allegiance to end conflict within nations." With 242 participants from various countries, mostly African, and with funds provided by an array of foundation, university, and government sponsors, a five-day seminar was conducted during September 1987 in Kampala, Uganda. After an opening address by the president of Uganda, five "plenary sessions" were held at which a prominent person first expressed a theme, followed by two speakers and a general discussion. The theme of the third session was "The African Traditional Concepts of Human Rights." Thereafter a day and a half was devoted to four "working groups," interrupted by what was listed as a "cultural evening." On the next day each group provided its report; the headings of the first groups devoted to "International and Regional Implications of Internal Conflict" were "Centrality of the State," "Peace/Stability as Goals," "Irrelevance of Military Solutions," "People's (Mass) Movements/Organizations," "Silence of the Ethnic Factor," "The Broader Regional Environment," and "Economic Reconstruction and Development." There was of course a "closing reception."[28] Although the practical and immediate consequences of such specific open interventions are unknowable, it may be guessed that they influence if only minutely those in power to be a little less ready to wage war and to strive to achieve lasting peace in another century or so.

Whether or not leaders and followers approve of war as a mode of intervention, "Military Science" raises its own problems concerning the feasibility of this method. Variables here concern one's own forces and those of the allies and the enemy: their number, training, availability, and equipment. Consideration is given to the site of the pending conflict and the weather. In addition, ideological issues may be raised, such as the potential damage to the civilian population and their homes. And what will the consequences of victory be in the short or long run?

Uncertainty

Without exaggeration, it seems clear that *the only certain guide to selecting a method of intervention is,* after being reminded of the ubiquity of uncertainty in human affairs,[29] *to postulate some degree of uncertainty.* Swim to reach the drowning child? Yes, but there may be a dangerous crosscurrent in the water; perhaps it would be wiser to throw him a rope and then drag him to safety. Or another child is frequently unruly and a therapist is sought; which treatment should be selected? The intervener may concentrate upon the child and try to discover the roots of his rebellion; on the basis of reports or observation, the recommendation may then be made that he be directed to another group of peers for recreation or to another school. Suggestions or even therapy may be offered to his parents so that they begin to treat him differently. Planned interventions follow a previously established procedure, yet the original plan may involve uncertainty: should there be mediation or arbitration whenever a disagreement arises; should there be mandatory or voluntary acceptance of whatever resolution is proposed; should third parties not intervene in the hope that the representatives of the groups will resolve the problem? And the most baffling, pressing, significant question of all during the early 1990s and beyond: how can the leaders of countries in Eastern Europe transform their urban and rural economies from what had been collectives supervised by the state to free markets in which private enterprise largely determines production, wages, living conditions, and personal security? The new leaders, the interveners—self-selected, newly selected, or elected—perhaps know what they wish to achieve, but how to do so?

Other illustrations of uncertainty are distressingly easy to locate. When a conscientious investigator extracted sixty-nine instances of third-party intervention in the Netherlands, he was of the opinion that no less than forty-eight different variables in these situations pertained to productivity, education, health care, social welfare, and government. In his language, the techniques included "raising personal matters," "expressing understanding," "giving interaction rules," "fact-finding," "external pressure," "impartiality," "improving the relationship," and "learning to live with the conflict."[30] Even the best of "solid" generalizations concerning intervention trail off on a sad note of uncertainty. A psychologist once squeezed three of them, which he modestly called strands and hunches, from "a few dozen experiments" in American laboratories that generally employed the usual American undergraduates as subjects. Such exercises could facilitate some form of resolution "without loss of face"; they may have proved effective when the conflicts were relatively "low" but less so or not at all when they were "high"; and there was a tendency for the principals to view the interventions "as an unwelcome and unwanted intrusion." Methodologically the conclusion can be criticized, as ever, from many standpoints ranging from the nature of the samples to the operational definitions of the concepts. Most significant with respect to uncertainty is the writer's honest admission that all three stem from "some contradictory and puzzling findings."[31] Ah yes, a perilous guide indeed but at least a guide.

The time to intervene in economic affairs may seem to be immediately, but both the practical means that governments can adopt and their consequences remain perilously uncertain. When inflation at a given moment is excessive and officials are determined to halt the trend, what intervening measures can or should they adopt? A country's currency is undervalued on international exchanges; possibly but not certainly that condition can be curbed by increasing exports and decreasing imports,[32] yet how can the changes be accomplished? An intervention here may have desirable or undesirable consequences for the economies not only of the particular country but also of other countries; hence the decision may be not to intervene at all. Indeed "the advantages of nonintervention," a scholar of international relations has noted, "have persisted over time."[33]

Specific persons can affect an intervention unexpectedly in ways difficult to anticipate. The most seasoned intervener may be unable even to imagine how a principal will behave, especially when the interaction makes him feel tense or insecure. Bystanders may suddenly intrude before, during, or after an intervention, as when a friend or relative interferes with the dual therapy being administered by a marriage counselor, when a surprise witness is called by the opposing side to testify during a trial, or when the enthusiasm of participants is later cooled by persons or officials who oppose the resolution they have achieved. So much of human judgment and behavior—but not all—is affected by individuals' so-called reference groups, the groups to which they belong or whose values they use to judge and guide themselves.[34]

Interveners are confronted with puzzles concerning the potential principals who agree or are dragooned to participate in an intervention. General information about them and their society is available, but specific facts may be lacking or the weights to be given whatever knowledge they possess usually are uncertain. The historical background of principals in an international dispute may or may not be one of the factors affecting their viewpoints: are they proud of what their ancestors once accomplished, do they believe that they have a responsibility to uphold or to perpetuate a set of traditions in their society, or are they only vaguely acquainted with that past and are driven toward objectives unrelated to it?

Both interveners and principals may feel impotent when they fully realize that some method must be selected. An individual who is ill realizes that he requires medical assistance, but does not know whether to consult the family physician, a specialist, or a homeopath. Someone who would persuade an acquaintance to cooperate with her does not or cannot anticipate beforehand whether flattery, bribery, threats, under- or overstatements, silence, or so on will be the best means to employ. Especially for societies like South Africa and others undergoing significant changes, leaders have no sure methods to achieve their newly emerging objectives. Historians offer no salvation because they themselves perforce must select the events, persons, and hence the interventions from the past which they consider significant. The "lessons" of that past in archives and textbooks must always be incomplete and somewhat arbitrary.

The uncertainties associated with many interventions, now so gloomily suggested, result in large part from the oft-repeated warning that the methods are "numerous and diverse" and reflect the banal but compelling fact that "human beings interact so variously."[35] Even the most experienced professional interveners know that short of shooting a principal success can never be completely certain (except temporarily in war?), regardless of the technique they choose or are compelled to utilize; like a very forthright social scientist, they realize that they must "muddle through" the situation that confronts them or that they create.[36] That guide, however, is not always so perilous; thus two professional boxers perform quite differently toward each other than do an experimental scientist and his laboratory assistant, though within limits it may be anticipated that each of the pair exhibits some unique behavior. In spite of all the perils, cannot some uncertainty be reduced?

Reduction of Uncertainty

Even if interventions teem with uncertainties, it does not follow that nonintervention is or should be the method. Like it or not, people constantly intervene regardless of uncertainties. Then, nonintervention has its own perils: doing nothing always means doing something. Although it may be true that the training desirable for lay therapists who would assist rape victims is uncertain and perhaps not completely effective,[37] nonintervention is not necessarily the resulting decision: the victims require comfort and direction which can be at least partially successful even when only trial and error guide the technique. At the very least, uncertainty regarding a particular method may induce a decision to employ one that is less decisive but that may be useful in its own right and even be less perilous. Before proposing surgery, a physician suggests that a drug be taken regularly; possibly that less drastic means removes the ailment. Consciously or unconsciously, it has been seriously contended, some Americans intervene against authority by plastering graffiti in public places or obscene forms of the same art in public toilets.[38] In the 1960s leaders of Mexican-Americans in the United States protested the status of their Chicano followers not only by forming protest organizations but also through their own "rhetorical discourse" that gradually was reported in the mass media. Such discourse had been part of their tradition and reached the many followers who were illiterate.[39] Here interveners reduced uncertainty by adapting the method to their followers' attributes.

If a crisis is or seems to be at hand, some method may have to be selected with dispatch regardless of its perils. The passerby or lifeguard must almost immediately plunge into the water and swim toward the drowning child; there is no time to undress or find a boat. Professional interveners believe they know which method has been successful in their past experience, they do not hem and haw concerning its application right now. Principals, when and if they have the opportunity to select a method, favor the one that in their opinion, correctly or not, is likely to enable them to achieve their objective; it matters not that they have a limited number of choices, as in some legal systems in which litigants decide whether a decision is to be rendered by a judge or by an intervening jury of peers.

In many situations, particularly those with pressing problems, interveners carry on even in the absence of certainty that they will succeed. What can, must, should be done by a dual intervention when someone threatens suicide? Community centers have been established that try to deal with the problem when and if a principal establishes contact with them; even in the absence of completely adequate knowledge concerning suicide—so many different and diverse factors are at work, including the possible cultural ones mentioned earlier in this chapter—personnel at the centers intervene and attain some success.[40] The American Psychiatric Association once indicated that therapists "in the present state of the art" cannot foresee whether their patients will commit violence, they may overpredict such behavior, and they are more often wrong than right; hence they should not violate their own code of professional confidentiality by warning potential victims or the police of their patients' expressed intention.[41] Nevertheless, psychiatrists continue to intervene for the prosecution and the defense by offering testimony against or for patients who are guilty of violent, criminal acts.

One guide to potential principals with an unresolved problem is provided not by their replies to questions or questionnaires requiring only yes-no replies but by their numerous relevant, real actions and interactions. Nobody but the shortsighted would oppose soil conservation, yet how is that objective to be attained? No single method of intervention suffices. Instead it is essential to have governments and private agencies that formulate, monitor, and enforce regulations and also foster research on the problem; perhaps to offer subsidies to those who cooperate; and to educate present and potential principals.[42]

Influenced not by feelings of futility resulting from uncertainties but by the conviction that minor assistance to principals may be effective, interveners may leave the initiative and hence the reduction of uncertainty to other persons or to the principals themselves. Facilitators bring principals together after they have made the necessary arrangements at the site where they are to interact. When the participants have assembled, the interveners themselves keep quiet, except to offer an occasional suggestion. In the United States "an evolving toolbox of techniques" has been given a flashing label, alternative (methods of) dispute resolution (ADR), the function of which is only to indicate to principals the various available methods at their disposal for settling disputes.[43] In a civil case, should disputants go to a law court or a mediation board; should their attorneys meet informally and arrive at a settlement; should they "caucus" alone or with social workers or other professionals? Within recent years another method, that of the ombudsman, has functioned throughout the world in countries as different as Sweden and Fiji. A designated office receives complaints concerning government agencies from individual citizens and then intervenes by communicating the complaints to the relevant authorities. This intervener is usually "appointed by and [is] responsible to a legislative body to insure independence from the executive."[44] Third parties can also provide a useful method in simple, dual interventions. Upon request a good friend offers advice concerning an action to be taken without participating in the intervention, such as suggesting that the principal consult a physician or an attorney.

Uncertainty may be at least decreased by planning to control some of the conditions under which the interaction occurs. As indicated earlier in this chapter, bystanders can be included or excluded through the selection of the intervention's site. Their almost total exclusion may be achieved through subtle diplomacy, which potentially has both advantages and disadvantages. If there is direct contact between or among participants, a decision can be reached concerning the precise number of persons who will participate voluntarily or through invitation or compulsion, a challenge also previously discussed (in chapter 3). Additional guides are available concerning numbers; is it sufficient merely to follow common sense or carloads of historical and empirical evidence indicating that all aspects of human relations, whether private or public, can be affected by intervention with other persons? Controversial experiments have been conducted, especially by North American social scientists, to obtain a definitive set of generalizations concerning the influence exerted by other persons.[45] These efforts lead to the profound guide that contact can produce change in any direction, no significant change at all, or a change in the intensity of previously held viewpoints. It is to be doubted whether the following statement from a psychiatrist, who once courageously intervened in an effort to reduce conflict among factions in the Dominican Republic, is universally true: "Contact and communication between members of groups in conflict will favorably alter the images which they hold of one another."[46] An effect, yes, but always favorable? In this instance the intervener, reporting half a dozen years after the intervention, may have in fact once observed an increase in intergroup understanding, an impression precisely similar to one this writer has had concerning his own experience with a limited number of multiple interventions; and it also seems to him that some of the hostility of the principals did not change at all or may have become even more intense.

Perhaps the precise details of the intervention's methodology can be fathomed if a helpful guide to the intervention is adduced beyond the prayerful hope that prolonged contact between persons promotes trust, understanding, peace, and other virtues. Always? Of course not: ethnic groups live side by side for generations, yet remain hostile. According to one psychologist, the desegregation required by the American law of 1954 did not promote good relations between whites and the underprivileged blacks or Chicanos in the state of Texas or elsewhere in the South: riots and fights occurred. He and his associates observed at that time the actual behavior of children in the integrated classrooms. The teacher would ask a question, the hands of those with an answer would be raised, and usually those hands were white; the underprivileged or less well educated blacks and Chicanos could not respond rapidly or at all. As a result the whites in the class over time began to consider the other two groups to be slow and stupid, and the latter believed the whites to be domineering and unsympathetic. The intervener, as he has breathlessly reported, then arranged to have teachers of the experimental groups introduce in their fifth-grade classrooms what he called a jigsaw technique; equivalent classes functioned as controls and did not have that experience. The children in the experimental groups were given a series of tasks, such as to learn the life history of a fairly famous person. They were divided into six subgroups, each of which was shown a paragraph containing one-sixth of the story (the subject as a child, a young man, and so on) and told to learn the contents of the section. Later the class put the pieces together in order to have the complete story. To do so, it became evident to the children that each subgroup could contribute vital information with which the others were unacquainted; hence its members merited both attention and respect. As the technique was repeated over a six-week period, the contributions of the blacks and the Chicanos, who had previously been considered and felt inferior, tended to be respected by the whites, and their own self-esteem tended to improve. Such changes are said not to have occurred in the control or "traditional" classrooms.[47] With the jigsaw teaching method the immediate interaction of the pupils may have been affected, but the lasting effects of the experience remain unclear. In Israel the same jigsaw method, although it seemed to increase the achievement of students from a Middle Eastern background, "provoked a more negative peer evaluation from their Western classmates."[48] Here the contact affected the principals but did not increase understanding and respect.

Interventions that urge changes in behavior may remain similarly unsuccessful until a meaningful and more direct communication is provided. Consumers of electricity are told that it is to their advantage to turn out lights in empty rooms and to utilize electrical appliances with discretion. To have them cooperate they may require more than such counsel or even the sight of their monthly electric bill. Samples of Americans once consumed less electricity not when told to consume less but when informed concerning their ongoing consumption by a conspicuously displayed meter, by being provided with continuous feedback regarding that consumption, or by noticing a blue light that was automatically turned on when the outside temperature no longer required indoor air conditioning.[49] Evidence of actual saving was thus close at hand.

When principals hold deep-seated views contrary to the objective of an intervention, a subtle or prolonged method may or may not succeed; thus efforts are made not to arouse such views. The leaders of all African countries who intervened successfully to obtain at least political freedom from their colonial powers retained, with minor exceptions, the old political boundaries. In most instances those boundaries had been arbitrarily and artificially established by the domineering powers, and hence ethnically homogeneous people were placed in more than one territory or nation. After independence discussions of the old boundaries were avoided. The assignment of a name to a collection of fairly distinct cultural groups, as in the case of the Union of Soviet Socialist Republics, Yugoslavia, Czechoslovakia, and other Balkan countries, did not cause the national or ethnic identities to disappear or produce unified countries.

The drinking of alcoholic beverages, whether or not alcoholism is a consequence, has been disapproved of by some Americans; eventually in 1919 the intervention of the Eighteenth Amendment was added to the Constitution and "intoxicating liquors" were banned. This amendment and the implementing Volstead Act sought to intervene and restrict people's heavily reinforced drinking habits; it was so unsuccessful that fourteen years later it was repealed. One of the organized groups very influential in fostering the original amendment was the Anti-Saloon League, which pointed to the evils not only of drinking but of every saloon that had been allegedly the "gathering place for the street gang, the pimp, and the prostitute, as well as a den of temptation for the young and a center of political occupation." Before Prohibition the saloon had also been an important "social center for the community"—at least for men; and so thereafter two women intervened and established in a rundown Chicago area the famed Hull House that included, among its many activities, a coffee room and gymnasium where many of the saloon's functions could be performed in the absence of potentially intoxicating liquor.[50] Hull House and its associations have endured because their intervention satisfied the needs of many working-class principals who had been frustrated during the Prohibition era.

Finally, as the last salvo in behalf of reducing uncertainty, once more *the potential uniqueness of every intervention must be emphasized*. Persons experienced in interventions or those who have reviewed the literature on the subject warn again and again that no single technique is likely to be successful in all situations and hence that there is more than one way to try to resolve problems. A scholar who has surveyed the "strategies of conflict resolution" merits unanimous applause: "The diversity of approaches to conflict management cannot be reduced to one major program of intervention designed to deal with conflicts in all settings."[51] This generalization is applicable to almost any intervention, including even one so specific as the effort to teach deaf children how to deal with novel tasks in a laboratory situation.[52] It is not surprising to learn from five individuals who had been mediators in 327 disputes concerning grievances between miners and management in the American coal industry that there was "more than one way to mediate disputes successfully" (that is, without the use of arbitration) and that the interveners "chose behavioral tactics based on the kind of outcome they wished to achieve"[53]: deal making, shuttle diplomacy, pressuring the company or the union. The one-word title of the next section is the best guide in this chapter: flexibility.

Flexibility

Many pages ago in chapter 2, adaptability was identified as a personal attribute related to the decision whether to participate in an intervention. Here flexibility refers to a similar attribute that affects the method of intervention to be selected or rejected. Interveners who record a voice or a sound in behalf of some objective possess zero flexibility after the recording has been made and is being transmitted. At the other extreme is the clever salesman who strives to intervene in an individual's personal budget by adapting his general sales pitch to what he knows, and then during the conversation to what he learns about the prospective customer and his reactions. Usually techniques of intervention are neither completely inflexible nor flexible, but somewhere in between. That flexible salesman is inflexible with respect to the language he uses—to an American he does not speak Swahili even if he knows the language—or the specific promises he can offer. In a less one-sided, dual intervention a physician can decide whether to provide patients with a medical name for their ailment, since labeling names may suggest symptoms that they may not have had and that consequently may appear.

When feasible, flexibility may reduce uncertainty and facilitate some but not all interventions. What can be done about very young children who live in poverty-stricken areas or about infants suffering from Down's syndrome or some other serious difficulty? Early identification of such problems is highly desirable, even though the action that can or may be taken is unclear;[54] and it is not easy to intervene effectively in behalf of "difficult" children whose parents are "weary, confused, and angry."[55] Dramatically it has been pointed out that "an 'ideal' preventive program" for all children would be to "ensure that every child will be born with a healthy central nervous system, that he will have a set of early experiences supportive of intellectual, emotional, and social growth, and that he will be protected from damaging physical and psychological trauma"; but "we are far from having reached the level of knowledge and practice that would permit us to claim even approximation of this Utopian state."[56] Interventions in these instances are not to be abandoned; rather, interveners are prepared to adapt their technique to the particular problem at hand. Although there may be "no standard procedure" to follow when an employer intervenes to reduce employee problems such as absenteeism or unfriendliness, she may deal with the individual on a person-to-person basis and first gently praise some aspect of his record before confronting him with the difficulty.[57] One analyst suggests that flexibility is required to identify and confront the issues at stake; to provide a favorable situation in which those issues may be confronted; to attempt to remove whatever has produced misunderstanding; to seek to establish an atmosphere in which understanding becomes possible; to probe possible solutions to the problem at hand; and to promote an agreement acceptable to the principals and perhaps relevant bystanders.[58] The decision then can be made concerning not only the method and its duration but also, when possible, the kinds of individuals who are asked or assigned to participate as principals.

No less than 198 different methods have been listed under the heading of "nonviolent actions," all of which have been known and indeed can be employed to achieve the objectives of all manner of interventions without resorting to force. "Nonviolent interventions" include forty-one methods that can be divided into five "somewhat arbitrary" subclasses and are here provided with a pair of illustrations in parentheses: psychological (disrobing, fasting), physical (sit-ins, invasions), social (overloading facilities, alternative social institutions), economic (strikes, blockades), and political (overloading administrative systems, civil disobedience). Many other nonviolent methods not classified by the author under "intervention" in fact involve intervention, such as display and wearing of symbols, parades, walkouts, boycotts, lobbying, listening to forbidden radio programs, and dumping produce in world markets below standard prices.[59] Even sports can be a violent method of expressing tensions nonviolently, particularly in national rivalries like in the Olympic games.[60] Believers in the morality of nonviolent intervention, confronted with another truly gigantic embarrassment of riches, may decide beforehand which of these methods is likely to be effective during a specific intervention.

Significant and not significant details of the method to be employed vary with the attitude of the intervener toward the principal. Parents who love their children may teach and dominate them more gently than those who resent their presence. Beliefs concerning the effectiveness of punishment types also affect the selected intervention. In wars the material at a country's disposal and the estimate of the enemy's strength in the same respect determine the mode of intervention at crucial moments and over time. Attitudes toward the enemy and their effect on the intervention vary: must the enemy be annihilated because he is "a symbol of strangeness, evil and danger to the community as a whole"; must he be simply subdued so that one's own side can be enriched politically, economically, or religiously; must war be waged for "glory and justice"?[61]

The relationships of persons in many social organizations are either so complicated or so subtle that interveners must be flexible in their search for the optimal method of intervention. Blacks who were members of a government department in an American city had no difficulty communicating officially *with* other departments when their complaints or suggestions were received by whites; but they tended to resent communications *from* whites who, they felt, "normally" ordered them about. The black mayor's white assistant, he once reported privately, intervened with these blacks by communicating his messages to the mayor who in turn relayed them to the black civil servants.

Up to a point the United Nations, through its General Assembly, the Security Council, and a host of its other councils and subsidiary organizations, has had to be flexible to achieve its objectives, especially the first two listed in its page-long preamble: "to save succeeding generations from the scourge of war" and "to reaffirm faith in fundamental human rights." Selected UN officials, especially the Secretary-General, make public statements in behalf of its objectives. In addition to passing resolutions deploring the violation of human rights, UN personnel have observed and investigated conditions violating its principals in countries such as Zaire, Lebanon, Yemen, Bahrain, Somalia, and the disunited Yugoslavia. Pointed discussions take place with local officials responsible for the violations; the findings are usually publicized by the UN and the international press and on occasion UN representatives have brought together the groups or regions in conflict and functioned as mediators or arbitrators. For the pressing problems arising from civil conflicts within a country or between countries, as indicated in the previous chapter, the UN Charter itself departs from advocating nonintervention in those affairs: "at any stage of a dispute" noted by UN members or brought to their attention, "appropriate procedures or methods of adjustment" may be recommended. Furthermore, the principals in conflict may be called upon "to comply with such provisional measures as [the UN] deems necessary or desirable." The measures not involving armed force include the "complete or partial" disruption or severance of economic, communication, and diplomatic relations. Even stronger actions are "demonstrations, blockades, and other operations by air, sea, or land forces of Members." Officials on the Security Council and other UN members invited to attend the council may be called upon to supply the necessary forces: "Members shall hold immediately available national air-force contingents for combined international enforcement action."[62] Even so, however, the council has not been able to react immediately because it has had no air or armed force of its own to enforce its decisions; it has been dependent upon members both to furnish and supply those forces. On occasion, at this intervention stage assistance has been provided by a private organization, the International Peace Academy, that approached countries informally to determine whether they would supply troops and equipment to a peacekeeping force; the fruits of its investigation were then submitted to the council for approval.[63] Indirectly but necessarily, any nation that is a member of the United Nations is lending its support to these expensive interventions in behalf of peacekeeping by paying its dues to the organization, even when in a particular instance its leaders do not approve of or vote against the council's decision. A crude, sad, but relevant note in passing: beginning in 1992, the peacekeeping as well as the regular budget of the UN was facing a financial crisis because its "leading members," particularly the United States and to a slightly lesser degree Russia (for the former USSR), had been delinquent in paying their dues;[64] flexibility was therefore threatened.

Planned interventions thus can be flexible. One intervener who has been both a formal and informal diplomat as well as an academic scholar advocates and has practiced what he calls "controlled communication" in the national and international workshops under his supervision. First, he functions as a facilitator and brings together principals or informed representatives from the groups in conflict. During the workshop he and a small number of social scientists speak up occasionally and spontaneously, as seems appropriate, without proposing a solution, to "explain conflict, its origins, its escalation, sometimes by reference to other conflicts, sometimes by analytical means, but within the context of a continuing discussion" between the principals.[65] As lay bystanders they thus try to provide the principals with knowledge concerning the situation and the principles governing the disagreements.

In 1985 this writer, on the basis of the experience of others and himself with workshops,[66] decided to provide selected Cypriots with an almost unlimited opportunity to interact as they themselves wished. This venture was his second attempt to intervene unofficially in that small but important country. He recruited principals from the Greek and Turkish communities without indicating or even suggesting to them the techniques that might be employed to promote understanding and possibly to discover ways to resolve or at least to mitigate the conflict. In fact, he functioned almost completely only as a facilitator: he sought to bring them together in a hotel located in the neutral crossing point between the two communities. Finally, when permission to hold the workshop had been obtained from both governments after aggravating delays, the principals assembled there one afternoon. As the intervener, he called them to order and suggested they take seats at a round table. After very brief, perfunctory, welcoming remarks by a United Nations official and by himself, they were told that the meeting was now theirs and that they could do whatever they wished. Being trained in the Western tradition that almost always resorts to conventional parliamentary procedure, they reacted with shocked surprise; they were told again to follow their own inclinations. One principal cracked the silence by telling a joke—a good one in my opinion—that seemed to highlight their conflict in a remotely metaphorical manner. Immediately thereafter they plunged into a discussion of the difficulties confronting Cyprus. Before going home that evening, they planned to have the group meet again the next week; and they did so during the next few months.[67] These Cypriots thus had the maximum flexibility the intervener had contemplated.

On a nonpolitical, compelling level looms the problem of improving children's intelligence. Suppose that intelligence is measured by means of a conventional intelligence quotient (IQ) test. Then the number of problems confronting interveners, as a most competent, lengthy review of relevant research in the United States once demonstrated,[68] is staggering. Which children should be the principals, preschool or those in school, those with low or average IQs, those from deprived or moderately wealthy households? Where should the intervention take place, in the home or the playground or the school? Who should be the principals: the children themselves, their mothers, their fathers, both parents, the teachers, or even their playmates? What are the attributes of parents who are able and willing to cooperate with interveners for the sake of their children? For the children as principals precisely what method should be employed: verbal instruction, manipulation of their toys, interaction with other children or adults? How long should the dual intervention last, a brief interval while the children are still young or continuously over the years until they reach adolescence? At what age is any kind of intervention likely to be futile, or is "intelligence" always amenable to change? Is a comparable group of children available for nonintervention so that changes in the children who are the experimental subjects can be attributed to the intervention and not some other cause? Do changes occur only when individuals with particular skills or personality traits become the interveners? Why are interventions successful with some children and not with others? These possible variables and variations, though indicating the complexity of the intervention, do not suggest that the situation is hopeless. By being somewhat reckless and admitting their inability to be concerned with all the questions and doubts just listed, interveners may plunge in and thus, first of all, affect advantageously the children they select as principals at a given time and with a particular method; and, second, at the very least provide guides for future interventions. Perhaps the best guide for the present American generation has been forcefully expressed by the same psychologist:

> The family is the most effective and economic system for fostering and sustaining the development of the child. . . the involvement of the child's family as an active participant is critical to the success of any intervention program. Without such family involvement, any effects of intervention, at least in the cognitive sphere, appear to erode rapidly once the program ends. In contrast, the involvement of the parents as partners in the enterprise provides an ongoing system which can reinforce the effect of the program while it is in operation, and help to sustain them after the program ends.[69]

Flexibility may be helpful and necessary to uncover the "deeper" layers of principals' personalities. People generally tend to conceal their "true" selves to create a more favorable impression upon others and thus perhaps to influence or control them; they also provide not necessarily accurate explanations of their own behavior.[70] In conflict situations, moreover, principals may shift their feelings of identity and hence their mode of expression in order to experience and demonstrate their loyalty to a group or a viewpoint with which they feel fully or partially identified.[71] During the tensions and excitement of interaction in many interventions such repressions may spring loose; but again it would be perilous to conclude in advance or thereafter that truth will thus always out or be the consequence of intense interaction.

Quite obviously many but not all principals are flexible as they contemplate participating even in nondomineering interventions. Ailing individuals, when the choice is theirs, select the kind of physician they believe to be related to their difficulty; they consult an otolaryngologist and not an opthamologist when their throat aches. Principals may deduce in advance something about the methods interveners employ on the basis of their status, profession, or reputation. And then interveners try to anticipate whether principals will or will not conform to whatever resolution is likely to result from the intervention.

From the intervener's standpoint, it may be necessary to decide at the onset whether a series of interactions over time is necessary or desirable. Psychiatrists know that a single session for most emotional difficulties may accomplish only a limited objective, such as establishing rapport, and that therefore patients must agree to return subsequently, sometimes over a long period of time. In multiple interventions, when groups are in conflict, interveners utilize what has been unjargonistically called a step-by-step approach: if limited agreements are perhaps achieved during the first interaction, then later more of the significant issues can be discussed. Henry Kissinger as American secretary of state employed this technique in the Middle East without appreciable success at the time. Later, in October 1991, representatives of Israel and Middle Eastern countries met in Madrid but settled none of their differences; at least they had agreed to meet and interact. They also agreed to meet again two months later in Washington, where once more no substantial issues were settled; yet the site of a third meeting, Moscow, was selected. Interactions continued, though progress toward a resolution of the major political problems remained painfully slow.

Moral consideration aside, a high degree of flexibility is essential when the intervention is covert, which on a national basis includes "secret propaganda, manipulation of foreign electoral processes, overthrowing of governments, secret financial assistance, paramilitary operations, and assassination of political leaders."[72] Such secrecy is important for two reasons. Through concealing the identity and purpose of the interveners, the enterprise's chance of being successful may increase: you do not warn an enemy leader that you are planning to assassinate him. Moreover, such activity is considered morally wrong and therefore is hidden. In less lethal interventions the identity of the intervener is not revealed: nasty rumors are deliberately spread concerning a political opponent, the ingredients of a competitor's product, or the amoral character of a professional athlete or of a rival in an affair of the heart.

Flexibility, however, cannot be the guiding panacea for all situations and for resolving all unresolved problems. Interventions backed by tradition or authority can be inflexible and successful. According to the stereotype, the stern, rigid parent or dictator intervenes to regulate or dominate a principal's behavior and tolerates only obedience. In a court of law the overall procedure is standardized; the order in which the prosecution and defense may speak out, the kinds of testimony that may be offered, the ways in which a verdict is reached, and the range of punishments in criminal cases are predetermined more or less in broad terms. In American labor disputes when arbitration is compulsory, procedures are established in advance that, though more flexible than courts of law, must also be somewhat standardized. Indeed, principals may regard flexibility as a sign of weakness and feel less respectful toward the intervener. They may be convinced that inflexibility itself has advantages: portions of the interaction can be anticipated and advance preparations can be made. In a Western-type court both the prosecution and the defense know that they will have an opportunity to present their cases.

In the final analysis, as the trite but appropriate phrase states, the selection of methods in advance depends upon pragmatic consider-ations.[73] Interveners may and do use those techniques that have been successful in the past; precedent is one of the acclaimed guides in the legal and everyday thinking in most, probably all, societies. But stare decisis may be a perilous guide because, as previously indicated, the legal precedents or past experiences may be so numerous that some selection to deal with the present event must be made. If the devil quotes Scripture to justify her (or his, if you insist) evil deeds, then participants, good or bad, may exercise the same privilege. Inter-veners, therefore, may ignore experience and do whatever seems sensi-ble to resolve the problem at hand. If participants are driven by a sense of urgency, they may select the most expedient method. Interveners in multiple interventions may grope to find the method that treats both sets of principals "fairly," and the principals themselves may opt for the method they believe increases their own chances of emerging suc-cessfully. Conceivably, too, inappropriate or unpromising methods may be sought by participants who, consciously or unconsciously, would not solve the problem at hand.

For an equally infinite number of reasons, potential principals may favor and decide upon nonintervention; and interveners may limit their intervention to proposing another form of intervention rather than their own. The ill person hopes he will recover without consulting a physician or the physician decides, on the basis of a brief conversation with the patient, that the ailment requires the services of another physician with skills different from his own. In most elections in the United States usually less than 50 percent of the eligible persons do not register to vote or, if registered, do not vote, which means that the nonvoters do not exercise the acclaimed privilege of intervening in governmental affairs by expressing their preference for one candidate or policy rather than another. For some persons such nonintervention is associated not particularly with low income and little education but with "attitudinal factors," such as the conviction that voting is irrele-vant to their existence or that elections do not affect government meaningfully.[74] In international affairs a third party who could have been the intervener recommends that the groups mediate their own conflict; that party may try, perhaps vainly, to point out the potential benefits of mediation or he suggests inducements resulting from the process or penalties from not doing so.[75] The potential intervener may convince himself that "values or beliefs that are deeply held" by principals in nations in conflict "are simply not negotiable because there is no room for concession making;"[76] and yet the Berlin Wall and its metaphorical equivalent elsewhere have come tumbling down so that this conviction is a truly perilous guide.

Inaction is often favored as a form of nonintervention concerning an actual resolution of the problem at hand: participants only issue warnings verbally or perform actions not related directly to the conceivable intervention, so that the intervention itself does not occur. The patient has an incurable disease; therefore the physician knows that surgery is futile or, whether or not the patient himself is convinced that his chances to survive are close to zero, nothing is done except to ease his existence as much as possible. Hatred between two principals is so intense that only a heavenly intervention might enable them to respect or love each other. A country's leaders are so irrevocably committed to a policy or an action that threats or diplomacy do not alter their determination to pursue their own ends.[77] In some situations interveners may not be available; the principals consider that intervention is too costly, too time-consuming, too risky, and so on. Nonintervention guides, nevertheless, are also risky; hope for an appropriate intervention may be abandoned too soon.

Record Keeping

For a number of reasons it is useful and desirable to keep a record of what occurs before, during, and after an intervention. Routinely physicians have such a record of their encounters with patients so that in the future, when necessary, they can remind themselves of details and also note ensuing changes in their condition. Records diminish the surprises and uncertainties when similar or different problems arise later, and in some instances may provide legal evidence concerning the resolution that has been reached. Morally it may be considered desirable and obligatory to inform participants beforehand that the interaction will be or is being recorded.

What kind of record shall there be? The memory of participants cannot be trusted usually, and when more than two persons participate, conflicting versions of intervention may be recalled. What is needed, as historians suggest, is an analysis that knits together the pieces of a chronology so that the reasons for the successes and the failures become intelligible. The give-and-take of participants may be so rapid that it may be impossible at the time to note the reactions of particular individuals. The ideal solution for recording is to tape or videotape the proceedings. Accuracy is thus increased, yet the presence of an instrument may make participants self-conscious and perhaps distort their reactions during the interaction. Such self-consciousness, however, may rapidly disappear since the presence of a recording device is quickly forgotten under most circumstances. In some interventions, particularly those of an international nature, recording the participants' words and actions may expose them to criticism or danger. The analysis of tapes after the interaction has ended, moreover, is time-consuming, expensive, and sometimes boring.

In this chapter and in the three preceding ones the principal factors have been delineated which indicate to the interveners, the principals, or both whether or not an intervention is feasible. Will the intervention actually occur when these factors have been considered and are thought to be propitious? No, what is thought to be feasible may not be morally satisfactory. This final stumbling block must now be surveyed.

MORALITY

Chapter Six

When deciding why, when, and how to intervene or to participate in an intervention, participants wittingly or unwittingly also face a set of moral questions or, in retrospect, they once did. For intervention in any form requires that interveners interfere with the judgment or behavior of other persons, the principals. Interveners may be convinced that the contemplated intervention will benefit the principals, who, however, may not agree with them at the moment or in the long run. The difference between interveners and principals then becomes a moral one. At the outset the most basic assumption behind interventions is that someone—a principal, a group of principals, and also whoever intervenes—but not necessarily everyone will gain by participating rather than not participating. Afterward someone is likely to find cheer in the outcome even though it may be without substantiation and even though it be asserted that "momentum toward a substantial accord"[1] has not been established. Gains and losses are evaluated morally.

The first page of this book offers a definition of intervention that presumes a moral value. The definition indicates that interventions arise when there is a problem. It slyly makes the moral (or ethical—let the words be considered synonyms) assumption that a problem is to be alleviated or resolved by the intervention and that therefore an unresolved problem is deplorable. Many interveners in Western societies seek to find solutions for unresolved problems that usually include some kind of conflict, and principals presumably seek peace and quiet rather than the continuation or consequences of the conflict. Ah yes, but some persons and those in some societies believe that unresolved problems or conflicts are highly desirable. You are stimulated by the presence or actions of an opponent, you surely do not crave an intervention to eliminate such inspiration. The definition of intervention, therefore, leaves open the problem of comparing intervention and nonintervention and permits moral considerations to be the guide:[2] is a particular intervention justifiable, is it good or bad? But perhaps you and certainly many philosophers and clergy would say, are there not universals that escape moral challenges; is not conflict either in the short or long run always detrimental; is not peace, at least in one's group or society, always better than war? The replies here are varied and, as ever, reflect the human moral predicament. Yes, the moral issue can be pushed so far that we must wonder whether all actions are selfish and hence subject to moral scrutiny and perhaps condemnation. Don't mothers who intervene and prevent their children from damaging themselves, and all other successful interveners, derive satisfaction or gratification from their successes?

"He didn't want me to do it, I did it for his own good." Here is a clash of values between the "he" and the "I"—and the latter assumes that his value justifies the intervention in spite of the opposing value of "I." Again and again intervening nations claim their judgment is morally superior to the nation with which they are interfering or which they are invading. Interventionists must often come upon a value that guides, explains, or justifies their action at least to themselves, whether or not their claims are rationalizations. In the West naked aggression is not respectable; it must be disguised, both for the victim and victimizer, behind a glorious-sounding slogan or value.

This chapter contains only a single guide, consequently, and it is not perilous: *every intervention or nonintervention raises moral questions even when they are not raised by the participants and when there is no time to do so,* regardless of whether the person passing judgment—a participant, a neutral, or a biased philosophical bystander—subscribes to an absolute or a relativistic system of moral values. A stranger intervenes and prevents a blind woman from stepping into a ditch; that intervention is called good because otherwise the person would be injured. American journalists are supposed to follow the idealistic, unrealistic tradition of reporting only the facts of an event and not their own prejudiced or unprejudiced views; when they deliberately inject a viewpoint into their stories—such as "subjective" accounts of actions by or concerning minority groups or blacks[3]—they are accused of being "unethical," immoral, or biased. If there is evidence that crime and violence in a society result at least in part from the kinds of stories appearing in television programs and from the ease with which ordinary citizens can purchase handguns and other lethal weapons, then surely legal authorities intervene: should television be carefully censored and should such weapons be outlawed for private citizens or at least more rigorously controlled? But then does one really wish to curb freedom of speech and action?[4] A geneticist shudders at the thought that very impressive scientific advances in his discipline and in other disciplines enable scientists to intervene in "the very blueprint of life to affect genetic functioning and hence significant aspects of behavior."[5]

Like the *Communist Manifesto* of 1848 that called upon the "workers of the world" to intervene in their own behalf and cast off their chains, similar documents provide moral justifications for the interventions they would foster. The 1955 Freedom Charter of the African National Congress in South Africa, before asking "black and white people together" to govern themselves, to demand equal rights, to "share in the country's wealth," and to possess additional spiritual and material benefits, includes among its reasons for intervening the statement that "our people have been robbed of their birthright to land, liberty, and peace by a form of government founded on injustice and inequality." In April 1990, an official of the Greek Cypriot government (which ruled one section of the country) stated that his community had rejected "occupation, invasion, intervention, violation of natural or human rights" by Turks from the mainland; the leaders of the Turkish community approved of the intervention by the military forces as well as the economic penetration against which the official was protesting. In the same month of 1990 the parliament of Estonia passed a resolution addressed to President Mikhail Gorbachev informing him that the republic decades ago had become part of the Soviet Union "as a result of military intervention and the occupation of the territory of the Estonian republic by Soviet forces";[6] obviously the parliament was using intervention in a derogatory sense in order to condemn the Soviet action in 1940.

Previously established moral principles may provide the guide for seeking to intervene or not to intervene. A crisp generalization related to observation and experimentation suggests that "perceived violations of procedural justice rules will lead to the perception of unfairness, emotional experience of distress and behavior designed to rectify the unfair procedural act"[7]—and here "rectify" is equivalent to intervention. In real life, Afrikaner scholars investigating the social and political role of religion in South Africa in the early 1980s noted that "at the centre of intergroup conflict is the perception by groups that they are being unjustly treated" and that whether that perception is "wrong or distorted . . . does not make the sense of being wrongfully treated any less real for those involved"; the problem in their country, they said, thus involved "political rights" and "the system" allowing those rights to be exercised.[8] Generally, as phrased in various sacred clichés, criminals must be punished by legal authorities, rascals should be thrown out of office, a crusade in behalf of righteousness must go forward regardless of sacrifices. The government of the Islamic country of Saudi Arabia, its crown prince once stated to an American audience, intervenes in the lives of its citizens in order to achieve "modernization" but not "Westernization."[9]

Moral issues concerning the aforementioned problems have been discussed, debated, and resolved or unresolved throughout the ages.

A branch of philosophy and these days special committees of attorneys, physicians, and government officials freely and abundantly pounce upon issues that are called "ethical." Almost always attention quite properly is directed to the question of "ought" or "should," auxiliaries that embrace the moral imperative. Immanuel Kant, when discussing the "speculative" and "rational" aspects of what he called pure reason, enlarged the moral problem by asking, "If I do what I ought to do, what may I then hope?"[10] Elsewhere, without at the time being aware of the Kantian reference to the future consequences of any action, the view was modestly advanced that among live human beings, as distinguished from the detached though useful abstractions of ethicists and moralists, additional questions must be raised and answered before moral judgments can be complete and give rise to moral behavior.[11] These questions include specific references to the capabilities of human beings as well as to the mandates of their society. It is useless or foolish—I am uncertain which—to pronounce a moral injunction without taking into account the present desires and propensities of the person for whom it is intended. Consider the moral judgments of an individual who is deciding whether to be a principal in an intervention. He favors a resolution of a conflict and not its continuation. He believes he has more to lose by not participating than by participating. He is convinced that it is "proper" to do so. He feels obligated to participate. He anticipates benefits rather than deficits from the intervention. He favors a resolution from his standpoint. He will really adhere to the resolution that is reached; and previous experience suggests to him that such an intervention will be beneficial.

A morally complete analysis is compelling when it considers a variety of *will, can, may, must,* and *should* issues. Should physicians intervene to keep terminally ill people alive?[12] The moral question concerning euthanasia arises now because the deed more readily occurs as a result of the impressive advances in medical technology. Must such persons be kept alive, is human life always sacred? May expensive apparatus be employed toward that end when it is needed for other patients in the hospital or the community? Should not the money and care being expended to keep these patients alive be utilized in other ways, for patients who are not suffering from an incurable illness, or for persons in general in order to prevent them from becoming ill? Should the relatives and friends of the patients be ignored when they would have those they love and respect be kept even vegetatively alive because—well, may not the prognosis of the physicians turn out to be wrong, isn't there always the possibility of a miraculous recovery? What might occur if medical students and physicians are not trained to accomplish such interventions and devote their energies to other medical problems? Finally, there is the moral question concerning who is entitled to make the decision concerning the prolongation of life: legal or religious authorities who permit or prohibit the practice; physicians or nurses; relatives of comatose persons; or the patients themselves who have signed a legal declaration before becoming ill. This last issue once came to a tragic climax for one patient who had stated previously that he wished to die if ever there was the possibility that he would suffer the "slow, agonizing" death he had witnessed in the case of his wife; later he had a debilitating stroke and was revived by a nurse; thereafter he was partly paralyzed, could scarcely speak, was confined to a nursing home, and was expending his life savings. He then filed suit against the hospital for saving his life.[13]

The extent to which potential participants consider moral values inherent in an intervention depends in part upon the time available to reach a decision. As suggested in chapter 4, their temporal perspective plays a role. They may hesitate to consider the moral factors, or concern for those factors may induce them to hesitate. Should you join a political organization that seeks to improve the city's parks by protecting and planting trees? To save that drowning child, there is no time at the moment for moral quibbling, but our rescuer may have previously subscribed to the view that human life is precious and that he will intervene when necessary to save it.

Ten Perilous Commandments

Let a simple assumption be made: when challenged or even when politely and gently asked, "normal" *people can almost always explain and justify or condemn an intervention they contemplate or have experienced.* They select one or more of moral issues as the guiding basis for approving or disapproving the justifications whose strength, according to a philosophical political scientist, varies from being considered "absolute," to being restricted only to oneself.[14] Whether they are expressing an eternal truth, a momentary or superficial declaration, or a well-considered rationalization is of interest, but is not the problem being addressed here. As our exciting drama of intervention unfolds, we know how most "laws," "principles," and "axioms" become outdated, such as the following distilled from the writings of Western sociologists pontificating in the last century and the first decades of the present one: "Each man is the rightful judge of his own desires and the appropriate protector of his own interests"; "Every restriction of competition is an evil, and every extension of it is always an ultimate good."[15] What people believe at the given moment of intervention—whether accurately or inaccurately from the viewpoint of someone else or of those supposedly competent to judge—is their reality, and the beliefs function as guides to behavior, even as a paranoid person murders an innocent person who, in his own distorted opinion, is about to attack him. Here the attempt is being made to list and briefly discuss prominent justifications that appear again and again in connection with interventions. The attempt is perilous and merits criticism by professionals, but it serves the function of alerting us to the ever-present assumption and ascription of morality.

The justifications are called commandments because whatever their origin, they serve as moral guides. But they themselves are also admittedly perilous because, like the ordinary mortals who adhere to such guides, they are incomplete: each one contemplates only a limited number of critical issues. They tend to concentrate on the *may* and *must* in order to derive the *ought*. I may do this or I must do this and therefore I ought to do it. In addition, no one of the commandments is absolute or without exceptions and the injunctions frequently contradict one another. In a given situation a commandment may be intoned by an intervener and then accepted or rejected for moral reasons by principals who are affected or by bystanders who would understand or analyze those reasons. No claim is being made that the commandments constitute a complete inventory, rather they would humbly illustrate the moral process. Why ten? There could be more or fewer; but, so help this writer, that number really happened to emerge from his notes and thoughts even before he considered calling them commandments and not because he deliberately sought to use Exodus 20 as a model. Admittedly they overlap, and thus portray the mode of thinking characterizing him and probably even you.

In the remainder of this chapter each commandment is illustrated but not thoroughly dissected with reference to the critical questions that might be raised. A loose distinction is drawn between Concrete Commandments, which refer to a particular aspect of an intervention, and Abstract Commandments, which refer to an intervention itself. These commandments, like eight of the ten in Exodus, are phrased negatively to highlight the potential disapproval inherent in interventions, and hence "moral outrage" is frequently invoked. Negatives imply positives and therefore the positive values of intervention are mentioned; thus there are absolutistic justifications (such as divine sanction, destiny, nature, humanitarian responsibility, freedom, security, justice, etc.) as well as those that can be called personificative (such as birthright, consanguinity, need, public opinion, etc.), all of which have been and are being employed in behalf of nationalistic interventions.[16] But such positive sermons on the mount would push the discussion into too numerous and fascinating tangents in their own right. The values of intervention cannot be buttressed with convincing evidence. Each can serve as a guide, yet like all guides, each is perilous since almost always exceptions not only occur but may also be favored.

Concrete Commandments

1. Disapproved in intervention is killing per se. Human life is sacred and hence an intervention that results in death requires an additional commandment to be justified. An insane person is about to shoot an innocent child; a desperate hijacker or a country's leader threatens to kill one or more hostages unless his demands are met—what should be done? This commandment is violated with approval when the goal of intervention is to prevent the killing of another human being or, especially, of oneself. For then the sacredness of existence is invoked, and the villain or criminal may be prevented from achieving his objective. Legal and factual arguments must be invoked in Western courts to claim the plea of self-defense.

Obviously wars involve killing and hence have received careful scrutiny from viewpoints ranging from unequivocal pacifism to the need for self-defense to a belief in the "just" war that is operationally and never satisfactorily defined because most persons are ashamed to kill another human being. When killing is respectable, however, elaborate explanations may be required to justify nonintervention. Shortly after an armistice in the Persian Gulf War was declared, a group calling itself Concerned Citizens of Japan, representing "numerous Japanese citizens" of various ages and in diverse professions, published under the heading INTERNATIONAL CONFLICT CANNOT BE SOLVED BY INTERNATIONAL FORCE a full-page advertisement in the *New York Times* to justify their country's failure to send combatants to help subdue Iraq directly. The declaration began as follows:

> Iraq's invasion and annexation of Kuwait was unjust, misguided, brutal, and opposed by the majority of the world's people. Many peaceful ways of bringing it to an end were proposed and were in the process of being enacted. All these efforts were swept aside, however, by the massive military intervention of the Multinational Forces and their swift victory.

After quoting from the Japanese constitution concerning the "Renunciation of War," the same document indicated that the Japanese learned from their own devastating experience in World War II "the horror of killing and being killed" and that "war isn't horrifying only when your own people are killed." Therefore:

> When the Japanese Government tried to send our already un-constitutional Self-Defense Forces to the Gulf, public opposition in Japan was massive. . . . The government was isolated and the first deployment of Japanese forces abroad since World War II was successfully blocked.[17]

In fact, the Japanese aided the forces against Iraq not with soldiers but with financial and material aid.

One writer has avoided this commandment against killing by excluding from the category of intervention all military coups "designed to uphold some established rule of law";[18] but surely an arbitrary definition of intervention in terms of some approved commandment does not affect persons who consider such coups a form of intervention that results in deaths. What of the coup that overturned the Ferdinand Marcos regime in the Philippines in 1986 when that regime, according to the victors and many outsiders, was guilty of graft, corruption, and the killing of opponents? Lenin and his associates, who seized power from the Mensheviks (who in turn had overthrown the czarist regime), likewise produced casualties while claiming to be acting in behalf of all the people in Russia and the attached or semiattached republics as indicated in their slogan of the "dictatorship of the proletariat," even though that proletariat may not have assigned them that role. What right has a small group, however motivated, to intervene allegedly for the sake of a larger group of principals who might not have made that decision if they had been consulted?

The same commandment is applicable to nonintervention in a different form: if intervention can save a human life, do the individuals have an obligation to intervene to rescue someone in danger? The child in the lake cries for help and the passerby does not respond because he cannot swim or because he is afraid that he himself will be caught in the current; a family in a burning building cannot escape unless a fireman risks his life and braves the flames. Recall, in addition, the moral debate concerning guides to euthanasia.

2. *Disapproved in interventions is damage to other persons.* Damages, less serious than killing, include not only property and other aspects of the physical environment but also the abuse of persons. Stealing is almost always condemned even when the motive is considered praiseworthy. Arson is a crime although individuals are not directly hurt; forests devastated by carelessness or stupidity may eventually flourish again, but in the interim people are deprived of solace, beauty, and timber. Psychiatrically, as emphasized in chapter 4, it is not always possible, in fact it may be impossible, to anticipate whether or when an individual will become violent. Actuarial reasoning here is not sufficient, though tempting to employ: if a person commits one violent act, will he repeat the performance in the future? To be socially safe, should he be guarded or imprisoned even though his personal freedom is thus damaged? A legal issue arises here, especially in connection with someone who has not committed a single crime but who, on the basis of some psychiatric criterion or of confidential information he himself has provided, is thought to be inclined to do so: should such persons be restrained in order to avoid considerable damage in the future? Should potential victims or even the police be warned, even though the warning may not be heeded or turn out to be unnecessary? At the very outset of a most thorough collection of struggling analyses by Canadian and American psychiatrists, criminologists, and legal and social science scholars, the editors have indicated that "the prediction of dangerous behavior has become a central topic in psychiatry during recent years" and that "there have been many patients, relatives, and professionals whose lives have been affected by recent key legal rulings on issues related to the prediction" of such behavior.[19]

By definition, whenever the issue of triage arises, interveners with power must make a difficult, painful moral decision: the medicine, the food, the allotted tickets, the luxuries, or the comforts are in short supply and therefore some persons must be deprived or sacrificed and others must be spared or will benefit.[20] Ultimately some triage is always inevitable; human beings everywhere are so interdependent that favoring some of them damages others.

3. Disapproved in interventions is the use of force. The prevention of killing and of damage may require force, a form of action that is more closely associated with multiple than with dual interventions and that is usually condemned. None of us presumably like dominating interveners: bullies who force us to do what we don't want to do or to sign on the dotted line. According to one political scientist, jurists in the classical sense and especially during the nineteenth century have tended to consider intervention "a forceful measure, involving the use of armed force but short of war, which is designed to coerce another state in the conduct of its own affairs"; preventive intervention thus had become action "not only in the face of outright attack, but also to counter a threat to a state's vital or essential interests."[21] A resolution of the UN General Assembly in 1970 labeled "Declaration of Principles of International Law" proclaims that "Every State has the duty to refrain from the threat or use of force . . . as a means of solving international disputes."[22] This agreement has been frequently violated by national leaders able or eager, or both, to foster the interests of their own country. Such interveners apparently have not been concerned with a strict interpretation of the UN's commandments against intervening; rather they have invoked other commandments such as those involving human rights or taboos against killing in general. The motive of revenge is rarely mentioned publicly: it is inspiring but not respectable.

There is a close relation between the first three commandments. The outstanding scholarly treatise on blacks in the United States before World War II suggests how all three of them were violated by some intervening whites: "It is the custom in the South to permit whites to resort to violence and threats of violence against the life, personal security, property and freedom of movements of Negroes [by exercising] a wide variety of behavior, ranging from a mild admonition to murder."[23] Over time such interventions have been outlawed and have disappeared, decreased, or been replaced by subtler, discriminatory interventions that violate other commandments concerning human rights.

4. *Disapproved in interventions is interference.* We must do as we like, we must obey that impulse, we must plan our own lives, we will not tolerate interference by others. The commandment here embodies an ancient cry, although it is immediately evident, as must be repeated, that interventions by definition presume interference by interveners. Commandment 4 is perilous since it slyly conceals the additional values that must be functioning before interference is tolerated. You have no right to interfere with me, have you? Under all circumstances? What about the three commandments just proclaimed, when I would kill or damage you, force you to do what you do not wish to do? Again a contradiction arises: if nobody except a psychopath questions the right of someone to intervene in order to try to prevent a raving maniac from committing mayhem, surely the same moral doubt arises when the government of another country is known to violate any of the items nobly expressed in the UN's own "Universal Declaration of Human Rights": "No one shall be subjected to torture or to cruel, inhuman, or degrading treatment or punishment."[24] One nation respects the rights of another nation to treat its own economy and citizens as it wishes, yet bystanders, including leaders but usually private groups and individuals in other countries, lodge protests when human rights of its citizens appear to be violated. As the wars in Vietnam and Afghanistan demonstrated, the superpowers have not been loath to violate the sovereignty of other nations in order to support the factions therein that received their approval:[25] they sought to justify the intrusion by references to one or more of the commandments that declaim human rights, ostensibly for the invaded inhabitants they would "protect."

From a slightly different vantage point: is it always essential to respect the territorial integrity of other nations, are the internal affairs of a nation of concern only to that nation even when they are thought to violate international law or some precious or respected doctrine involving human rights? The decision of bystanders to intervene here presupposes some higher moral right or responsibility, although selfish interests may also be paramount. Indeed, as the interdependence of all human beings on this planet is being increasingly appreciated, the decision to intervene outside national borders becomes more compelling. The destruction of a forest in one country affects the chemistry of the environment almost everywhere; consequently is the decision to intervene in that country morally justified?

In international affairs, this commandment is disobeyed when other principals are thought to be violating commandments to which interveners subscribe. In his 1985 State of the Union address President Reagan declared, "We must not break faith with those who are risking their lives on every continent from Afghanistan to Nicaragua to defy Soviet-supported aggression." According to a senior official of the Reagan administration, this declaration meant "the right to dictate the form of another country's government," inasmuch as "some rights are more fundamental than the right of nations to nonintervention, like the rights of individual people"; therefore the United States does not "have the right to subvert a democratic government, but we do have the right against an undemocratic one."[26]

Some citizens in newly independent states have been politically and socially disturbed by their own leaders' policy to retain or achieve a one-party state rather than to permit or encourage parties with diverse viewpoints. The contrary view, especially of Westerners controlling economic aid to those countries, has been that multi- rather than one-party states can achieve "democracy" when parties compete for political approval and power.[27] The proponents of one-party states insist—or used to insist—that at this stage in their development African countries cannot tolerate those parties: disaster would result but, more important, such parties would be likely to be organized along ethnic (or "tribal") lines and hence to retard the development of political unity and stability. Which objective is more important at present or in the long run?

This commandment, it now seems evident, expresses an unrealizable guide almost always, but one that shines brightly and gives us courage to struggle on.

Abstract Commandments

5. Disapproved are interventions that violate an esteemed principle.

Religion—the mere mentioning of this word is sufficient to recall the countless interventions undertaken by the followers of almost all organized religions to defend and extend their own beliefs and practices. Elaboration is unnecessary; a reference to concepts in one's vocabulary will suffice: holy war, missionary, sacrilege, conversion, Veda, blasphemy, Koran scriptures, paradise, sin. St. Thomas Aquinas advanced numerous objections to one form of interventionism, suicide, the ultimate method of intervening in behalf of oneself. Suicide, he thought, is "contrary to the inclination of nature, and to charity whereby every man should love himself"; it "injures the community" of which "every man is a part"; and it "sins against God" who "alone" may "pronounce sentence of death and life."[28]

Ordinarily most persons respect their own religious and political authorities, who are considered legitimate interveners in everyday thinking and existence, and therefore they are to be obeyed. Intervening to disobey them is usually condemned, and so penalties ranging from disapproval and ostracism to fines and jailing are imposed. To intervene in order to produce change requires not only courage but also a principle indicating that customary obedience and nonintervention violate a significant principle: one's conscience does not countenance continued obedience. The claim of legitimacy is denied: "If legitimacy rests on an electoral process, a power holder who came into office through a military coup may be objectively defined as illegitimate" and be disobeyed and toppled from power.[29]

Participants' doctrines concerning inevitability, whether they take the form of determinism, fatalism, or destiny, not only affect their intention to participate in interventions, as previously indicated in chapter 2, but also may be expressions of moral doctrines that they treasure and draw upon to appraise interventions. To assert that all interventions are futile or that a specific one will accomplish little or nothing is a violation of a principle seldom accepted completely by human beings. Somehow we must and can intervene, they think, if only to avoid injustice, which, someone probably has said, may be more meaningful and easier to define than justice itself. "God's will be done" suggests that it would be sacrilegious to intervene and hence that nonintervention is the more sacred course. This view of events is thus related to the participants' conviction as to whether they actually are able to intervene or seek an intervention. In addition, the moral value of intervention results from a reconsideration of past events: was it my duty then to keep silent, should I have helped, was I spared by destiny not to have been present or to be born after the tragedy occurred? Every doctrine pertaining to inevitability, whether its moral overtones are explicit or implied, thus tolerates or requires an exception or at least some degree of intervention. The most determined determinist eventually admits that we do not know enough to be absolutely certain at the moment or that another principle must be invoked to account for the event in question; and the most devout fatalist will rescue that drowning child, whether or not he thinks the child was fated to drown. From a practical standpoint, a paradoxical observation is apparent: "We seek inevitability, but we would also intervene."[30]

Similar words can indicate political interventions that did, do, and will secure approval or disapproval: *democracy, communism, development, dictatorship, parliament.* In most interventions, potential principals may consider the justice of the proposed procedure or method, definitions and conceptualizations of which vary considerably from society to society and from person to person, as philosophical and legal thinkers have suggested since ancient times. For some, justice may be procedural: they would have the intervention and the outcome be fair, honest, and unprejudiced. Others seek equality when benefits or goods are in dispute and are to be distributed as a result of the intervention. Still others may wish for equity: the benefits, they believe, should be distributed according to the contribution of the disputing principals to the resources at hand. Perhaps their value is that of need, which means that disputing principals should receive shares as a function of what they require to survive or to survive satisfactorily. There is, finally, "restorative justice" which, according to one psychologist, may involve retribution or some form of revenge; restitution or righting a wrong in proportion to whatever damage has occurred; compensation; or even forgiveness. The active form of justice anticipated from the intervention may depend upon the nature of the problem, the relationship of the principals, and ways in which the principals characterize each other.[31] Some interveners may be able to distinguish between legally required and morally responsible actions, and they may believe that a legal requirement receiving their approval must also be morally justified.

Questions arise concerning the significant details to which attention must be paid as guides to this commandment of justice. Principals consider the rules governing the intervention and their "fairness" or "reasonableness," including the opportunity to express their own viewpoints.[32] In multiple interventions, the principals of both sides must have equal or nearly equal access to interveners before and during the actual interaction; and the interveners themselves must not favor one side over the other. Governmental bodies in contrast with private citizens, and large corporations in contrast with groups seeking to protect the environment, are likely, particularly in the United States, to have greater resources at their disposal; hence they are in a more advantageous position to afford the costs in planning and participating in mediation, especially when the process is prolonged or required by custom or law.[33] Contrary to some of his legal colleagues, a jurist argues that principals who submit their disputes to mediation may reach a settlement that produces peace but not justice. In contrast, civil litigation in a court of law is "an institutional arrangement for using state power to bring a recalcitrant reality closer to our chosen ideals": the relation of the case to precedent and future implications is taken into consideration.[34]

6. *Disapproved are interventions that violate "truth"*. Truth is one of those virtues that is not supposed to be contravened during an intervention, but still this commandment must be intoned. Interveners who have lied in the past lose credibility in the present and future. But truth may be concealed, or downright lies may be necessary or encouraged in tracking down a criminal or in waging a war. A

quick personal note: Although this writer believed himself to be a staunch believer in truthful communication, as a government official he did not blink when he and others in the American Office of War Information during World War II implemented what they boasted publicly to be a "strategy of truth" by deliberately slanting the news their mass media communicated throughout the world; also they and I willingly cooperated with the Office of Strategic Services in planning "black propaganda" (for example, spreading false rumors). We were not morally disturbed because it seemed much more important—and moral?—to win the war against the Nazis and those responsible for bombing Pearl Harbor than to follow the commandment concerning honesty.

Personal matters, such as the love letters of a deceased person, are not to be cited as evidence in an intervention; yet the sexual peccadilloes of prominent candidates are sometimes publicized in American political campaigns. An authority orders a principal to be arrested because what he has written is obscene or blasphemous and hence allegedly likely to damage the young or because it is clearly immoral; yet its author believes he is telling the truth.

Utilizing what is considered to be a wrong method of intervention violates this commandment. To diminish juvenile delinquency, it has been argued, it is better not to follow the medical model that focuses upon patients but to concentrate upon families and schools, especially because "our knowledge of causes of delinquency is not sufficient to permit making early accurate diagnosis of the condition."[35] Here the sincerity and motivation of interveners addicted to the model are not being questioned; rather they are said to be misleading principals and themselves. But subsequent evidence may vindicate them and not those with an agnostic, defeatist viewpoint. Ah yes, one does and must ask throughout eternity, what is truth?

7. *Disapproved are interventions that violate human rights.* In modern times references to human rights are frequent and appear in varied contexts. A parent who abuses his child is violating a human right, but at what age and under what circumstances has the child the right to disobey a parent whose intervention, according to that inter-

vener, is for the immediate or the ultimate welfare of the child? The problem of abortion, intervening to prevent the growth of the embryo and the eventual birth of the infant, is an especially tense issue in many countries. So-called pro-choice groups contend that every woman has the right to control the inside of her own body and so to decide to abort or not to abort; hence the state should follow a policy of nonintervention. The antiabortion groups, when not invoking a doctrine such as a taboo stemming from theology, assert the right of the unborn to live and to be born on the assumption that its life begins at the moment of conception. Whether or not "life" truly begins at that moment may be in dispute or a matter of definition, but the pro-choice group contends that the pro-life group has the right to subscribe to its own belief without imposing that view upon others.[36]

Rights are attributed to groups, often by invoking a commandment of sovereignty that is not supposed to be violated. Even as each of fifty states comprising the United States has two senators in Congress regardless of its size, so every nation has a single representative in the General Assembly of the United Nations, regardless of its size or strength. As the United Nations was established, however, another principle, that of population size, was recognized in one instance: the Soviet Union as well as two of its republics secured membership. That principle also determines the number of seats for each of the fifty states in the American House of Representatives. The UN Security Council adheres to a mixed principle: it is composed of a representative from each of the five principal victors in World War II and ten nonpermanent members elected by the General Assembly for two years.

References to human rights appear frequently in contemporary international conflicts. Again the divided country of Cyprus has stepped forward as a clear-cut illustration. At the beginning of 1990 and thereafter when its two communities were deadlocked in their effort to reach some kind of settlement concerning the division of their small island into two separate and isolated states within a federation, each side claimed rights to justify its policies in the negotiations.

Turkish Cyprus: The separate right of self-determination of each of these two peoples [has been] recognized internationally since the 1950's.[37]

Greek Cyprus: What is at stake in Cyprus is whether states made up of more than one ethnic community can survive intact within secure boundaries or whether they will be allowed to fragment as each community claims that the only way to safeguard its rights is to secede under the banner of self-determination, with the backing of military intervention by a foreign power.[38]

In the same context the use of the words *imperialism* or *aggression* always suggests that one or more powerful nations is interfering in the affairs of another country or invading its sovereignty for some mercenary or selfish reason, whether or not the principals in the invaded country become slaves or semislaves and whether or not they reap material benefits from the intervention. Bystanders, moreover, may agree that the rights of the invaded country are being violated, or they may applaud the invasion when they believe that the aim of the intervening country is to protect the rights of persons in the invaded country because those rights have been violated by its own rulers. Moral commandments once again may be promulgated as rationalizations for other objectives. Indian writers have maintained that the powerful nations of the West have intervened in the lands bordering on the Indian Ocean not for humanitarian but for military reasons, especially during the period of Soviet-American rivalry, and also for economic motives involving trade, raw materials, and oil.[39]

8. *Disapproved are interventions conducted without the principals' consent.* This commandment assumes that interventions are permissible, possibly also desirable, without the consent of those being affected when and only when the principals are very young children. In fact, the exceptions raise problems in their own right which the commandment does not consider. The four concrete commandments specify in effect that consent has not been obtained, but there are also

situations in which commandments, may be violated without concern for them. Consider a methodological problem in many research investigations designed to provide benefits to mankind. Competent objective investigators immediately recognize the procedure to be followed: they select a sample of the relevant population and without their consent divide them randomly into a so-called experimental and control group; they measure both groups before beginning the investigation; they subject the experimental group to the intervention (such as a form of guidance or a drug); and they leave the control group alone. After the intervention they again measure both groups and discover whether there is a difference between them. Since members of the two groups have been randomly distributed, presumably they did not differ at the outset with respect to whatever is being investigated; but if they differ afterward and the experimental group exceeds the control group in the direction the intervention has been designed to test or achieve, then the conclusion may be drawn that the intervention was probably successful. But moral questions must be raised. Did the treatment also affect the experimental group adversely in ways that had or had not been anticipated; was their privacy invaded? Were those in the control group informed that they were serving that function, were they deprived of the benefits the experimentals may have received? Being forthright and providing truthful information to both groups, moreover, introduces information that can contaminate the design of the intervention. These are only the most pressing moral issues raised by research with human beings in real settings.[40]

Competent observers may agree that the methods of an intervention meet standards that have been established and that are praiseworthy. In modern societies many disposable wastes can and must be recycled if expensive or carelessly expedient methods of disposal are to be avoided and if natural resources are to be conserved. Municipal or other authorities then intervene and require all families to separate their recyclable waste from that which cannot be recycled before disposing of it or preparing it for collection. Many persons may be unaware of the problem and the manner in which it is being solved; they voted for the officials who have enacted the regulations without knowing their views concerning the problem; in fact, the candidates themselves may have been equally ignorant when they were elected. Should such an intervention be condemned or approved because the beneficiaries were unaware that their decision in the voting booths would have this favorable environmental consequence? Persons who have not consented to be principals may feel antagonistic toward the intervener: they are being treated like guinea pigs who have had no opportunity beforehand to decide whether they wished to submit themselves to the procedure. Possibly, however, a Western bias is being expressed. Principals in some societies may show less or no concern for this value of consent—but provided their own leaders have given their consent? They may agree to participate in a multiple intervention without being able to anticipate the difficulties they will experience during the exercise itself. Here we have consent, not informed consent. Then it is to be wondered whether completely informed consent is possible.[41] In the few workshops with which this writer has been associated, every sincere effort was made in advance to communicate the methodological details and objectives as the principals were being recruited; yet, I confess now and did so at the time, we did not always succeed in communicating verbally the discomfort that the interaction would entail, so that the principals had only partially and inadequately consented.

9. *Disapproved are interventions that ignore future consequences.* As indicated during the discussion of temporal perspective in chapter 4, it is very difficult, often impossible, to renounce a present gain for the sake of one in the future. Commandment 9 suggests that nevertheless, the future should not be ignored. At first glance it seems desirable to crush "evil" by any means, including violent ones, without seeking a peaceful settlement through mediation or some form of intervention. The war is "just" or "necessary," all other means have been exhausted. But what will be the consequences in the long run for the families of those who have been killed, for the economies that have been destroyed, for the survivors who harbor hatreds for generations, for peoples not embroiled in this conflict and affected by it? In 1938 to 1939 Hitler and his advisers obtained complete control of Czechoslo-

vakia peacefully after negotiating the Munich agreement with Britain and France; within a year his armies invaded and annexed that country. At the time of the pact it seemed that war had been avoided by a "legal" and an illegal ploy, but our profound commandment was disobeyed: one war was circumvented but a more deadly war eventually resulted.

Interventions may be morally shortsighted when they stem from only a limited number of the relevant moral questions. Should parents always intervene to prevent their children from injuring themselves? Yes, they have the duty to do so, and they surely anticipate that the potential injury will be unpleasant both for the children and themselves. In terms of the immediate behavioral issue, however, the intervention may be considered desirable or undesirable. Good, perhaps the children will avoid such dangerous activity in the future; yet commanding them to stop doing what they are doing may contribute to the development of a subservient or dependent trait that later will be condemned by their peers, maybe their psychiatrist, possibly themselves. Is such a trait, then, desirable? A husband and wife whose religious affiliation is opposed to divorce discover that they are incompatible and therefore contemplate a divorce. Should a clergyman or a mutual friend intervene and attempt to reconcile them; what right has a third party to intervene, should not the principals settle their own affairs? Suppose it is true that in the 1970s violence, according to estimates, occurred in "50 percent of American families"?[42] Here the evil can be condemned without hesitation, and intervention to prevent its occurrence is immediately considered desirable on the basis of every imaginable criterion—including, once more, divorce? Why not, then, always use the identical moral judgment for war? And then to traverse the same circle: a plea of self-defense is employed by police and civilians alike who have launched an attack when their life seems to have been threatened, so that the end of survival clearly justified the means of killing a would-be assailant. What "good" does it do to argue that the assailant was a human being who with patience and funding and under the proper conditions might have been reformed or then educated and later have contributed mightily to his family or community?

This commandment, like all the rest, may be inextricably linked to other decisions concerning intervention, particularly the method to be employed. Authorities in a developing country wish to improve the health of the population. Should they increase medical facilities and the supply of medically trained personnel; should they take measures to combat poverty so that people can afford better food and housing and hence be less likely to fall ill; or should they change the school curricula so that pupils and students at an early age learn practices that promote health?[43] The use of "or" in that long question points to a moral problem when funds are limited and therefore intervention cannot achieve all three objectives. Unless adequate emphasis is placed upon all three methods, the future consequences of neglecting one or both of the other methods may be serious and interfere with the overall objective.

The consequences of interventions may be unforeseen or ignored and therefore justified by a reference to their immediate goals. Let colonialization and subsequent interventions of Western powers in developing societies provide the sermon. On the surface the goal of the interveners has been clear. Governments and individuals have sought economic advantages. Missionaries have had theological interests in promoting their own beliefs and usually in saving the heathen from everlasting damnation. Certainly, as a result of these activities, roads have been constructed, life expectancy has increased, more persons have been educated in schools and have become literate. In thus spreading their ways of thought and behavior, however, the Western interveners have also intentionally or unintentionally produced suffering resulting from exploitation and domination. On a subtler level the non-Western principals have learned or been taught to guide themselves less by the past and the present and more by deferring present gratification for the sake of the future. Likewise, in Western societies and in other parts of the planet, such as South Africa, a policy of affirmative action has followed the moral and economic wrongs associated with the injustices inflicted upon minority groups in the past and present. Members of such groups, as distinguished by skin color, culture, and gender, are supposed to be given access to positions formerly occupied or monopolized by members of the "superior" group. Such a policy then has had consequences for that dominant group whose present generation may be suffering discrimination for wrongs their ancestors but not necessarily they themselves have committed. The efficiency of an enterprise may be lessened when and if positions are allocated to the less qualified members of the group suffering discrimination. It may be difficult as well as costly to enforce the new policy. But are such consequences important; does not the nation or the society as a whole benefit from the changing policy?

The ultimate consequences of an intervention can seem obvious and yet be different from what is anticipated. The Roman Vegetius declared twenty centuries ago, "Let him who wants peace, prepare for war"; and in this century Albert Einstein declared, "You cannot simultaneously prepare for and prevent war."[44] Both interveners were seeking peace, but differed with respect to the recommended consequences. Equally challenging during the present century again has been the problem of sustaining life on the planet, which proclaims the interdependence of all other problems ranging from the pollution of the atmosphere to the condition of homeless people wandering through the streets of wealthy nations. In the late 1980s there were almost half a million refugees in the eastern Sudan. These people began gathering wood for fuel and for their houses. The local authorities as well as international experts were convinced that the forests would thus be depleted, the lasting consequences of which would be disastrous. One set of principals themselves wished to survive, the other to have the forest survive: the refugees were intervening to obtain the wood, the local authorities to prevent the refugees from doing just that. There was thus interference with the local economy and interference with the struggling refugees;[45] for which should the authorities have intervened?

This commandment, it thus seems, is violated when participants fail to note the inevitable relation between a part, some parts, or many parts and the whole; their failure may be intentional or—as suggested in chapter 2 during the discussion of planning—innocent and unintended. A change in one aspect of an individual's behavior cannot be evaluated in isolation because what he does or does not do may affect the organization that is his personality as well as other persons' evaluation of that personality. A tradition or an institution may appear unimportant, but a shift in that area may have far-reaching repercussions on the society as a whole. Yes, a new highway is needed to facilitate transportation between the city and the outlying areas, and hence citizens sign petitions and officials exert pressure upon the legislature to obtain the necessary funds; but what effect will the road have upon the land it will traverse, upon the homes located close to its route, and upon the social and economic life of the communities it will bring closer together?

10. *Disapproved is nonintervention when interventions are feasible and desirable.* Since nonintervention is zero intervention, it is evaluated by means of one or more of the same critical guides and other commandments applying to intervention. According to the First Amendment of the U.S. Constitution, "Congress shall make no law respecting an establishment of religion, or prohibiting the free exercise thereof; or abridging the freedom of speech, or of the press; or the right of the people peaceably to assemble, and to petition the Government for a redress of grievances." Over the years, however, American federal, state, and local authorities have felt compelled to abridge this right of nonintervention in a variety of ways, including the nonintervention expressed even in the Second Amendment concerning "the right of the people to keep and bear arms"; of the police to arrest persons who appear to be engaging in unlawful acts; and of so-called pornographic communications in a variety of forms. In these instances the values embodied in the First Amendment have become less morally pressing than the consequences of adhering literally to its consequences.

Certainly it is not always easy to follow Commandment 10. Beggars and homeless people, unless they are pathological, crave the interventions that can bring them comfort; why, then, are hosts of persons, ranging from passersby to government officials, unable or unwilling to help them? In the Genovese case previously mentioned—the woman being murdered in the distant but safe presence of 38 persons—this commandment points to an obligation to intervene in behalf of "good" causes or of persons who require assistance. It is clear that discharging the obligation depends upon a large variety of factors that include impulses, moral and religious values, the presence or absence and the evaluation of other persons, and very personal factors such as status, wealth, and previous experience.[46] The charter of the United Nations, as must be repeatedly but often reluctantly recalled, frowns upon one nation's intervention in the local affairs of another nation, although exceptions to this commandment are numerous. A less drastic form of intervention than the use of force occurs when supposedly neutral individuals designated by the Security Council or by private organizations, such as those sponsoring former President Jimmy Carter, monitor elections in foreign lands. Here the interveners are presumably ensuring that the country's own regulations are enforced, although those seeking to engage in the locally illegal practices must privately protest at such interference in their quest for power.

Nonintervention as a result of one principle is disapproved when a "higher" or more "significant" principle is violated. In chapter 4 reference was made to the Americans who were distressed in 1991 when television and the printed media made them aware of the suffering of the rebellious Kurds and the Bangladeshis: they themselves did not intervene and instead tried not to witness the horrors and to forget them. On the same day in the same newspaper an epidemiologist defended the view that the principle of nonintervention in the affairs of another nation in need is morally unjust. Hence he stressed the peril of Commandment 10 as a guide:

> We believe this intervention will have greater historical importance than the coalition's war against Iraq.
>
> The right to intervene, as defined by Doctors of the World, the French humanitarian group, means that a request from

those who are suffering is sufficient to justify crossing a boundary without authorization from a nation's leaders; the humanitarian imperative takes precedence over noninterference and sovereignty.[47]

De gustibus non est—no, no, there must be a dispute.

REALITY

Chapter Seven

Up to this point attention has been conscientiously riveted upon decisions determining whether interventions are or once were feasible and desirable. If it has been decided to reject nonintervention—deliberately or impulsively, slowly or quickly, superficially or profoundly—then what actually occurs, should occur, might have occurred during the actual interaction of the intervention? The reality that emerges from past experiences, present moods, and the participants' interaction is a favored subject of the avalanche of reports impolitely mentioned in chapter 1. Some highlights are provided here, those stemming from the decision to intervene and more or less directly affecting the outcome of the intervention. The four "stages" in which mediations were once said to "unfold" (setting the stage, defining issues, examining issues, and resolving those issues)[1] are useful guides for mediators and perhaps for all interveners and analysts; they cannot and need not be reported here in detail, inasmuch as they vary more or less uniquely from situation to situation. As a guide it is sufficient to know that principals provide or communicate information to interveners and, in multiple interventions, to one another; thereafter they resolve or do not resolve the problem originally stemming from an event that provoked the intervention.

Participants in interventions emerge from contact of any kind. Whoever intrudes by randomly approaching us on the street or over our telephone is usually treated with some degree of politeness. Bitter enemies who are compelled to appear before an arbitrator are able, at least at the outset, to force themselves to restrain their enmity. The participants may or may not believe that the beginning of the interaction now at hand will produce a solution. The physician will tell you what to do to relieve the pain; the strike cannot be avoided; we shall win the war.

Surprises

Writing on the subject of mediation, an anthropologist with experience in developing and developed countries has pitched the interaction problem in a manner applicable to most interventions: "What a mediator can do, what he chooses to do, and what he is permitted to do by the disputing parties are all much affected by who he is in the particular context and why he is there at all."[2] Like negotiation generally or the negotiating that may occur between groups during a multiple intervention, possible interactions include "bargaining, wheeling and dealing, compromising, making deals, reaching agreements after disagreement, making arrangements, getting tacit understandings . . . mediating, power brokering, trading off, exchanging . . . engaging in collusion."[3] Such a statement is yet another way to express and justify the reference to "chaotic behavior" proposed and endorsed at the end of chapter 1 in this book. One guide with the fewest perils, therefore, suggests that *under almost all*—note the qualification—*circumstances, surprises occur during the intervention.* Human beings are difficult to grasp completely and therefore participants themselves or outside observers do not or cannot anticipate in detail precisely how other people will react in specified situations. Public meetings, such as those in behalf of peace mentioned in chapter 5, may have their set agenda, but once they are open to discussion from the floor, the unexpected may occur as a cantankerous or aggressive individual stands up to speak. During the interaction participants may be surprised that time seems to be passing so slowly or quickly, and they have differing judgments concerning the actual duration.

A change in the procedure of the intervention, in short, is almost—no, absolutely—inevitable: every situation is unique in some respect. Let your and my favorite sagacious quip of Robert Burns be recalled: "The best laid schemes o'mice and men / Gang aft a-gley." And again for reasons to be traced to events in his milieu or to his own conscious or unconscious impulse, every individual unintentionally acts differently from what he had planned earlier or even immediately before the actual action: unintentionality is a good clue to the existence of the many perils that accompany most guides.[4] Even in dual interventions the particular participants' role may change; unwittingly their facial expressions, posture, body movements, or type and color of clothing may reveal thoughts or feelings at variance with what they have been intending to express verbally. In any intervention, the sudden perception of traditional proverbs, metaphors, flowers, flags, animals, or music can affect momentary responses. A principal may resent and attack a proposed resolution to the problem at hand and thus suddenly or unexpectedly can become the intervener as he resists or makes a counterproposal. Many surprises are avoided when interveners are acquainted with the cultures of the principals. A knowledge of their folklore, of their beloved values (that may or may not be recognized as metaphysical), of the persons or institutions that are respected or have authority, and of the prevalent taboos provides guides to diminish misunderstandings during a multiple intervention.

Surprises are often, maybe usually, anticipated. Interveners who have privately or publicly formulated the goals they would achieve, as indicated in chapter 5, may realize that they will change their objectives after principals have interacted with them or with other principals. In all interventions, except perhaps for those involving domination with consent, they presume that principals will make surprising demands and will cooperate fully, partially, or not at all.

When it is stated that by definition "the mediator is not responsible for solving the problem,"[5] such a view is only a perilous guide to surprises that are expected. Mediators, however, may change their anticipated role during the interaction and contribute to the resolution.

Other surprises are more unexpected and require changes in method. Before and during early phases of interventions, interveners may believe they are attempting to determine what principals "really" think about a problem or how principals "really" feel toward one another; later they discover that the principals appear unwilling or unable to disclose what they "really" believe. The interveners then decide to ignore the basic attitudes and to achieve superficial assent, which nevertheless appears sufficient to lead to the appropriate action—amazing, those persons were actually willing to compromise! The members of one ethnic group truly dislike contact with members of another ethnic group, yet to produce cooperation within a community and perhaps even to achieve less segregation it may be sufficient not to expose their hostility but to achieve halfhearted support for some democratic principle such as having equal access to goods or services. At first, principals' attitudes as expressed to themselves and even to others may undergo a "Socratic effect"—"the tendency for cognitions to increase in consistency once they have been made salient"[6]—and then later they are not disturbed by inconsistency between those attitudes and the proposed or actual resolution.

Even interventions governed by tradition can be surprising, and hence the resulting actions conform only partially to moral commandments. Topics are discussed in accordance with unwritten codes of etiquette: one person listens, wholeheartedly or perfunctorily, while the other expresses himself or herself, and neither one shoots the other; yet the possibility of an outburst is recognized by the anticipation that verbal or legal punishment will be administered to whoever is gauche or makes a slanderous remark. Although individuals are pleased when they perceive evidence for their preexisting beliefs and attitudes, they also can find contradictory evidence "more interesting,"[7] even or particularly during multiple interventions.

Gypsies in the United States have their own traditional ways to settle disputes among themselves concerning offenses varying from adultery and sexual intercourse with a non-Gypsy to theft and assault; minor problems are settled within the immediate or extended family. Disputes between members of different families and those of a more serious nature require intervention by the equivalent of judges selected for the occasion and a jury. Although the purpose of the procedure is "to find the truth," Gypsies know that the outcome also depends on the rhetoric they employ, rhetoric that is "colorful and flamboyant, filled with lengthy and poetic arguments, exaggerated claims" as well as with "frequent analogies to nature, day-to-day life, mythology, and folktales."[8] Within the cultural pattern of intervention, individual principals then produce the unpredicted. Similarly, principals and attorneys as well as the judge in an Anglo-Saxon court case anticipate roughly the events during a trial, yet the unexpected may occur after a judicial ruling or the testimony of a witness. Likewise, a competent physician foresees the components of a syndrome after the patient has revealed one or more symptoms; nevertheless, slightly or markedly different symptoms may be discovered in a particular patient after closer examination.

In well-planned interventions, interveners can be surprised by what occurs. At what point is it propitious for them to speak up and contribute whatever they can to the resolution of the conflict? They may have to decide at the spur of the moment, and regardless of experiences they have had in similar situations, they may discover that they have selected the right or wrong time. Then, interveners may be convinced that multiple interventions produce more surprises than dual interventions: the larger the number of principals, the greater the possibility that their interest will be complex and hence unpredictable. Still, how often are interveners surprised by the reaction of a friend or a client?

Both during and after interventions, surprises are considered a peril or a bounty, even as "excitement" generally is viewed either unfavorably as a stressful interruption of peaceful adjustment or as a desirable experience deliberately cultivated in sports and in many other so-called leisure-time activities.[9] Surprised interveners may subsequently become aware of what they have been doing or what they did. "Sorry, I beg your pardon, I didn't mean to do that." Tongues slip, don't they? Someone who is angry during an intervention wishes to conceal that feeling, which unwittingly is revealed by a strained facial expression. Principals look as though they have understood a resolution and they may say that they have done so, but in fact they have not grasped its full implications. To increase productivity, the manager of a plant makes a minor change or adjustment in working conditions, as a result of which the workers feel uncomfortable, contrary to his original intention.

One or more phases of unplanned interventions are likely to be both unintended and surprising. That metaphorical passerby who rescues the drowning child had been simply walking or exercising. He was not near the lake in order to perform an heroic act; his intention became salient only after he heard the child's cry and quickly realized that he was capable of accomplishing the deed. Mediators plan to remain "objective," yet in the course of an intervention they may gradually come to sympathize only with one set of principals and thus unwittingly affect the outcome.

Among all "the many activities aiming to create, maintain or restore the state of harmonious constructive competition and just living together we call peace," an activist Quaker indicates, "all that we do is to establish and nurture social and economic systems that nurture and minimise the inequality and want that generate conflict."[10] What most of us do in that role is to be interventionists: as citizens we vote for one candidate rather than another; we contribute to a charity; our life-style functions as a model to others; these actions of ours occur in response to innumerable pressures upon us of which we are not completely aware, and hence as principals we unintentionally intervene in such minor ways in order to improve the existence of everybody.

Within recent times new phrases such as "the tragedy of the commons" and "social traps" have called attention to the possibility that the separate actions of individuals may eventually damage their own long-term interests as well as those of their peers.[11] If each inhabitant allows his or her cattle to graze an unlimited time on the commons that is open to all, eventually the land is overgrazed and becomes useless for the entire community. Metaphorically the intentional intervention of each person has been not to destroy the commons, yet unintentionally that outcome is a consequence unless members of the group or an authority intervenes to regulate the actions of everyone. The components of an ecological system are also interrelated so that a change in one of them may have unintended and even undesirable consequences upon one or more of the rest; protecting one endangered species of plants or animals can have disastrous consequences for another species unless the system in which both are embedded is managed as a totality.[12] From the standpoint of the historian, the journalist, or the sociologist it is facile and tempting to refer abstractly to the diffusion of an innovation within a group or society or from one society to another, yet of course the assumption is thus being made that there is "a change agent who attempts to influence adoption decisions in a direction that he feels is desirable."[13] Nothing diffuses "automatically" like those ripples on a pond: one or more interveners adopt and then advocate the change; many principals comply or do not comply with its requirements.

The individuals and the organizations that conduct public opinion polls and publicize their findings aim to provide insight into how people in general and electorates in particular view and react to the issues and public figures of their time; they are paid by whoever employs them and utilizes their findings. Their reports are often influential and thus they intervene in the political process: give them what the polls say they want, don't give them what they don't want. In democratic societies when surveys indicate that a candidate for public office is in the lead, he and his supporters may be convinced that he will win; he may relax his efforts during the campaign and they may become too confident to go to the trouble to vote. If the opposite finding is reported, the candidate and his supporters may resolve to work all the more strenuously to win, and so they view actually voting as the effective way to counteract the trend revealed by the polls.

Efforts have been made in the United States to prevent computer projections from samples of voters who are questioned as they emerge from voting booths—so-called exit polls—from being publicized lest such early estimates, unintentionally or intentionally, affect those who have not yet voted or who live in later time zones.[14]

The validity of many items reported even by systematic surveys may be questioned. On some issues of vital concern to them, respondents may refuse to reveal how they "really" feel either because they fear it might be dangerous to do so or because, like some Africans in the colonial days, they wish only to offer the opinions they believe are anticipated or respectable. For the same reason they may simply say the have "no opinion" or "don't know" which may also be true. Even when they easily and perhaps glibly express an opinion, they may be unacquainted with some or many of the relevant issues; their conviction concerning the issues can range from weak and unreliable to strong and steadfast.

If interveners were to know all there is to know about principals, including the kinds of data gathered after the occurrence of an intervention, there would be fewer surprises. What has happened when public officials in the United States have intervened to warn principals concerning impending disasters resulting from floods or the derailment of trains or trucks carrying hazardous materials? Do they continue their normal routine, engage in some kind of protective actions, or heed the warning and evacuate where they have been living or working? Common sense might suggest that their general attitude toward risks and the particular risk would affect them. But how do such factors operate among whites, blacks, and Mexican-Americans? Even when the answers to such questions are available on the basis of American research conducted in the early 1980s,[15] there is no guarantee that the same reactions will occur a decade or so later. But at least the earlier investigation provides a basis for anticipating what may happen in the future and hence to diminish the possibility of a surprise.

176

Prearrangements

Although surprises cannot be eliminated, some aspects of interventions can be prearranged and then a designated plan without too many substantial deviations can be implemented. For easily diagnosed medical difficulties, the physician and patient follow a customary procedure anticipated by both participants; and specialists know how they will treat particular ailments before patients consult them. Both the analysand and the analyst contemplate what will happen during psychoanalysis, regardless of who initiates the encounter; yet the precise details of the sessions depend upon the analysand's problems as well upon the analyst's particular techniques, his own theoretical assumptions, and also the ways in which the subject or patient behaves during the sessions.[16] Courts of law that intervene in criminal or civil cases also follow a standardized adjudication procedure, more or less. In the West parliamentary routine is so well known that its use in mediation and especially in mandatory arbitration enables participants to anticipate in advance more or less the interactions during the interventions; and reality conforms to that plan, again more or less.

Prearranged plans for interventions permit a specified amount of flexibility. Principals decide to cooperate, to sabotage the effort, or to remain neutral or uncommitted throughout an intervention without specifying in advance how such action will be accomplished. On the basis of a dozen "arbitrated hearings," a British psychologist has observed that in mandatory arbitration some elasticity was evident: at one "stage" in the hearings, arbitrators offered their own suggestions whenever it seemed sensible to do so.[17] Likewise three dozen mediation cases in an American city, each occurring in three sessions, were once carefully examined by observing the interactions and by interviewing the mediators. It was found that "setting the stage" by indicating the procedure and gathering information occurred in the early session, "problem solving" by posing the issues and facilitating alternatives in a later session, and "achieving a workable agreement" by suggesting feasible methods and urging agreement in the last session.[18]

Plans almost certainly are modified somewhat in the course of most interactions. In civil suits one principal may modify his demands in the hope that his opponents will also make a concession, which may or may not be forthcoming.[19] Diplomats pursue the economic interests of their countries and ordinarily cannot be induced to abandon slices of their territory or members of their own ethnic group unless special circumstances require that such restrictions be abandoned in favor of some other goals. In time of war each side hopes that its human casualties will be light, but the military and political leaders may be wrong, and they cannot anticipate the precise individuals who will be killed or disabled. There were exceptions to the changes in the three mediation sessions mentioned in the previous paragraph. Lessons from the past, therefore, can be of fallible assistance in planning interactions. They can be guides, yes, though always somewhat perilous.

Transforming Principals

Interventions follow a procedure that seeks to facilitate a solution to the problem or to reduce the conflict at hand. Patients must allow their bodies to be examined and must reply to the questions of the physician who is making the diagnosis. During mediation, arbitration, and the proceedings of a Western-type court, experts or witnesses are afforded an opportunity or are summoned to present relevant evidence. Skillfully or crudely, successfully or unsuccessfully, interveners can try out and then accept or reject varying approaches during the intervention, even as they contemplated available methods beforehand (chapter 5). Shifting arguments are advanced to persuade a friend to adopt a course of action; to strengthen one's cause in a legal brief; to elicit background and personal data from someone consulting a therapist.

All the nuances of human communication may be observed during the actual interactions. Psychiatrists, having numerous methods at their disposal, pick and choose in the midstream of an intervention the approach most suitable to the patient at hand or at the moment during the therapy: direct questions, free association, dreams, challenges, diaries, praise or criticism, medication, and so on, all of which can be carefully adapted to the person being treated. *Warning:* the remainder of this section deliberately wanders from one method of transformation to another without providing systematic links between them; it would thus reflect the trials and errors of many interveners as they seek promising solutions to their methodological problem.

A basic guide to all methods suggests that *inevitably some learning occurs during interventions, and hence both sets of participants change their approach or behavior in minor or major respects.* Diplomats anticipate the response of an adversary whom they would influence, their anticipation may turn out to be correct, and they thus learn a tidbit useful during the current and a future intervention. The learning and the change may also pertain to a mixture of the principals' knowledge about themselves, the problem at hand, and the ways in which human beings think, feel, and act. The degree to which they attach their central values or welfare to practices and actions influences their readiness to change. Although the goal of intervention in behalf of a new brand of toothpaste may be easier to attain than shifts in national or religious affiliation, during an interaction it may be less difficult to link human welfare than toothpaste to a proposed resolution. In the course of interacting, principals can discover that the resolution of the problem at hand requires them to abandon or modify a dearly beloved moral commandment as a result of extenuating circumstances; then the next step may be to invoke another commandment to justify the original one.[20] What should devout pacifists do when their own country is threatened or invaded?

Principals can be transformed when they come or are somehow induced to appreciate how the symbols they employ affect the ways they conceptualize their own problems and the solutions thereto. Clarifying the role of symbols is generally useful and especially necessary when principals clothe their objectives in abstract terms: "A word is already a theory," a Russian psychologist once said.[21] Consider one concept particularly prevalent in multiple interventions:

"democracy." Almost anywhere in the last years of the twentieth century there have been references to that concept as a goal to be attained or a practice to be retained. The "requirements" of democracy include, according to one political scientist, opportunities of people to formulate and signify their preferences (such as freedom to form and join organizations, the right to vote, the right of political leaders to compete for support) and to have those preferences weighted equally in the conduct of government. In addition, reference may be made to "the proportion of the population entitled to participate on a more or less equal plane in controlling and contesting the conduct of government."[22] And is it not essential to add to the referents of democracy the need for a market economy rather than one centrally controlled; for a rule of law rather than regulations promised by a wise or a foolish authority; or for a multi- rather than a single-party state or organization? Democracy likewise involves political and moral values that may be difficult to specify, such as safe working conditions or an equitable distribution of wealth or resources. Recently, still other concepts such as "free enterprise," "privatization," "central planning," and "authority" have been similarly bandied about.

It is not easy to induce principals to realize that such verbal and other symbols are so embedded in particular values that they cannot be quickly or glibly devalued or transformed. Your mother may have died decades ago, but now you refuse to tolerate any slur upon her character even when the slur does not reflect upon you: her memory is "sacred." In every society similar symbols cannot be denigrated or dishonored. The audience stands at attention or at least keeps respectfully quiet when the national anthem is played. Statues and other portrayals of the deceased or living personages considered to be heroes dare not be desecrated. The nation's flag, in actuality a piece of colored cloth, must not be trampled upon without fear of punishment or censure; when governments in Eastern Europe and the Soviet Union were overthrown or changed in the late 1980s and early 1990s, the ending of a regime was symbolized by dispensing with all or parts of Communist flags. The guardians of the state concern themselves with their version of history that is taught in symbols or otherwise communicated. In a classical treatise (one that is incisive and challenging and, despite its age, still frequently cited or useful), it is stated that ideology as a concept "reflects the one discovery which emerged from political conflict, namely, that ruling groups can in their thinking become so intensely interest-bound to a situation that they are simply no longer able to see certain facts which would undermine their sense of domination."[23] Adding to the difficulty in changing the symbols and ideologies is the fact that other interveners in a society seek to perpetuate them.

Decades ago one mediator brilliantly suggested why and how such symbols and ideologies can be related to psychological reality if individuals are to be transformed in some specific respect.[24] You and I, she wrote in effect, are seated in a room and you wish to open a window and I want to keep it shut. The two of us need not quarrel or compromise by opening the window less than halfway. Instead we must discover what you "really" want is some fresh air and so you would have the window open; what I "really" want is to avoid a draft and so I wish to have that window shut. Then at this more basic level we may agree to open a window in another room, so that you will have your fresh air and I shall not endure a draft. A friend and perspicacious mediator can intervene to help both of us obtain the insight and the solution. One or both of us, however, may be stubborn and may cling to our original verbal demands; or the third party may have to demonstrate to each of us that the integrated solution is satisfactory by actually opening the window in the other room. During the process of arriving at this resolution of our conflict, both of us may also generalize from the experience and in the future avoid fixating upon formalities by plumbing beneath the verbal level.

But then suppose that you and I wish to marry the same person and that both of us truly believe there is no one in the world or at least among our acquaintances quite like the one each of us deeply loves. Or suppose any two countries of your choice (North and South Korea not long ago) instead of going to war had preactively sought the assistance of an intervener who, in the words of an experienced mediator, had enabled them to distinguish between the "principles" they were advocating and the "interests" that "really" motivated them.[25] The difficulty here would have been to have them agree to sit down with an impartial mediator and to allow him or her to help them discover what each side "really" sought: economic security, prestige, power? Then they might have uncovered an arrangement "really" satisfactory to the two groups and have lived not happily forever after but at least without bloodshed or wasting their energies. This window-open-window-shut approach, therefore, may be a theoretically and psychologically sound approach to transformation, but too often it remains unrealistic or unrealizable, however compelling it remains as an ideal guide to less ambitious interventions. The conceptions of principals concerning themselves, the groups and subgroups with which they identify themselves, and their vital interests may be the basic premise of existence that individuals "really" seek. You wish fresh air directly from the outdoors and not from that other hypothetical room because you know from experience and from your family that only such air seems really fresh; and so you prefer the compromise of a window half opened.

Another difficulty with the window guide arises when principals are reluctant to reveal their "real" objectives: it is not having the window open or shut that they really want, rather they would dominate the other person. Workers may argue for higher wages, but when the time is more propitious, they actually may seek to play a greater role in formulating the company's decisions. Somehow in multiple interventions interveners must seek to have principals explore in their own minds and also most concretely what their concepts mean in practice. The immediate objective of a diplomat may be to defend the rights of a minority group belonging to his culture or of the same persons in another country, yet a deeper motive may be territorial expansion or his own prestige. International relations in particular are clouded with misperceptions that are both unconscious and conscious,[26] so that their recognition and removal among interventionists or ordinary principals are impossible to achieve. Recall, nevertheless, the splendid dimunition of hostility between the French and Germans after World War II. Finally, an intervener who appreciates the existence of a discrepancy between declared and deep objectives may or may not seek to expose the discrepancy and hence to allow the problem to be judged or resolved on a less basic level.

Interveners may wonder whether during a multiple intervention they should somehow steer the discussion toward the abstract or the concrete. Is it better to concentrate upon lofty principles or upon specific projects? There is no eternal answer. The concrete can eliminate symbolic jargon and abstract commandments, but that very jargon and those commandments are necessary if principals are to reach a resolution that transcends and transforms the particular problem inspiring the intervention in the first place. A bill of rights provides for unforeseeable contingencies, yet a discussion of specific violations can lead more easily and quickly to agreement.

Transformation, however, can be on a purely verbal level when during the interaction principals come to attach different labels to relevant referents. Kenyans in our workshop on the conflicts in the Horn of Africa learned from their Somali counterparts that the Somalis who had been moving in and out of an adjoining area of their country were not "bandits" as they were being called on Radio Kenya but nomads who with their cattle were following seasonal changes in the weather.[27] Similarly but on a more general level, principals may be able to learn or can be taught that they function ethnocentrically as they assess other groups, opponents, individuals, or themselves. Certain concepts, when incorporated both meaningfully and emotionally into their vocabulary, can help them secure that insight. *Projection* offers such a guide. We all have a tendency to project our own feelings, prejudices, and modes of thinking upon other persons. They must be like me because that is the way I feel. But you may be wrong. Are those principals projecting their own insecurities upon their opponents? The intervener may tell them that they are doing just that; but his words, being "only" words, may not be heeded; instead he may help them recognize the ways in which projection functions before they interact concerning the conflict at hand. Likewise the expressive label of "snapping" has been applied to "a phenomenon that occurs when an individual stops thinking and feeling for himself, when he breaks the bonds of awareness and social relationship that tie his personality to the outside world and literally loses his mind to some form of external or automatic control."[28]

A term quite common and frequently used somewhat broadly and carelessly is *stereotype:* the tendency to characterize the self, another person, and especially a group with a string of chichés such as honest or dishonest, lazy or hardworking, decent or indecent, immoral or moral—and many others. The stereotypes of in- and out-groups can be associated with age, social class, ethnicity, nationality, culture—and again a string of demographic attributes in this context. Events can also be stereotyped. Such stereotypes exist in all societies and persist over generations because those holding them have had what they believe to be confirming experiences with the persons and situations so stereotyped or because they have unwittingly learned them in the course of being socialized. Some stereotypes have probably originated in a group whose members have been motivated to justify themselves and their own position in a society by the use and abuse of distinguishing labels. Whether or not stereotypes are partially accurate and hence contain a "kernel of truth" and whether or not the behavior of persons so characterized tends to be affected by conforming to or rebelling against the stereotypes others attribute to them are fascinating problems in their own right. But for a fruitful intervention it may be essential only to make principals conscious of these sweeping characterizations and their probable or possible inaccuracies.

On a deeper level, transformation can occur if and when principals engage in experiential learning: somehow they are induced to be meaningfully active not only by speaking and listening but also by becoming emotionally involved in the changes they experience.[29] This intervening approach, derived from Sigmund Freud and his deliberate and unwitting followers, suggests that insight into the genesis of one's problems may provide some or even total relief. Compulsive behavior becomes less demanding when the adult realizes that he continues to react as if his parents were commanding him to obey or not to disobey.

In our workshop held in Scotland for fifty-six principals from Northern Ireland, the interveners believed that the principals should learn that much of what one does or even thinks at the moment depends upon the group in which one happens to be participating. A lecture on the subject was not hurled at these men and women from Belfast and vicinity; we had them experience the guide. In one of several exercises, they were first divided into small groups of seven or eight based upon age: a young group, a slightly older one, a group still older, and so on. We directed the groups to go to separate small rooms. There they were given no instructions and a parliamentary procedure was not prescribed; an intervener, one of the organizers, told them to do whatever they pleased and then he kept quiet. Being together, they simply talked to one another on topics they themselves selected. After an hour or so of chatting, they were told to return to the large room where they usually met. There they were again immediately assigned to small groups, this time on the basis of gender—all women, all men in a group—and once more they interacted in separate rooms, however they wished, for roughly the same period of time. After lunch, still on the same day, the procedure was repeated a third time, with the small groups then being based upon religion. By the end of the day, when these principals were asked to reflect upon how their behavior changed as they participated in groups based upon age, gender, and religion, perhaps they could appreciate the inclination for each of them, as a result of their experiences, to feel and behave somewhat differently as they moved from group to group. Experiential learning transcended the verbal level.[30] The interveners' objective was to enable principals to become conscious of their own modes of thinking, feeling, and behaving but only thereafter in the same workshop to have them utilize this insight as they sought to resolve the conflict in their home territory. Thus, it was hoped, they would realize that the hostility they felt concerning an opposing group was likely to have been stronger whenever they were conscious of membership in their own group rather than pondering what they really believed in the quiet of their own contemplation.

Another strategy that may transform principals is to aid them to appreciate the viewpoint and perhaps even the feelings of their opponents; then in a multiple intervention they may be better able to appreciate why a conflict has arisen. Instead of listening to the opponents or the intervener explain the opposing viewpoint, the principals may be instructed to engage in what is termed reverse role-playing. In our workshop with the two territorial conflicts in the Horn of Africa (Ethiopia versus Somalia and Kenya versus Somalia) a succession of principals was asked to make believe they were not themselves but someone else from the opposing side and to offer as effectively as possible the claims of that other person's country to the disputed territory.[31] The presentation may have been only a bit of play-acting, yet it was performed in front of the other principals in the workshop and hence required the players to be somewhat serious and not supercilious. They consequently became the devil's advocates and presented the strongest or at least the most dramatic case of their opponents; to do so, they had to internalize the opposing viewpoints and appreciate them to some degree. Not only reverse role-playing of this kind but also role-playing in general has the important if only potential advantage of requiring persons to behave rather than just to think, and hence it can inspire them to gain insight into themselves and the feelings of others.[32]

A risky, sometimes useful method is to have groups in conflict express their hostility or their emotional view of the conflict. To some extent, a cathartic explosion may not only release some of the aggression but also reveal to other principals and interveners the barrier to overcome and some of its subtle nuances. That barrier, however, may appear insurmountable and hence its expression can make a resolution less likely. On the other hand, the confrontation by less powerful principals both during and outside the intervention through verbal and bodily protests may frighten the more powerful principals and induce them to seek a solution more vigorously.[33] Hostility in forms ranging from mild aggression after frustration to enduring hatred may also intrude, especially during multiple interventions. One group becomes increasingly hostile toward the other group either for personal or ideological reasons, and the feelings endure after the intervention has ended.

Somehow in face-to-face multiple interventions it may be essential to create an atmosphere in which principals feel less anxious and recognize their similarities rather than their dissimilarities.[34] Then they are less likely to be prejudiced and misinformed about one another. Some form of communication is necessary, including prompting by the intervener.[35] One writer has proclaimed, without evidence but probably on the basis of past experience during one decade, the following "Principle #1": "Movement toward resolution will occur when the parties communicate directly with each other about their conflict for a sustained period of time."[36] And yet—the usual *but* to every guide—even though principals in multiple interventions grow to respect, perhaps even love, one another as a result of the contacts and of a subtle, very "psychological" procedure, and even though at the time they truly believe that they have resolved the conflict at hand, some principals may have been only "seduced" by the interaction to suppose that a solution is at hand; the disillusioned awakening comes later. Intimacy, however, may also provoke hostility, especially over time. Freud himself observed that "there are present in all men, destructive, and therefore anti-social and anti-cultural, tendencies, and . . . with a great number of people these are strong enough to determine their behavior in human society,"[37] as well as during the interaction of an intervention. Then, as must be oft repeated, the solution securing agreement may be only perfunctory or face-saving: again it may not be acceptable in reality, namely, to the persons in the society who wield power or who have been the agreement's targets.[38]

The precise verbal expression employed before and during the interaction in multiple interventions leads to varied reactions among the participants. Suppose that one participant makes an insulting remark which could hinder the achievement of a resolution. Hong Kong Chinese and American students were once asked to indicate what action they would take when one person at a fictitious business meeting had insulted another person in the company; they also rated the personality traits of the insulter. Among the Chinese but not among the Americans ratings of the insulter were less unfavorable when the *he* or *she* had been portrayed as the manager than as the assistant manager.[39] Aside from these perilous factors of cultural background and status, puzzling questions remain if the effect of the insult upon the interaction is to be ascertained. Why the insult? What does the insulter hope to accomplish; would he injure that other person or cause her to change her behavior, or does he simply wish to punish her through this form of aggression? Does the target of the insult consider that she has been insulted; and, if so, does she think the insult trivial or serious? Can the insulter modify or retract the insult and will his intention to do so be successful? Insults dramatically raise such questions, but less dramatically almost any communication during interventions can evoke responses that will affect the outcome. A slip of the tongue—really not intended at least on a conscious level—hinders or assists a resolution to the problem at hand, or goes unnoticed.

Again there are no magic guides to achieving understanding or consensus among principals in multiple interventions, no more than infallible techniques can be recommended to a dual intervener who would intervene by first convincing another person to adopt his point of view. The goal, however, is clear: a method must be found either before or during the interaction that enables participants to "talk sensibly to each other without being blinded by such emotions as anger, fear, and suspicion."[40] Then transformation may be possible. Ego and ethnocentrism, however, are unavoidable. Understanding may come slowly. Conflict reduction may not be achievable in a long weekend—the favored time period of academic and political interveners and their busy principals—when those principals appear friendly to one another, particularly when they come from different cultural or national backgrounds that have had limited or superficial contacts with each other in the past.

Initiatives

Interveners can assume the initiative by proposing and facilitating an intervention at the outset, by being active to some degree during the interaction, or by performing both functions. They may be responsible for determining the techniques described in the previous sections of this chapter, yet in that role they can avoid intruding during the interaction and refrain even from expressing their own view concerning the problem at hand. If they wish, however, and all else is "equal," they may take the initiative and even propose a solution. Covertly or overtly, especially in multiple interventions, their aim then is to have all participants, including themselves, identify the issues at stake to which the intervention-producing event has given rise and to analyze or dissect them and eventually, *Deo volente,* to resolve them.[41]

Information can be deliberately obtained concerning questions such as what are the facts?, what do principals seek?, what are their stereotypes and commandments? Principals may be asked to engage in exercises that reveal such beliefs and values. Or the intrusion can be relatively simple and even unobtrusive: "What do you mean by that?" "Could you tell me, please, your reasons for believing that?" Nonverbal behavior—principals appear relaxed or tense—may provide clues, perilous or not, to their internal state or to the progress of the intervention itself. Although an intervener is likely to function effectively when he is acquainted with the facts, viewpoints, and ideologies related to the problem at hand, still there is the danger that he may prejudge the situation "on the basis of his own experiences and prejudices" and hence sometimes "the less, and not the more, the third party knows in advance of the 'facts' of the situation to be approached, the better."[42] It is helpful, nevertheless, for interveners to be aware of the questions they seek to have answered in order to induce principals to reveal vital information or values that perhaps will cause them to refocus their demands or viewpoints: "How can I bring up and explore questions of compatibility without sounding too clinical, doubtful, or demanding?" or "How can a division of labor be defined without too much rigidity and without scaring people?"[43]

Interveners can provide principals with a guide to themselves or their own actions not in the abstract but in the context of their interaction during the intervention. In multiple interventions it may become evident that distrust inhibits progress toward a solution. Interveners then indicate directly or subtly that the mistrust has been feeding upon itself. Group A, they suggest, believes that it does not mistrust Group B, but that Group B mistrusts them; and Group B also believes that it does not distrust Group A, but that they are distrusted by the A's. A skillful or alert intervener may be able to indicate the inhibiting interaction at hand. Again knowledge of a very general principle may be helpful. One of the consequences of frustration but not the only consequence, according to this principle,[44] is that some form of aggression is likely to occur; and the aggression may be turned against the alleged cause of the original frustration or can be displaced upon oneself, some other person, or the situation at hand. Knowledge of that principle as provided by the intervener may possibly enable principals to recognize the source of their hostility or anxiety and thereafter *perhaps* be in a mood to resolve the conflict with an opponent.

A deliberately conscious philosophy or procedure concerning a particular intervention may not be the precise method to be employed during the interaction. In the semislang phrase, is it useful for interveners to speak up at some point? The question is too broad. Mediators may be active or passive during the interaction. They decide at the spur of the moment whether they should offer a suggestion or be quiet;[45] they believe it necessary to disrupt "destructive communication patterns" displayed by principals.[46]

In the midst of the interaction of a multiple intervention, according to a jurist and an anthropologist, it is useful to try to induce the disputants, as the title of their book suggests, to move in the direction of "getting to yes." Some agreement, however insignificant, can lead to more significant agreement. The same authors also provide a host of undocumented, undocumentable useful suggestions concerning ways to achieve agreement among principals. In particular, they themselves deliberately depart from what might seem to be a rational, debating-society approach and emphasize the importance of the principals' emotions: "Often, one effective way to deal with people's anger, frustration, and other negative emotions is to help them release those feelings. . . . Letting off steam may make it easier to talk rationally later. . . . A brainstorming session is designed to produce as many ideas as possible to solve the problem at hand . . . people need not fear looking foolish since wild ideas are explicitly encouraged."[47] From that viewpoint, emotions are counterproductive unless they can be expressed freely; if principals recognize this tendency in the midst of being emotional, they may be more eager to find a solution to the problem concerning which they have been interacting with another person or group.

Obviously interveners cannot remain silent when they are consulted unless they would avoid responsibility. Convention and tradition during multiple interventions may specify the occasions when offering a hint or suggestion is desirable and permissible: when principals request them to do so, when clarification is required, or when the proceedings have reached a turning point. If they are active on other occasions or speak up too frequently, they may be considered a nuisance or they can lose rapport by departing from their expected roles. They themselves may require patience to keep quiet when they recognize or believe they recognize that one group of principals is bluffing concerning the information they possess, the objective that they really seek, or their announced intentions.[48] Tact, diplomacy, discretion, skill—and all the other words in a generous thesaurus—are needed.

Interveners may suggest, politely or abruptly, that the principals' discussion of a particular point is no longer useful and hence that it might be wiser to turn to another aspect of the problem. Should interveners remind principals that time is elapsing and that the interaction, as perhaps agreed at the outset, must end at a particular hour or day? The reminder may accelerate the discussion but may not necessarily produce a better resolution: the case for either leisure or pressure can be made.[49]

Interveners can function as third parties for principals who have difficulty communicating with one another. With good reactive timing, mediators can facilitate the emergence of a resolution by escalating or decreasing the expression of conflict among principals, who consequently can then perceive or create the resolution.[50] At the spur of the moment, interveners alter the ways in which they communicate their objectives.

In the course of an intervention, interveners may find it necessary to enlist the assistance or cooperation of other persons. A self-appointed committee of union members, peace advocates, and citizens in a Massachusetts community once sought to have a local shipyard convert more of its production to civilian uses rather than constructing new ships for the U.S. Navy. Their objective could be attained only by enlisting the cooperation of the parent company, other union members, and the state government.[51] A union's intervention in behalf of its members may succeed only when other unions assist by striking or exerting pressure directly or through "public opinion" upon owners. Britain and the section of France not under German domination, even after the entrance of the Soviet Union into World War II in 1941, were actively eager not only to have the United States provide material assistance but also become a belligerent.

Nonimpulsive actions usually require careful preparation. After many initial obstacles, the ones emphasized in chapter 5, the Security Council of the United Nations has been able to assemble peacekeeping forces in non-Western areas as diverse as the Congo, Cyprus, southern Lebanon, Namibia, and Kuwait-Iraq. These forces, however, have always encountered unanticipated events. In the Congo they became embroiled in the local disputes and suffered serious casualties; in the Middle East during the middle 1950s they prevented conflicts, for example, between Israel and Egypt, but eventually withdrew without facilitating a permanent settlement there.[52] Dual interveners in most areas of health, being or thought to be experts, make the initial decision to intervene, although principals may also play a role. Americans and perhaps other persons who wish to lose weight may first be determined as interventionists to submit themselves to a regimen; but external factors must be favorable,[53] including other interveners—relatives, companions, restaurant owners—whose assistance and cooperation fluctuate with the behavior of the dieter.

Those interveners must be similarly innovative when they would affect the health of principals in other respects, perhaps by changing their beliefs (through fear or additional knowledge), by modifying their behavior (through self-observation, desensitization, or reinforcement), or by functioning as models.[54] Physicians who indicate various regimens for patients to follow may or may not suggest that they change their way of living. They may indicate one and only one course of action. Or in the interests of public rather than private health they advocate measures to follow in schools and other public buildings, whether or not community authorities are notified and can take legal action to enforce them.

Action?

After the interaction, what happens? Is the child rescued? Do the workers who threatened to strike go back to work? Does the country declare war and begin advancing its troops and bombing its enemies? Or is there nonintervention: the child drowns, the workers strike, peace continues? The concern here is to determine the action that does or does not occur after the interaction; *action* is used in the broadest possible sense. A political scientist has provided a platitudinous guide that is likely to be valid for all eternity: *"The relationship between what people think and how they behave is not unambiguous."*[55] Over and beyond such a guide, it is immediately clear that the principals who are to take action must be specified. The action in a dual intervention may be taken either by the intervener (the rescuer of the child) or by the principal (the patient who follows the advice of the physician); or both intervener and principals participate in a multiple intervention (binding arbitration requiring the arbitrator to oversee the actions of the principals, who are compelled to act by implementing the decision).

It is well to be reminded that some hesitation, if only in milliseconds, precedes all action.[56] Even your reflexive impulse to yawn audibly is repressed if you are in the presence of others who will be offended by that harmless action. In fact, hesitation concerning whether or how to intervene may lead for the moment or indefinitely to another form of intervention. Scholars in their writing or in academic meetings; clergy in the private tyranny of their own thoughts or in their public sermons; journalists concerned with a particular problem or stationed in a foreign country—respectable interveners such as these certainly wish to improve human existence and formulate plans to do so; but they themselves do not expect to take appropriate action, rather they may be content to pursue personal glory and renown with their proposals concerning possible interventions. Nonrealizable plans may be utopian, yet their very existence can affect others and eventually lead to appropriate action.

The action may point to another interaction in the near or far future: we must meet again. Such a decision is necessary when either of the participants subscribes to step-by-step interventions; it may also result from procrastination or from the conviction of principals that they wish to think or feel through what has occurred during the interaction. Or they are obliged to consult bystanders, such as parents or officials in power, to secure their consent. At my initial workshop in 1985 at which small groups of Greek and Turkish Cypriots assembled at a neutral site between the two communities as described in chapter 5, the first interaction ended not with any proposals to improve relations between the two communities but with what seemed to be an enthusiastic agreement to meet again at the same place the very next week. Regular meetings then were held for three months, during which time the principals in the absence of the original facilitating intervener by and large came to respect and even to trust one another; proposals emerged to improve relations between the two communities.[57]

Before participants take action, certain conditions must be present, many of which are similar to those determining whether or not there can be an interaction in the first place. Interveners may wonder if the time is propitious; professionals await a call from principals or from their own organization. Permission may have to be obtained from local authorities before a demonstration can be staged. Money may have to be raised to pay for the expenses associated with the intervention. Lay interveners may seek additional training concerning the solution of practical problems. Principals may lack the courage to carry out the decision reached during the interaction; are you really willing to walk the dark streets at night to persuade drug addicts and prostitutes to seek psychiatric assistance at some clinic? Again and again individuals wish they could intervene to help the homeless or the malnourished, to promote greater equality in their society, or to prevent riots and wars; yet, correctly or not, they feel powerless to intervene effectively: what can I do to help? Nowadays many communications in modern and not-so-modern countries point to damages in the natural environment resulting from human intervention. Principals learn about the greenhouse effect of chemical emissions from factories and cars, and they may come to treasure bits of wisdom such as Francis Bacon's view that the only way to command Nature is to obey her. The action they take, sorting their rubbish or collecting plastics and old newspapers for recycling, may or should appear trivial in comparison with what might be accomplished by controlling pollution and destruction at their sources.

Interveners may assume or believe they can assume that principals have already participated in some kind of interaction and merely must be told which action is appropriate or necessary. Members of a congregation within a church presumably belong and subscribe to the order's precepts; during the service and especially in the sermon their beliefs become salient and actions are demanded or recommended. "How to Do It All," the World Federalist Association proclaimed in the early 1990s. By "all" was meant in its own words the following: "abolish war," "protect human rights," "promote economic and social progress," and "build a new world order." These objectives could be attained by demanding "a *new* United Nations"; and the specific ways to achieve the changes were indicated. More specifically, those receiving the circular were told that the changes could be facilitated by signing an attached petition to the American president asking him to take the initiative to "Strengthen the United Nations" ("All Signed Petitions Will Be Delivered Directly to President Bush") and to join and contribute money to the association. Similarly, in many dual interventions the expert intervener tells the principal the action to be taken to improve his physical or mental health, to curb maladaptive tendencies in his children, to increase the productivity of his land, or to protect his home and himself against criminals.

Moral issues can delay or preclude action when interveners would act upon their inclination in international affairs. Such interventions involve the seemingly contradictory procedures in theory provided by the UN Charter as previously mentioned and the "conflict between two fundamental principles of international law": mentioned by a political scientist: "the right of self-defense by the intervening state and the right of independence on the part of the target state." The same writer indicates the different situations in which international law during the present century has permitted interveners in practice to violate that right of independence or national sovereignty. Recognized governments may receive outside assistance when their country is plagued by a civil conflict. Intervention is justified to protect the interventionist's own nationals or, more generally, what is vaguely or concretely called human rights. Outside assistance may be given a country when it is being attacked by another country, whether that aid comes from one other country or a group of countries. The intervening country may be requested to intervene under specified conditions or as a result of a standing treaty of "friendship and cooperation." Intervention may be tolerated when conditions in the country being invaded appear to disrupt conditions in neighboring countries.[58]

International law thus provides moral bases for military action. From somebody's standpoint, however, particularly that of the invaded country, the justification being invoked may be considered invalid or wrong or a rationalization of some other goal. In 1991 when representatives of President George Bush and of the leaders of a few other countries voted in the Security Council to send military forces, principally American, into the Persian Gulf in order to force the Iraqi leader to withdraw his forces from Kuwait, the interveners may also have had motives related to their oil supplies in that region; and the president may have sought to draw attention away from his tarnished domestic policies. If the Security Council in the future is to prevent and quell conflicts more effectively, probably it must have sufficient funds available to recruit and direct a standing force that is adequately armed for the sole purpose of self-defense and that can be rapidly deployed to enforce its decisions.

EVALUATION

Chapter Eight

The intervention has ended, at least for the time being. One or more interveners have interacted with one or more principals; appropriate action has or has not taken place. The participants themselves, academic theorists, journalists, and the rest of us now evaluate what has happened, especially with reference to the problem originally initiating the intervention after a precipitating event. Was that problem solved or not? Evaluations are important not only because they inevitably occur but also because they indicate the reasons or the alleged reasons for the success or failure and can be used as guides for future interventions.

Criteria for assessment, like all other aspects of intervention, are most varied. Participants, especially principals, judge an intervention in terms of their own goals or needs: in the short or long run have those goals or needs been achieved or satisfied? The outcome is considered to be the meaningful criterion. Another judgment involves the procedure of the intervention, the value of which is praised or condemned. Outcome and values, then, are the leitmotivs of this chapter.

Outcome

Questions concerning the solution of the original problem are crucial. The intervention was a success, it seems. That lad was rescued. The patient was cured after being treated by a physician. The two persons who had been having an argument shook hands and agreed on a solution to their disagreement after a mutual friend indicated possible reasons for their misunderstanding. The Security Council of the United Nations passed a number of resolutions; its forces—especially those from the United States—bombed Iraqi forces, then began an invasion of Kuwait; and the Iraqi government quickly called for an armistice and began to withdraw its forces from Kuwait. In these instances were the interventions successful?

Three guides to evaluating the outcomes of interventions are essential: perspective, consequences, and the evaluator's own judgment. A single or even a number of successes or failures of particular intervention modes does not necessarily augur a similar outcome for the future. Yes, the lad is safe and the patient's temperature is normal. But that mutual friend may be later ignored by his two acquaintances.

Three scholars have sought to provide perspective concerning the efforts of the United Nations and other international agencies to settle disputes between 1945 and 1970. Their analysis indicates that about half of these conflicts were settled successfully either by stopping the hostilities or isolating the conflicts. Such a balance sheet, however, is insufficient; it is important to determine under what conditions success or failure was achieved. From the summary of this study, three statements—expressed in the present tense but referring to those two and a half decades—concerning the United Nations are arbitrarily quoted:

> While no single leadership pattern shows marked success in the U.N., success is least often scored when leadership is exercised by the weakest nation.
>
> In the U.N., conflicts that are never formally discussed are often managed successfully by the Secretary-General.
>
> In the U.N., . . . the higher the intensity of the conflict, the

more active is the organizational response, the more energetic the field operations, and the greater the degree of success.[1]

In addition to the leadership of the Secretary-General, the intensity of the conflict, and the actual action of the interveners, other factors that affected outcomes were cooperation with a superpower, the type of resolution by the Security Council, the attitude of the nation being admonished, and the presence of a UN peacekeeping operation.[2] On this actuarial basis, therefore, success has depended on a variety of factors, so that the utilization of intervention could not guarantee success and, if successful, would be attributable to a complex pattern of factors. Perspective is thus needed not only to determine the reasons for the outcome of interventions but also to view them as they will be judged later. The Iraqis were driven out of Kuwait in 1991, but you and I must wonder what historians will say in 2041 concerning that intervention. And the "victories" of the Crusaders in the Middle Ages? An objective American political scientist has recorded instances in which opposing groups concerning environmental issues, including government agencies, have been either satisfied or dissatisfied by agreements reached as a result of mediation;[3] but of course the battle to preserve the environment and to protect profits continues on and on.

Second, all the consequences of interventions must be considered before they can be judged to have succeeded or failed or to have been somewhere in between. A multiple intervention, as in international affairs, that fails to reach an agreement can be a partial success: the very effort to do so prevents the conflict from escalating, so that no action rather than destructive action is taken and the possibility of resuming the effort to reduce the conflict remains. Certainly for years after the intervention of the Turkish army in Cyprus in 1974 and the cruel fighting that broke out between the Greek and Turkish communities, the presence of the UN peacekeeping force there helped to prevent renewed warfare between those two communities. Both sides profited from the prolonged if restless peace and strengthened their own economies without reaching an agreement concerning a more enduring settlement, consequences not anticipated generally or in detail at the outset of the UN operation. Peacekeeping there—and, woe is me and all of us, elsewhere in the Middle East, Asia, and Africa— has not led to peacemaking. On a less pessimistic but not a magnificent note, although our unofficial workshop in the Horn of Africa obviously did not solve the problems between Somalia and her two neighbors, the Kenyan principals did inform their authorities, as reported in the last chapter, what they had learned in the workshop, namely, that the Somali intruders were not bandits. Hence, we were subsequently told, the Kenyan radio station ceased referring to them as bandits in its Somali-language programs.

And now third: the evaluation of the participants in the same intervention may differ. Principal A and Principal B submit their problem to an apparently unbiased arbitrator who decides in favor of A. At the moment of decision, A calls the intervention a success because he won; B calls it a failure because he lost or because now he is obliged to make concessions or compromises; the intervener calls it a success because he apparently settled the dispute; and a neutral observer calls it a failure either because he sympathizes with B or because from his standpoint the decision was unjust or immoral.

Either then or later, A and the intervener may feel distressed because both of them "really" preferred a compromise. Or A may believe that he did not merit the victory or that he did not obtain the gratification he had anticipated therefrom. After other experiences or additional guidance the intervener believes he made a mistake: B was treated unfairly. Then there may be an additional complication: the public statements of A and B at any time may not be expressions of what they "really" think.

Interveners in multiple interventions like labor-management disputes may believe that a successful resolution has been attained; externally their judgment appears correct, but one or more of the principals may continue to harbor resentments that lead again to future conflicts. From the standpoint of the intervener, of the groups and persons affected by a company, and perhaps of the general public, the intervention has been successful. Since the two groups of principals, however, have had to modify their demands somewhat or make concessions to reach the agreement—the union did not achieve the absolute wage increase it had initially demanded and the company agreed to a partial increase and hence a decrease in profits—the success was incomplete for both sides. Within the company or the union, there may be persons pleased or displeased by the settlement: some rejoice because the strike has been averted; others are happy because wages have been increased; still others rejoice less joyously because they consider the increase to be too small. The arbitrator may be disappointed because the goal he postulated was not attained; thus he believes that no lasting reconciliation between labor and management has been achieved, yet the intervention may have reduced tension between the principals and at the very least have enabled them to explore possible solutions to future conflicts.[4]

Oversights

After appreciating the surprises concerning interactions solemnly tolled in chapter 7, it should come as no additional surprise to anticipate that errors of evaluation likewise occur. *Since interventions involve interveners and principals, and since often more or many persons are affected, faulty judgments concerning the success or failure of the interaction are likely.* Either participant may wish to believe that his or her efforts have been successful and then be ready to make such an evaluation.

A patient follows a physician's advice, swallows the medicine regularly as prescribed, and the ailment disappears. The intervention has been successful? No, the same laudatory result may have been achieved without the intervention after the passing of time. What is required is some form of methodological control: another person with a similar ailment who does not take the medicine; a recurrence of the ailment in the same principal who this time has no medicine; or, as mentioned during the discussion of Commandment 8 pertaining to principals' consent, large numbers suffering from the ailment, with half assigned randomly and obligatorily to the experimental or medicine-taking group and the remainder to the control group without the medicine.

The need for a control may appear irrelevant, as when a mediator between a union and management averts a threatened strike as a result of an agreement reached during the intervention. Even then, however, evaluation is perilous if and when future interventions are planned on the basis of that success, for then it is necessary to know which ingredients during the interaction produced the agreement: the particular company, the union, the principals, the procedure that was followed, the skill or charm of the intervener? Caution may also be required even when both an experimental and a control group have been observed or measured. During or after the period of the intervention experienced by the experimental group, the control group may have had uncontrolled experiences that affected its members in a manner similar to the intervention that they did not experience. With a single experimental group, moreover, the statistical measure of change must be carefully selected. To reduce gun-related crimes the Massachusetts legislature once passed a gun-control law; an examination of the raw data and one statistical analysis at first indicated a decrease in such crimes in one city after the passing of the new law, but a reanalysis of the same data concluded that the apparent change was "not statistically significant."[5]

An evaluation of a dual intervention is too sweeping when many principals participate: their average may go up or down, yet those deviating from that average may merit special consideration. Forty depressed women in Great Britain were once assigned to social workers for counseling; an equivalent number of controls were not assisted. All the women were reassessed six and twelve months later on a psychiatric schedule. Some but not all were found to be less depressed according to the findings of the later assessment, and more of the experimental than the control group had improved; but in both groups those with marital problems tended to continue to be depressed.[6] When American college students—and less intensively their parents and other adults—were queried in the late 1960s concerning their participating in and attitudes toward protests such as those concerning the Vietnam War or civil rights, their responses varied along a continuum, at one end of which was indifference or failure to support the cause or opposition to it, in the middle sympathy or some concern shown by making only easily executed gestures of support, and at the other end active support.[7] In both studies the deviating exceptions disturbed the guides and merited special attention.

What appears to be a successful intervention can lead to overconfidence in that success and hence the possibility of a different evaluation in the future. Curricula can be imposed on schools, but the hope that the students will be permanently affected by their experiences in the classroom can be illusory. A discrepancy between school learning and the contents of the mass media as well as the experience of reality in society can produce dissatisfaction either with what has been taught or with the society or system that imposes it. Perhaps the portrait of communism previously taught in the schools of Eastern Europe under domineering Communist regimes was so different from everyday living that some of the disillusionment with the system can now be traced perilously to that contradiction.

The interventions of one country in the affairs of another are especially difficult to evaluate, and hence oversights are likely. Volumes have been and will be written on the effect of sanctions on South Africa by other countries during the 1980s and the early 1990s. They were imposed, as indicated in chapter 4, in order to express disapproval of apartheid and also to bring about reform. Were sanctions effective? Many South African whites must have perceived the disapproval symbolized by that measure; some may have felt chagrined that their country was thus being excluded from the family of nations; others protested that the action involved interference in their own political system. Divestment—the withdrawal of foreign companies from South Africa—often accompanied sanctions, but their plants and offices were purchased at bargain prices by South African whites who thus profited from the intervention. Both measures resulted in the loss of jobs by non-Europeans, only some of whom hoped that this loss would be temporary and would result eventually in ending apartheid and in a better society and hence greater prosperity for themselves. Likewise, it is difficult to draw a general conclusion concerning the effectiveness of sanctions per se as domineering interventions: when employed elsewhere, they function in different economic and political systems. Again we see the same perils regarding the location of causes when many variables interact.

Additional errors may be unavoidable in such complex multiple interventions. Below are the problems discussed in two volumes of papers originally presented in 1985 at the annual meeting of the International Association for Impact Assessment in the Netherlands, attended by 170 persons:

increasing or decreasing birthrates
economic growth
manufacturing of fertilizer
pubic transportation, including railways and roads
pipelines
pollution and hazardous wastes
nuclear power plants and other technologies
telecommunications
water supply
"an artificial island in the North Sea for industrial activities"

Solutions of such problems through intervention, the contributors to the volumes insist, require the skill and experience of trained natural and social scientists, legal authorities, and managers before even a tentative assessment can be made and also because monitoring is essential. Even when it is recognized that warnings about technological impacts are both necessary and desirable, the inability to make value-free assessments of these and other changes also introduces into decisions about future interventions "an unavoidable element" of uncertainty which then plays "a major role."[8]

Possibly, too, evaluators do not or cannot take into account consequences that have not been intended or foreseen. A solicitous mother intervenes in the socialization of her daughter by functioning as a parent. When the child matures and guides children of her own, she may try to socialize them in a manner in accord with or contrary to her own childhood experience—and her mother may not have intended to bequeath such deliberate, self-conscious, domineering intervening. Unintended consequences become more probable as the number of principals affected by the intervention increases. Indeed, parents of children whose traits or actions they have modified discover later that such successful socialization is maladaptive in situations they could not possibly have anticipated.[9] During their lifetime, significant religious, political, and military persons intervened in the lives of their followers and others, but only a team of godlike historians, few of whom have ever existed, can indicate definitively the influence they actually exercised upon their own and subsequent generations; and in what sense are they responsible for a future they did not experience?

Most political interventions inside a country have repercussions that transcend the original intentions of the interveners and hence are overlooked at their inception. Such insight is especially prominent in developing countries. When once some of these indigenous peoples acquired a useful object from the West like a bicycle or benefited from a Western practice like a particular medicine, many but not all of them subsequently have been motivated to obtain additional products and to adopt other Western practices until eventually they or their descendants have become more completely westernized.[10] The initial interveners, their own peers, the colonizers, and the commercial companies who introduced them to the new ways, thus unintentionally initiated the changes.

Finally, it may be premature to assess interventions on the basis of current evidence when new evidence in the future can change the evaluation. The patient may be immediately "cured" after taking the drug, the overweight person follows the fad and eats less, the strike is called off after a resolution has been mediated, the two political or ethnic factions agree not to attack each other. But what happens subsequently: does the ailment recur, does the person abandon the diet, is there another strike after a period of peace, do hostilities break out again? The resolution of an intervention may even be accurately recalled, yet the details concerning why and how it was achieved are subject to distortion, just as children who, though they know the outcome of a fable like Jack and the Beanstalk, experience suspense many times during the retelling of the same tale.[11]

Past interventions may be difficult or impossible to describe or analyze accurately in the absence of adequate archives, yet the archives themselves may be inaccurate for many reasons: the events have not been accurately recorded, the participants have emphasized activities more favorable to their future reputation than to truth, legends glorify or vilify actual events. Participants can have afterthoughts concerning themselves; a questionnaire devoted to misgivings contains items such as "Were there things that you would have liked to have said or done . . . but did not?" and "How satisfied were you with tonight's session?"[12] In the short run, principals may be displeased by the outcome of an intervention, but later criticize themselves for the role they played in selecting the intervener or for agreeing initially to participate; in retrospect, they find fault with the system when the choice of intervener was not theirs or when they were forced to participate.

Throughout the years since it was first assembled in 1959, the Dartmouth Conference has produced joint reports in which Soviet and American principals reached understanding on problems of interest to their two countries. They met in both countries, even though Soviet officials once insisted that such meetings could not replace formal diplomatic relations.[13] Likewise Pugwash Conferences provided similar exchanges of ideas between the same two countries. During the summer of 1988, the members discussed "Global Problems and Common Security" and were greeted by a statement from Mikhail Gorbachev. Papers were presented on nuclear disarmament, the proliferation of nuclear weapons, chemical warfare, European security, global environmental problems, and alleviating underdevelopment.[14] The principals at such conferences were attempting to intervene to obtain the objectives stated in the titles of their presentations. Talk, talk, talk? A prayerful guess: at the very least the talk increased understanding among the powerless principals who attended and may also have influenced those who read or heard about their views as well as some of the policymakers who helped bring about the apparently significant changes in the relations between the two countries that occurred in the late 1980s and early 1990s.

Moral Values

Without exception *evaluations of interventions are incomplete* and hence guilty of some oversight *unless they are referred to the moral values inevitably embedded in the goals that are or are not achieved.* Charitable and religious organizations intervene in developing countries to allay starvation and disease and do so successfully during a limited period of time; yet such seemingly benevolent interceptions may contribute close to zero to remedying poverty, which together with climate, political and economic exploitations, and corruption has probably produced the misery in the first place.[15] Criminals are restrained successfully by being incarcerated in prisons; there they may or may not acquire desirable traits that make them respectable citizens when and if they are released. In World War II South Africa and the United States were among the countries that intervened successfully in behalf of Britain, France, and the Soviet Union; after the defeat of Germany and Japan all the victorious countries continued to be plagued with domestic problems of poverty and inequality that raised perplexing moral challenges.

Interventions may resolve problems arising from specific events, but in the longer run it is both necessary and desirable to wonder whether ultimate values are achieved by or accompany the actions of participants. Are they unwittingly answering the pleas ascribed to St. Francis of Assisi, "Where there is hatred, let me sow love; where there is injury, pardon; where there is doubt, faith; where there is despair, hope; where there is sadness, joy; where there is darkness, light"?[16] Feasible, possible, probable?

Both in the last and first analysis the evaluation of interventions is referred to the evaluator's own values. You immediately agree. But there are subtleties. A concrete example is extracted from an interview during World War II between a Mennonite and the Saskatchewan War Board in Canada:

Q: Why do you object to bearing arms?

A: Because we are taught to love our enemies.

Q: Do you love the Nazis and the Japanese?

A: I love their souls.

Q: Do you love their acts?

A: No.

Q: Do you think they should be restrained in their acts?

A: No. Because we are told to resist not evil.

Q: In the event of this country being invaded, what [are] you prepared to do?

A: I would pray.

Q: Is that all?

A: Yes. I have nothing to gain and nothing to lose here. I serve the Lord. I have been promised that if I am faithful I shall have a crown of life forever.

Q: And that is what you are fighting for?

A: Yes.[17]

How is one to evaluate the sentiments of this young man who was intervening in behalf of his faith by resisting conscription? His interrogator would conclude that he was a conscientious objector who would have to be assigned to some "alternative service" such as working in a hospital or on a farm or forest. Many Canadians would have condemned him for avoiding military service at a time when the Germans and Japanese were threatening enemies. From this temporal distance half a century later, you or I might be intrigued and praise him for consistently following his beliefs, and then one of us might wonder whether he may have been setting a laudable or dangerous example for you or me right now. He himself, all Mennonites then and now, and pacifists would contend that the intervention, although it did not halt World War II or any subsequent war, at the least communicated a relation between religious faith and action or the contradiction between brotherly love and war.

Evaluators, whether they be interveners or principals, may appraise a decision by referring to some transcending principle they apply to the problem at hand. The patient and his physician invoke an obvious principle: has the patient been helped or cured, can the change be attributed to the diagnosis and the subsequent treatment? When a dam is constructed to prevent floods, to improve navigation on a river, or ensure a steady supply of water for irrigating fields or for animal and human consumption, the evaluation is more complicated. Consideration must be given not only to the stated purpose but also to whatever distress results among families who have been evacuated from the land flooded by the water behind the dam as well as to the cost-effectiveness of the project.

In addition to evaluating the outcome of a multiple intervention, experimental and historical evidence indicate that participants employ empirical, pragmatic criteria that invoke one or more of the commandments concerning intervention versus nonintervention revealed in chapter 6 as well as the following:

1. *Is the outcome just or fair?* Having achieved or not achieved their own objective, participants decide whether that outcome conforms to a moral value. Winners are more likely to offer a favorable assessment than losers. Likewise, bystanders who lean toward one group of principals rather than the other may be similarly disposed, but those with no identification may be in a better position to render a judgment stemming from a value not associated with their own objectives.

2. *Have the principals had an adequate opportunity to present their viewpoints?* If members of one group believe they have not been able to defend their objectives fully and if they live in a society that promotes or encourages such expression, their assessment will be unfavorable. "Procedural justice processes operate in all social settings," it has been hypothesized on the basis of systematic studies, common sense, and intuition,[18] which here must mean that interventions, however trivial and incidental, are assessed with reference to the method through which they have been achieved. You interrupt my train of thought to convey crucial information; I may not like your

method, yet I excuse you because that was the only procedure you could have followed to come to my assistance. After an interaction, principals may wonder whether they have been treated respectfully, politely, and fairly as they assess the decision and, if feasible, question whether they should abide by it.[19]

3. *Who has made the decision regarding the outcome, and what role have the principals played?* In mandatory and especially in binding arbitration the principals know preactively that they themselves will not make the ultimate decision and hence that they may not approve of the resolution. Therefore they assess formal rules and their own relation to them: Did one's own side have an equal opportunity to contribute to the outcome, or was there disproportional representation so that the opponents' side had an advantage? Was the evaluation being made by the intervener, the principals, or an outsider?

4. *Is the outcome in accord with the participants' anticipation before and during the intervention?* Various emotions may be evoked, depending on whether the outcome is consistent with the expectation and, if inconsistent, whether it turns out to be a pleasant or a unpleasant surprise.

The evaluation of an outcome is important not only because it brings satisfaction or dissatisfaction to the participants, but also because it may have important consequences for future interventions. Interveners who have achieved their objective are motivated to repeat the method they have employed, and those who have failed may strive to improve it if they intervene again. Principals who are pleased seek to be guided by the same or a similar intervener and to participate in interventions following a similar procedure. Intervening institutions such as arbitrating societies and international associations thus acquire different skills and reputations with the passing of time. The modes of assessment are related and hence may be confounded: you think the intervention was fair because you won or unfair because you lost.

The failure to raise moral questions is likely to result in an incomplete evaluation. In the early 1980s, a scrupulously careful statistical analysis of available data revealed the following:

In 25 countries young men are eligible to go to war at an earlier age than they are eligible to vote.

The cost of a single new nuclear submarine equals the annual education budget of 23 developing countries with 160 million school-age children.

In a year when U.S. farmers were paid to take nearly 100 million acres of cropland out of production, 450 million people in the world are starving.[20]

Dominating governments thus charged with intervening affected the lives of people by compelling young men to be soldiers and also, as a result of other priorities, by curtailing educational and nutritional resources. The value judgments behind each of the three interventions may seem praiseworthy until the indicated alternatives are considered. When the background of a particular governmental decision is examined in detail, such as President Lyndon Johnson's decision to intervene in the Vietnam War in 1965[21] or President George Bush's 1991 excursion into Kuwait and Iraq, it appears that such decisions have resulted from a variety of factors, including the traditional policies and prejudices of the nations, the leader's personal views, the recommendation of trusted advisers, and the availability of relevant military and overall information,[22] the value of each of which must be considered and weighted in context. Likewise, the policy of "multiculturalism" confronting the Canadian government raises a moral question: should ethnic communities like those of Canadian aborigines, and French-Canadian, Chinese, European, and West Indian groups retain their own cultures which they themselves value, or should such communities be discouraged so that eventually Canada can become more unified from a cultural standpoint?[23]

Unraveling

Let it be imagined that a semimiracle has occurred: in spite of perplexing perils, it is possible to judge that a particular intervention has been not only definitely successful or unsuccessful but also indisputably good or bad. The evaluator rejoices: the child has been rescued, the threatened strike has been averted and both sides find the settlement satisfactory. Or the evaluator is gloomy: the patient died, the good offices of a third government were unable to avert the outbreak of the war. The evaluator, however, is a perfectionist and is not content. Another question is raised: why was the intervention a success or a failure?

There is no easy answer to such a question, even when there is agreement concerning the value of the outcome. That value-oriented assumption can be disputed: if the patient no longer wished to live (remember the person in chapter 6?), from his standpoint the unsuccessful operation might have been called a success. For the sake of the present analysis, nevertheless, the challenge to the intervention's value is gently and temporarily pushed aside.

In every imaginable intervention, the least perilous guide is that *the explanation for an outcome cannot be forever unraveled and ascribed to one or even more than one decision leading to the completed intervention; all of them must be evaluated.* The rescuer of the child had to be near the lake, the child had to be visible or audible, the rescue would have been futile if it had been delayed, and so on. Possibly the surgeon was inexperienced or made a mistake, the patient waited too long to seek medical assistance, therapy less drastic than surgery might have produced a cure, and (again) so on. In every instance the outcome depends upon all of the steps.

Some unraveling may sound feasible. The conclusion is drawn that the brilliant mediator certainly facilitated the resolution, someone else would not have succeeded, compulsory arbitration would have been a disaster. The war would not have broken out if the intervention had been preactive rather than reactive and if there had not been an economic depression in the more aggressive of the two countries. Unraveling points to crucial steps in the specific intervention by assuming that other steps, would not have been propitious.

Such weighting suggests that limited unraveling of one or more of the decisions is possible and desirable. A less brilliant mediator might also have inspired a successful intervention—but not a prejudiced intervener. Even if the depression in the aggressive country had been less severe, the war would have occurred—but maybe not if there had been prosperity or if the government had been somehow compelled to respond to public opinion. Within the range of variability, it is absolutely necessary to proclaim that "other things" must be equal, which means also within some range.

The guide concerning unraveling need not be utilized if and when the purpose of the explanation is to unravel only the leading reasons for the success or failure of past interventions. Many of the actions of a Caesar or a Napoléon can be ascribed—even in large part—to their talents, but other events in their lifetime may not be neglected. The guide, however, is essential when future interventions are planned. It would be best to have a brilliant mediator again, but what should we do if one is not available?

Unraveling in behalf of future interventions offers only a tentative guide. Also tentative must be judgments concerning success or failure and the value achieved or not achieved. Consequently, tentativeness itself must be assaulted as a final guide.

Tentativeness

"We may search for the last word," one writer has profoundly commented, "but so long as human thought continues, the last word should be unattainable, for there is always more that can be said."[24] That statement inevitably recalls both the methodology and the philosophy embodied in the definition of chaotic behavior provided in chapter 1. Likewise, *judgments concerning evaluations remain forever tentative.* Interventions in the future affected by the memories and images retained and recalled by participants concerning other participants are likely to be imperfect: sometimes consistent, at other times inconsistent impressions become salient. The disruption of a human relationship, such as a divorce, whether achieved through intervention or not, may seem gratifying at first, but then guilt lingers and leaves "a residue of grief and depression."[25] If the already elastic meaning of intervention may be stretched for the last time, intervening in a living language by creating a neologism, enlarging a word's connotations, or giving a turn to a phrase may not win adherents in the short run, yet the linguistic innovation can gradually become part of popular or scholarly discourse. Planners and naturalists achieve their objective of preserving a wilderness area, and then later the trees are ravaged by animals, pests, or fire; eventually the forest recovers, provided other hazards are not introduced in the meantime by a new generation of loggers. A surgical operation turns out to be only a temporary success after the patient has been discharged from the hospital. Smokers who seek help from physicians, therapists, and others who claim to utilize ingenious or sure-fire methods may smoke less or smoke not at all during the treatment, but then later some of them drop out and return to their normal habit.[26] Obese, neurotic, or fashion-conscious persons may be helped at first by the interveners they consult and later regain their lost weight because they are unable to resist tempting foods.

Many studies concerning interventions to raise the so-called intelligence of children (the ones mentioned in chapter 5) also reveal that the effects may disappear as the children grow older.[27] An individual feels satisfied that he or she has achieved his momentary goal, perhaps at the expense of someone else, then later suffers from feelings of guilt.[28] Leaders and managers intervene and improve the functioning of organizations; yet, as suggested by a political scientist who defines organizations very broadly and surveys them historically, most organizations usually "die" as a result of their inability or "failure" to adjust to new problems that arise. The explanation for those that survive "for great lengths of time is largely a matter of luck."[29] In addition, morally approved interventions fail over centuries in part because methods of intervention apparently cannot cope with recurring and unavoidable problems. "The war against war is going to be no holiday excursion or camping party," William James conceded as he sought "the moral equivalent of war," his provocative phrase that has been too frequently misinterpreted.[30]

Presumably the success of interventions may thus depend upon "luck," when luck includes a set of fortuitous circumstances not anticipated or controlled by interveners. The invocation of luck, however, produces a hesitant, perilous evaluation. In the long run, as previously indicated, interventions may be appraised as valuable in contrast to judgments rendered after their immediate termination, and of course vice versa. Think again of great religious figures whose influence both lingers and inspires. Wide-sweeping interventions, such as the new institutions (parliaments, courts, schools) introduced into developing countries after liberation from colonial rule, require not only the capability of satisfying the needs and aspirations of citizens but also the potentiality of stimulating their imagination (which probably means their central values): "It works and it thrills me." Transcendental patience, however, may be required to achieve such perspective; at the moment or shortly thereafter, the verdict concerning any accompanying sacrifice may be different. The various forms of protest during the pogroms of 1881 to 1882 by Russian intellectuals and in the European and American press did not halt the killing of Russian Jews, but in the longer run their flight to Palestine and especially to the United States[31] had repercussions that facilitated the eventual establishment of the state of Israel and may have contributed to the decrease of anti-Semitism elsewhere.

The evaluation of interventions in temporal perspective may not be final at a given moment. The strike is averted, but either side feels so dissatisfied that future interventions become difficult and appeal to neither group of principals. Toward the end of World War II an official of the American Office of Strategic Services made the following declaration: "Our interests require the maintenance of a policy designed to prevent the development of a serious threat to the security of the British Isles (and of the United States) through the consolidation of a large part of Europe's resources under any one power."[32] The policy in effect was implemented and the resulting interventions helped produce, if unintentionally, the cold war that eventually led to unanticipated changes in many European countries, including the Soviet Union. For the moment and beyond, a disease is cured, yet eventually the patient is weakened and succumbs to a more serious ailment.

Another patient does not follow a physician's advice. There is a deadlock between management and union, and the strike takes place.

Such failed interventions, however, can have beneficial consequences in the future. The patient conforms to medical advice a second time because he or she has learned that nonconformity brought discomfort or pain. During the strike principals from one of the contending groups become convinced that little or nothing is being gained from prolonging the action and then recall favorably one of the proposals that had been made but rejected during the interaction. Failure contributes to success, yes, but what about wars, what have officials and the rest of us learned from conflicts that occurred when negotiations or interventions failed?

Valid evaluations of historical interventions, especially after a long delay, are especially elusive. What influence did Aristotle or Vladimir Lenin have upon their contemporaries? Scientists ranging from biochemists to psychologists are baffled when they weight the contributions of genetic or physiological factors to atypical phenomena ranging from genius to insanity. Deciphering the rationale of political decisions is likewise puzzling. There may be a paucity of information: the private diaries of decision-makers, even if they are truthful, are usually not available; when interviews are feasible, the subjects may conceal more than they reveal for the sake of their personal privacy or public relations; those with valuable and relevant information are unlikely to speak out. The public statements of leaders that explain or justify interventions in the affairs of other nations must be viewed not with a grain but with a ton of salt; in the calm words of a German political scientist, there is "barely another area where the hypocrisy of states is as great as here, i.e., where there is such a disparity between solemnly professed principles and the necessity of state behavior."[33]

The reasons for waging or not waging a war in the formal or informal sense are often displayed in memoirs of the participating interveners or their associates, yet these sources too are not necessarily valid or reliable. Serious scholars are able to subsume judgments of political interveners under catchy phrases such as "preserve group harmony," "the self-serving rule," "rely on gut feelings," "seat of the pants," and so on,[34] which thus serve as satisfying, journalistic classifications that are superficially brilliant but probably only anecdotal and hence perhaps unenlightening. For diplomats, journalists, and curious citizens as well as scholars there is no end to the appearance of stimulating clichés that give rise to useful checklists enabling them to label the judgments of policymakers and conclude, "Ah ha, that's what made him think." Maybe his military staff told him that the armed forces were not in a state of readiness or were inadequate to deal with such an adversary: maybe their advice was heeded; maybe not.

Yet another approach is to speculate, wisely or otherwise, from experience or intuition concerning the reasons for the "defects in the governmental decision process," in this case the United States. It is said that "fundamentals" are ignored, "original suggestions" are in short supply, "improbable alternatives" are inadequately considered; the "decision-maker" wonders how his own career may be affected by the decision; "one decision" can damage the principal's relation to other decision-makers; and "trial balloons and planted stories" are difficult for officials to launch.[35] Inasmuch as particular decisions may also possibly spring from the temporary mood of the participants, it is not surprising that an extremely competent review of studies by psychologists and other social scientists who have sought to provide advice to officials concerning foreign policy concludes with the following guide: "Formidable conceptual and methodological obstacles exist simply to extrapolating solutions to particular problems from general theory or aggregate data"[36] (translation: such research is perilous, be skeptical concerning its practical utility). Scholarly delays in explaining the guides to intervention thus may not contribute to the validity of what is finally conjectured.

Efforts continue to extract principles from past experience as guides to future interventions. Such guides are tentative and must contain the usual perils of ifs and buts. In an interpersonal intervention, the stronger participant always wins; yes, but not if the weaker one has a figurative gun he is able to discharge. After surveying real and experimental studies of mediation, largely in the United States, two psychologists indicate that mediation has tended to be effective under the following conditions: when the conflict has been "moderate"; when the motivation to resolve the conflict has not been low; when the principals are committed to utilize mediation to settle their dispute; when resources, including financial ones, are available; when the principals do not consider that "issues of principle" are involved; when both groups appear to have "equal power" from a realistic standpoint; and when each group in conflict is not itself torn by disagreement.[37] To be noticed is the fact that even such a stimulating, long-winded generalization is perforce cautiously phrased; it may not be valid in other cultural contexts.

Patience, therefore, is necessary, especially when the cost-effectiveness of an intervention, in whole or in part, is to be determined. Diplomatic staffs and their administrative machinery require a slice of a nation's budget, the cost of which is both economically and morally much lower than the losses resulting from the absence of such staffs that can range from economic waste to war itself. Early interventions to prevent later interventions that include dealing with children at high risk or the social and political conditions that account for the risks are themselves costly; yet the costs are impressively less than the savings that result from not having to imprison the principals if as adults they commit criminal offenses which an intervention might have prevented.[38]

Ideologies, whether the traditional beliefs of a society or those formulated by reformers and revolutionaries, are usually difficult to change even over a long period of time. Principals may pay lip service to new beliefs they have learned during an intervention, yet then later their experience or their interpretation of that experience pushes them backward toward what they had previously believed. In September 1990 the reigning Pope reminded his Polish compatriots of the Holocaust: Jews there "were taken to the gas chambers, they underwent death—only because they were children of the people of the Patriarchs, of Moses, and the Prophets, the inheritors of the faith of Abraham." The cardinal who was Primate of Poland then stated in a pastoral letter that was read during Mass in all Roman Catholic churches in that country:

We expressed our sincere regret for all the incidents of anti-Semitism which were committed at any time or by any one on Polish soil . . . all incidents of anti-Semitism are contrary to the spirit of the Gospel and—as Pope John Paul II emphasized—"remain opposed to the Christian vision of human dignity."

. . . The most important way to overcome the difficulties that still exist today is the establishment of a dialogue which would lead to the elimination of distrust, prejudices, and stereotypes, and to mutual acquaintance and understanding based on respect as well as opening the way to cooperation in many fields. It is important, moreover, that while doing this, we learn to experience and appreciate the proper religious contexts of Jews and Christians, as they are lived by Jews and Christians themselves.[39]

This program proposes an intervention in the ideology of Poles and of many Christians as well as Jews elsewhere. It would affect, as indicated in the same letter, long-standing ideologies. The Church is confronted with a difficult objective that is likely to be achieved only after a large number of interventions (via mass media, religious organizations, and workshops) repeated not only in Poland but also in other countries.

For some time after the completion of an intervention, it may appear that only judgments have been affected, with no corresponding change in behavior. During the interaction, however, the information that has been communicated concerning either issues or the participants can become relevant and affect action in the future. The fruitful assumption must be that an interaction produces some change, especially in multiple interventions. On the surface principals may appear unchanged, and indeed the content of their judgments and actions can be momentarily unaffected; yet the experience of the interaction probably reinforces some past tendencies and thus future interventions may be influenced.

Even a careful evaluation of an intervention can be changed in the future. Evaluations of the Munich agreement between Neville Chamberlain and Adolf Hitler in 1938 have shifted over the years. At first many non-Germans greeted that event with joy because apparently war had been averted; then when war came and as their joy faded, Chamberlain was deposed; and now more than a half century later perhaps those oldsters still alive view it in perspective and realize that the British were thereby given the opportunity to rearm before the outbreak of war. Without the nervous peace that lasted slightly less than a year they might have been defeated.

In the late 1930s it looked as if a dual intervention program for boys between the ages of five and thirteen, extending over a period of about five years, would be or had been successful. One set of 250 received almost every imaginable assistance, such as being provided with counseling, tutorials, medical attention, and vacation at a camp. A matched control set of 250 was not treated. Thirty years later, an analysis was made of the court and other records of both groups as well as the replies to questionnaires distributed to as many of the individuals who were alive and could be located. Those who had been principals tended to remember the intervention and the interveners in glowing terms. As adults both groups, however, were very similar with respect to marital status, percentage being classified as unskilled and blue-collar workers, political orientation, and ways of spending their leisure time. In comparison with the control group, very slightly more—*not* less—of those who had been treated, moreover, had committed more than one serious crimes, were engaged in occupations with lower prestige, had died at a younger age, had experienced serious mental illnesses, were alcoholics, and derived less satisfaction from their use of leisure time. Possibly the intervention had created among the principals in the intervention, the treatment group, a sense of dependency, the anticipation that they would continue to be helped, too high expectations in general, or internal conflicts resulting from comparing themselves with their interveners. "Interaction programs," the evaluator herself concludes, "risk damaging the individual they are designed to assist"[40]—another ethical issue concerning research on intervention to be piled upon those already mentioned.

The various methods to produce experiential learning mentioned in the previous chapter may successfully change principals without affecting the problem that has initially inspired the intervention, even when cordial rapport is established among those confronting one another who come to peer beneath their own verbiage and locate a basis for resolving the problem. Multiple interventions may also produce resolutions without effecting "basic" changes within principals, who may continue to distrust or dislike one another while still agreeing to the proposed solution. In all interventions, dual and multiple, action to be followed from the verbal resolution may remain stillborn.

More specifically, the interaction-produced changes may be ineffective in "real" life back home. The dreams from the interaction, let us agree once more, can be punctured by those with power to implement a proposed resolution. The walks in the woods, as the private talks between an American and Soviet official in July 1982 near the French border in Switzerland have been called (though usually the singular *walk* is used), apparently enabled the two diplomats to reach an understanding regarding arms reduction by their own countries, but their superiors subsequently rejected the "packages" (the designation by the American).[41] Again and again, American scholars in academic institutions and those in research institutes who emerge with brilliant plans of action to resolve current problems, especially those with an economic-political flavor, learn to their own dismay that government officials ignore their relevant recommendations concerning interventions and file them away after providing their authors with perfunctory or profuse thanks. The researchers may not have been trained to present their reports in a manner that is intelligible or appealing to the officials who have not provided a channel to receive them. An aside: it is conceivable that these thinkers and others do in fact possess sufficient knowledge to reduce the probability of wars and other intergroup disputes, maybe even to eliminate them, if only their recommendations were heeded—conceivable, but possible? In addition, events may render an intervention's resolution inappropriate or irrelevant; when the Somalis in our workshop concerned with conflicts in the Horn of Africa returned home in 1969, their own government was overthrown and hence they were compelled to communicate—unsuccessfully it seems—with a different and less sympathetic set of leaders.[42]

In such multiple interventions, the principals may then be compelled to function as interveners when they confront those in power and would have them adopt at least some of the ideas resulting from a walk in the woods or a workshop. They communicate their recommendations in language their superiors may comprehend. Their "nonofficial contacts" may have provided "an opportunity to try out new ideas"[43] that they themselves at least can communicate to their peers and thus have some effect upon public opinion. In general, however, the effect of that opinion upon policymakers in turn is difficult to ascertain. When the two leaders of the Soviet Union and the United States met at Malta in December 1989, could the cordiality of Mr. Bush have been affected by surveys which showed that the percentage of Americans having favorable opinions of the Soviets increased from 15 to 30 percent and the percentages having unfavorable feelings decreased from 41 to 13 percent during the ensuing twenty-two months?[44]

The organizers of a half dozen workshops in the 1970s involving Arabs and Jews in Israel suggest that the enterprises achieved both focus and flexibility. The principals focused upon the conflict between the two communities but also changed their beliefs as additional information was acquired. The principals affected one another creatively, and there emerged perhaps "a useful addition to the tool of international conflict resolution," although subsequently the interveners forced themselves to admit that these workshops were "no panacea" for the basic conflict at hand.[45] Some observers of the step-by-step diplomacy undertaken in the Middle East by Henry Kissinger for almost two years after the October War of 1973 believe that "the central and most thorny problems were left untouched and no easier to address (perhaps even more difficult to address) at a later time."[46] There is, alas, no way of knowing—at least to anyone not having access to the participants' files or their minds—whether the interactions so evaluated and the academic workshops may have contributed to the resumption of interactions among the same principals in 1990 to 1992. Similarly, large public meetings in behalf of worthy causes, such as those delicately favoring peace rather than war, conclude by passing resolutions, by having rapporteurs write and even publish concise, brilliant reports, or simply by adjourning on a high or a low note; and then subsequently nothing happens: wars and the threats of wars continue. Nothing happens? Some members of the audience may well have been influenced and begin or continue what they consider to be the good fight, and so eventually they may be influential in some related or unrelated respect.

Both in the short and long run, participants' reactions to an intervention affect their expectations concerning interventions in the future, including their attitudes toward participating again. Aside from the success or failure of the actual experience, they retain impressions of what has occurred. A careful study of thirty-four technical interveners who had been employed overseas by the Agency for International Development once revealed that their principal source of frustration during the intervention had been "the American organization" that employed them; less frequently mentioned were "attitude and feelings of the host nationals and the professional situation" they had encountered.[47] Clients probably consult the same attorney who has won their case or secured a satisfactory settlement for them in the past when new difficulties arise, provided they believe he or she has not changed or is equally competent to function in the new conflict.

Perhaps the most tentative judgments of all concerning intervention are those that would seek to forecast future actions. One can jump from past experiences or history and extrapolate: she has always sought advice from her elders, that political party has continually espoused the conservative or the liberal position, the nation has a long record of interfering in the affairs of other nations when it believes its own interests are being threatened. But the past is not an infallible guide to the future, obviously: she has become an adult and has not found a substitute for her elders, most of whom are now dead; the political party may decide to shift its strategy in order to gain more seats in the parliamentary body; and the nation may be able to achieve its objectives because it has joined a common community of nations and hence its citizens are better able to promote their own interests without assistance from the state. On the international front, perhaps the greatest change that is affecting the relations between modern nations has been a shift in the attitude toward the use of force to settle disputes and hence the branding of all wars, in the terminology of the Nuremburg and Tokyo trials after World War II, as "crimes against humanity"; principals perhaps are turning to interventions by third parties, such as a friendly country or the United Nations, to settle disputes.[48]

Above all, in the final analysis, when all is said and done, as everyone agrees, without fear of contradiction—select whichever phrasing you wish—evaluations of interventions remain tentative and perilous because human beings, like it or not, are engulfed in ever-changing events for which they are, or consider themselves, responsible or not responsible. They and their society inevitably experience these changing events, and therefore they seek to become or do become interveners and principals in interventions as they try to anticipate or resolve the ensuing problems. What's next? We must continue to believe that there is no surefire path to absolute or everlasting truth and that we are doomed or inspired to engage in trial and error in order to uncover the ways of living most satisfactory to ourselves. We dimly or brightly perceive guides to push us forward. And yet . . .

APPENDIX: CHECKLIST FOR ANALYZING OR ANTICIPATING INTERVENTIONS

Since the past is ever an uncertain guide to the future, since guides to interventions are always somewhat perilous, and since almost all interventions reflect a large number of variables, the best and probably the most useful procedure is to have available a checklist displaying those variables. Such a list appears in the following pages. For interested readers it may function as a convenient notebook or a reminder of the factors and variables to be considered in planning or evaluating a specific intervention.

The two checklist pages can be photocopied so that they may function usefully again and again.

The checklist is divided into eight sections that correspond to the eight chapters of this book; fuller explanations can therefore be found in each corresponding chapter. Herewith more detailed instructions after a title is given to the intervention at hand.

Chapter 1: Name the EVENT and the ensuing PROBLEM that have given rise to the intervention. *Specify* both PARTICIPANTS after "Dual" or "Multiple," whichever is applicable. *Encircle* the one PROCEDURE used in the intervention. For SEQUENCE in the parentheses *number as "1"* the step that has given rise to the intervention and then number in order others that may also have been relevant.

Chapters 2–5, 7–8: *Encircle* "Y" (yes), "N" (no), or "?" (don't know or irrelevant) whenever possible. With three exceptions, two or three of the trios of "Y," "N," and "?" should be judged and the appropriate choice encircled. As indicated, the first set always applies to the intervener; the second to the principal in a dual intervention or to the first principal or group in a multiple intervention; and the third set to the second principal or group in a multiple intervention. The three exceptions in chapter 5 refer to Salience of Cultural Setting, Peace, and Record Keeping, which apply to all participants.

Chapter 6: Select one or more of the commandments concerned with MORALITY and applicable to the intervention; in the parentheses place a "+" if the intervention conforms, a "−" if it does not conform, or a "±" if it conforms in some ways but not in others.

TITLE:

Event:

Problem

Participants: Dual:

Multiple:

Chapter 1 Foreground

Procedure	Consultation	Domination	Adjudication
	Consent	Mediation	Arbitration
Sequence	( ) Participants		
	( ) Rationale	( ) Timing	
	( ) Method	( ) Morality	
	( ) Reality	( ) Evaluation	

Chapter 2 Participants

	Intervener			Principal 1			Principal 2		
Power	Y	N	?	Y	N	?	Y	N	?
Experience	Y	N	?	Y	N	?	Y	N	?
Planning	Y	N	?	Y	N	?	Y	N	?
Confidence	Y	N	?	Y	N	?	Y	N	?
Adaptability	Y	N	?	Y	N	?	Y	N	?
Knowledge	Y	N	?	Y	N	?	Y	N	?
Trust	Y	N	?	Y	N	?	Y	N	?
Availability	Y	N	?	Y	N	?	Y	N	?

Chapter 3 Rationale

	Intervener			Principal 1			Principal 2		
Selection	Y	N	?	Y	N	?	Y	N	?
Alacrity	Y	N	?	Y	N	?	Y	N	?

Chapter 4 Timing

	Intervener			Principal 1			Principal 2		
No Delay	Y	N	?	Y	N	?	Y	N	?
Strong Motivation	Y	N	?	Y	N	?	Y	N	?
Resolvability	Y	N	?	Y	N	?	Y	N	?
Single Session	Y	N	?	Y	N	?	Y	N	?

Chapter 5 Method

	Intervener			Principal 1			Principal 2		
Salience of Cultural Setting	Y	N	?						
Site	Y	N	?	Y	N	?	Y	N	?
Peace	Y	N	?						
Uncertainty	Y	N	?	Y	N	?	Y	N	?
Reduction of Uncertainty	Y	N	?	Y	N	?	Y	N	?
Flexibility	Y	N	?	Y	N	?	Y	N	?
Record Keeping	Y	N	?						

Chapter 6 Morality

1. Killing ( )	2. Damage ( )	3. Force ( )	4. Interference ( )
5. Principle ( )	6. Truth ( )	7. Rights ( )	8. Pro-choice ( )
9. Consequences ( )	10. Nonintervention ( )		

Chapter 7   Reality

	Intervener			Principal 1			Principal 2		
Surprises	Y	N	?	Y	N	?	Y	N	?
Prearrangements	Y	N	?	Y	N	?	Y	N	?
Transformation	Y	N	?	Y	N	?	Y	N	?
Initiatives	Y	N	?	Y	N	?	Y	N	?
Action	Y	N	?	Y	N	?	Y	N	?

Chapter 8   Evaluation

	Intervener			Principal 1			Principal 2		
Positive Outcome	Y	N	?	Y	N	?	Y	N	?
Oversights	Y	N	?	Y	N	?	Y	N	?
Moral Values	Y	N	?	Y	N	?	Y	N	?
Unraveling	Y	N	?	Y	N	?	Y	N	?
Tentativeness	Y	N	?	Y	N	?	Y	N	?

NOTES

Chapter 1 Foreground

1. See, e.g., Urs Schwarz (1971). *Abkehr von der Gewalt,* p. 113. Düsseldorf: Econ Verlag.

2. See William Damon (1983). *Social and Personality Development,* pp. 20–26. New York: Norton.

3. William Austin and Joyce M. Tobiasen (1984). "Legal Justice and the Psychology of Conflict Resolution." In Robert Folger, ed., *The Sense of Justice,* pp. 227–274. New York: Plenum.

4. Arthur S. Berger and Joyce Berger (1991). *The Encyclopedia of Parapsychology and Psychical Research,* pp. 330–331. New York: Paragon.

5. Philip Kunig (1981). *Das Völkerrechtliche Nichteinmischungsprinzip,* chap. 3. Baden-Baden: Nomos.

6. Richard Little (1975). *Intervention: External Involvement in Civil Wars,* pp. 15, 24, 57–58. Totowa, N.J.: Rowman and Littlefield. See General Assembly Declarations, 2131 (Dec. 21, 1965) and 2625 (Oct. 24, 1970).

7. Jean Dubost (1987). *L'Intervention Psychosociologique,* pp. 280–286. Paris: Presses Universitaires de France.

8. Bruce L. Smith, Harold D. Lasswell, and Ralph D. Casey (1946). *Propaganda, Communication, and Public Opinion*, p. 121. Princeton: Princeton University Press.

9. Laura Nader and Andrée Sursock (1986). "Anthropology and Justice." In Ronald L. Cohen ed., *Justice*, pp. 205–233. New York: Plenum. Jeffrey Z. Rubin and Bert R. Brown (1975). *The Social Psychology of Bargaining and Negotiation*, pp. 43–48. New York: Academic Press.

10. See, e.g. Dubost, *L'Intervention Psychosociologique*, p. 151.

11. See Clyde H. Coombs and George S. Avrunin (1988). *The Structure of Conflict*, p. 4. Hillsdale, N.J.: Erlbaum.

12. See James A. Schellenberg (1982). *The Science of Conflict*, p. 236. New York: Oxford. John Thibaut and Laurens Walker (1975). *Procedural Justice*, pp. 12–13. Hillsdale, N.J.: Erlbaum. Joseph A. Scimecca. "Conflict Resolution in the United States." In Kevin Avruch, Peter W. Black, and Joseph A. Scimecca, eds., *Conflict Resolution*, pp. 19–39. Westport, Conn.: Greenwood.

13. See P. H. Gulliver (1979). *Disputes and Negotiation*, p. 209. New York: Academic Press.

14. See Jeffrey Rubin (1981). "Introduction." In Jeffrey Rubin, ed., *Dynamics of Third Party Interventions*, pp. 3–43. New York: Praeger.

15. T. Hanami and R. Blanpain (1984). "Introductory Remarks and a Comparative Overview." In T. Hanami and R. Blanpain, *Industrial Conflict in Market Economies*, pp. 1–20. Deventer, Netherlands: Kluwer.

16. J. Macaulay and L. Berkowitz (1970). *Altruism and Helping Behavior*, chap. 1. New York: Academic Press.

17. John E. Hunter et al. (1982). *Meta-Analysis*, chap. 1. Beverly Hills: Sage.

18. Kurt Kraiger and J. Kevin Ford (1985). "A Meta-Analysis of Ratee Race Effects in Performance Ratings." *Journal of Applied Psychology* 70: 56–65.

19. Robert Tolles (1991). *Meta Analysis: Reporting for the Russell Sage Foundation*, n. 13; 1, 4, 7.

20. Jeffrey M. Schneider (1990). "Research, Meta-analyses, and Desegregation policy." In Kenneth W. Wachter and Miron L. Straf, *The Future of Meta-Analyses*, pp. 55–60. New York: Russell Sage.

21. Tolles, *Meta Analysis*.

22. David Lowenthal (1985). *The Past Is a Foreign Country*, p. 187. Cambridge: Cambridge University Press.

23. Alex Robertson and John Gandy (1983). "Policy, Practice, and Research." In John Gandy et al., eds., *Improving Social Intervention*, pp. 241–289. New York: St. Martin's.

24. See, e.g., Kenneth Thomas (1976). "Conflict and Conflict Management." In Marvin D. Dunette, ed., *Handbook of Industrial and Organizational Psychology*, pp. 889–935. Chicago: Rand-McNally.

25. See Richard E. Walton (1969). *Interpersonal Peacemaking*, p. 143. Reading, Mass.: Addison-Wesley.

26. Sheila Kessler (1978). *Creative Conflict Resolution*, pp. 25, 30. Fountain Valley, Calif.: National Institute for Professional Training.

27. See, e.g., Francis A. Beer (1987). "War Cues and Foreign Policy Acts." *American Political Science Review* 81:701–715.

28. See, e.g. James G. Blight (1987). "Toward a Policy-Relevant Psychology of Avoiding Nuclear War." *American Psychologist* 42:12–29. E. Allan Lind and Tom R. Tyler. *The Social Psychology of Procedural Justice*, pp. 203–206. New York: Plenum.

29. Gerald L. Nieremberg (1973). *Fundamentals of Negotiating*. New York: Hawthorn.

30. See, e.g., I. William Zartman and Maureen R. Berman (1982). *The Practical Negotiator*. New Haven: Yale University Press.

31. David Suzuki and Peter Knudtson (1989). *Genethics*, p. 342. Cambridge: Harvard University Press.

32. Quentin Skinner (1985). "Introduction." In Quentin Skinner, ed., *The Return of Grand Theory in the Human Sciences*, pp. 3–20. Cambridge: Cambridge University Press. Charles E. Lindblom (1990). *Inquiry and Change*, p. 65. New Haven: Yale University Press.

33. Sybil P. Parker, ed. (1989). *McGraw-Hill Dictionary of Scientific and Technical Terms*, p. 329. New York: McGraw-Hill.

Chapter 2 Participants

1. S. B. Kar (1971). "Individual Aspirations as Related to Early and Late Acceptance of Contraception." *Journal of Social Psychology* 83:233–245.

2. Donald W. Cole (1981). *Professional Suicide,* pp. xi, 142–147. New York: McGraw-Hill.

3. Clyde H. Coombs and George S. Avrunin (1988). *The Structure of Conflict,* p. 4. Hillsdale, N.J.: Erlbaum.

4. Edmund Jacobson (1963). *Tension Control for Businessmen,* p. 77. New York: McGraw-Hill.

5. See Jamshid A. Momeni (1986). "Introduction." In Jamshid A. Momeni, ed., *Race, Ethnicity, and Minority Housing in the United States,* pp. xxi–xxx. Westport, Conn.: Greenwood.

6. Leonard W. Doob (1988). *Inevitability,* chap. 5. Westport, Conn.: Greenwood.

7. C. E. J. Whiting (1940). *Hausa and Fulani Proverbs,* pp. 105, 107. Lagos: Government Printer.

8. Hazel Markus and Paula Nurius (1986). "Possible Selves." *American Psychologist* 41:954–969.

9. Cited by Joan V. Bondurant (1971). *Concepts of Violence,* pp. 36, 115. Berkeley: University of California Press.

10. Maureen R. Berman and Joseph E. Johnson (1977). "The Growing Role of Unofficial Diplomacy." In Maureen R. Berman and Joseph F. Johnson, *Unofficial Diplomats,* pp. 1–33. New York: Columbia University Press.

11. Sheila Kessler (1978). *Creative Conflict Resolution,* p. 5. Fountain Valley, Calif.: National Institute for Professional Training.

12. Dennis J. D. Sandole (1984). "The Subjectivity of Theories and Actions in World Society." In Michael Banks, ed., *Conflict in World Society,* pp. 39–55. New York: St. Martin's.

13. Lloyd C. Gardner (1989). "The Evolution of the Interventionist Impulse." In Peter Schraeder, ed., *Intervention in the 1980s* pp. 17–30. Boulder, Colo.: Lynne Rienner.

14. Leonard W. Doob (1940). *The Plans of Men,* p. 6. New Haven: Yale University Press.

15. See Glenn H. Snyder and Paul Diesing (1977). *Conflict among Nations,* p. 203. Princeton: Princeton University Press.

16. C. H. Mike Yarrow (1978). *Quaker Experiences in International Conciliation,* chaps. 3 & 4. New Haven: Yale University Press.

17. Leonard W. Doob (1981). *The Pursuit of Peace*, pp. 239–241. Westport, Conn.: Greenwood.

18. Leonard W. Doob (1976). "Evaluating Interventions." In G. E. Kearney and D. W. McElwain, eds., *Aboriginal Cognitions*, pp. 53–68. Canberra: Australian Institute of Aboriginal Studies.

19. William Damon and Daniel Hart (1988). *Self-understanding in Childhood and Adolescence*, pp. 110–113. Cambridge: Cambridge University Press.

20. See Arnold Sameroff and Barbara H. Fiese (1990). "Transactional Regulation in Early Intervention." In Samuel J. Meisels and Jack P. Shonkoff, eds., *Handbook of Early Childhood Intervention*, pp. 119–149. Cambridge: Cambridge University Press.

21. David Anderson and Richard Grove (1987). "Introduction." In David Anderson and Richard Grove, eds., *Conservation in Africa*, pp. 1–11. Cambridge: Cambridge University Press.

22. Susan T. Fiske (1989). "Examining the Role of Intent." In James S. Uleman and John A. Bargh, eds., *Unintended Thought*, pp. 253–283). New York: Guilford.

23. William James (1902). *The Varieties of Religious Experience*, pp. 430–433; in original. New York: Modern Library.

24. Ronald J. Fisher (1990). *The Social Psychology of Intergroup and International Conflict Resolution*, p. 214. New York: Springer-Verlag.

25. See Leonard W. Doob (1964). *Patriotism and Nationalism*, p. 17. New Haven: Yale University Press.

26. Frich Fromm (1964). *The Heart of Man*, chap. 2. New York: Harper & Row.

27. D. J. West (1966). *Murder Followed by Suicide*, p. 46. Cambridge: Harvard University Press.

28. OSS Assessment Staff (1948). *Assessment of Men*, p. 12 & chap. 10. New York: Rinehart.

29. John Baynes (1967). *Morale*, pp. 84, 253–254. New York: Praeger.

30. Alexander Abdennur (1987). *The Conflict Resolution Syndrome*, pp. 13–15, 32, 41. Ottawa: University of Ottawa.

31. Ibid., pp. 57–62.

32. Mark H. Davis (1983). "The Effects of Dispositional Empathy on Emotional Reactions and Helping." *Journal of Personality* 51:167–184.

33. See Leroy C. Gould et al. (1988). *Perceptions of Technological Risks and Benefits*, chap. 2. New York: Russell Sage.

34. Anthony de Reuck (1984). "The Logic of Conduct." In Michael Banks, ed., *Conflict in World Society*, pp. 96–111. New York: St. Martin's.

35. C. Peter Rydell (1986). "The Economics of Early Intervention versus Later Incarceration." In Peter W. Greenwood, ed., *Intervention Strategies for Chronic Juvenile Offenders*, pp. 235–274. Westport, Conn.: Greenwood.

36. Karl Marx (1935). "The Eighteenth Brumaire of Louis Bonaparte." In Emile Burns, ed., *Handbook of Marxism*, pp. 116–131. New York: International Publishers.

37. Orlando Patterson (1982). *Slavery and Social Death*, p. ix. Cambridge: Harvard University Press.

38. Herbert M. Lefcourt (1982). *Locus of Control*, appendix 4. Hillsdale, N.J.: Erlbaum.

39. Jerome J. Tobacyk (1992). "Changes in Locus of Control Beliefs in Polish University Students before and after Democratization." *Journal of Social Psychology* 132:217–222.

40. Anne L. Milne (1985). "The Development of Parameters of Practice for Divorce Mediation. In Leonard L. Riskin, ed., *Divorce Mediation*, pp. 209–219. New York: American Bar Association.

41. Richard E. Walton (1985). "Toward a Strategy of Eliciting Employee Commitment Based on Policies of Mutuality." In Richard E. Walton and Paul R. Lawrence, eds., *Human Resource Management*, pp. 35–65. Boston: Harvard Business School.

42. Leon J. Saul (1967). "Preventive Psychiatry and World Problems." In Stuart Mudd, ed., *Conflict Resolution and World Education*, pp. 34–38. Bloomington: Indiana University Press.

43. Raanan Lipshitz and John J. Sherwood (1978). "The Effectiveness of Third-Party Process Consultation as a Function of the Consultant's Prestige and Style of Intervention." *Journal of Applied Behavioral Science* 14:493–509. C. R. Mitchell (1981). *The Structure of International Conflict*, p. 292. New York: St. Martin's.

44. Adam Curle (1971). *Making Peace*, p. 175. London: Tavistock.

45. Indar J. Rikhye et al. (1974). *The Thin Blue Line*, p. 11. New Haven: Yale University Press.

46. C. H. Mike Yarrow (1977). "Quaker Efforts toward Conciliation in the India-Pakistan War of 1965." In Berman and Johnson, *Unofficial Diplomats*, pp. 89–110.

47. Richard K. McGee (1974). *Crisis Intervention in the Community*, pp. 252–253. Baltimore: University Park Press.

48. Lydia Rapoport (1975). "Crisis Intervention as a Mode in Brief Treatment." In Sanford N. Katz, ed., *Creativity in Social Work*, pp. 83–124. Philadelphia: Temple University Press.

49. De Reuck, "Logic of Conduct."

50. Karl Menninger (1963). *The Vital Balance*, p. 33. New York: Viking.

51. Sonia M. Livingstone (1990). *Making Sense of Television*, p. 101. Oxford: Pergamon Press.

52. Allen R. Dyer (1988). *Ethics and Psychiatry*, pp. 113–114. Washington, D.C.: American Psychiatric Press.

53. George H. Mead (1934). *Mind, Self and Society*, pp. 322–325. Chicago: University of Chicago Press.

54. John Dollard et al. (1939). *Frustration and Aggression*, pp. 1–11. New Haven: Yale University Press.

55. Edward F. Zigler (1990). "Foreword." In Meisels and Shonkoff, eds., *Handbook of Early Childhood Intervention*, pp. ix–xiv.

56. Thede Perdue (1980). *Nations Remembered*, pp. 102–103. Westport, Conn.: Greenwood.

57. Janice A. Roehl and Royer F. Cook (1989). "Mediation in Interpersonal Disputes." In Kenneth Kressel et al., eds., *Mediation Research*, pp. 31–52. San Francisco: Josey-Bass.

58. See Morton Deutsch (1973). *The Resolution of Conflict*, pp. 167–169, 183, 202–203. New Haven: Yale University Press.

59. Donald B. Straus (1981). "Kissinger and the Management of Complexity." In Jeffrey Z. Rubin, ed., *Dynamics of Third Party Intervention*, pp. 253–270. New York: Praeger.

60. Jack Rothman (1974). *Planning and Organizing for Social Change*, p. 71. New York: Columbia University Press.

61. Ernest A. Haggard (1949). "Psychological Causes and Results of Stress." In Panel on Psychology and Physiology, ed., *Human Factors in Undersea Warfare*, pp. 441–461. Washington, D.C.: National Research Council.

62. See William Ury et al. (1988). *Getting Disputes Settled*, p. 68. San Francisco: Josey-Bass.

63. Jeffrey Z. Rubin (1981). "Introduction." In Rubin, ed., *Dynamics of Third Party Intervention*, pp. 3–43.

64. Leonard W. Doob (1987). "Adieu to Private Intervention in Political Conflicts?" *International Journal of Group Tensions* 17:15–27.

65. See Kenneth Thomas (1976). "Conflict and Conflict Management." In Marvin D. Dunette, ed., *Handbook of Industrial and Organizational Psychology*, pp. 889–935. Chicago: Rand-McNally.

66. Max Habicht (1967). "Conflict Resolution by Peaceful Means." In Stuart Mudd, ed., *Conflict, Resolution, and World Education*, pp. 98–103. Bloomington: Indiana University Press.

67. John Rawls (1971). *A Theory of Justice*, pp. 3, 235. Cambridge: Harvard University Press.

68. Larry Ray (1982). "The Alternative Dispute Resolution Movement." *Peace and Change* 8:117–128.

69. Jerold S. Auerbach (1983). *Justice Without Law?* p. vii. Oxford: Oxford University Press.

70. See Douglas J. Amy (1987). *The Politics of Environmental Mediation*, chaps. 1, 3. New York: Columbia University Press.

71. Owen Fiss (1984). "Against Settlement." *Yale Law Review* 93:1073–1090.

72. Richard K. McGee (1974). *Crisis Intervention in the Community*, p. 133. Baltimore: University Park Press.

73. United States Strategic Bombing Survey (1947). *The Effects of Strategic Bombings on German Morale*, p. 77; *The Effects of Strategic Bombings on Japanese Morale*, pp. 125, 127. Washington, D.C.: U.S. Government Printing Office.

74. Cited by Jerome D. Frank (1968). *Sanity and Survival*, pp. 232–233. New York: Vintage Books.

75. Emily H. Mudd (1967). "Conflict and Conflict Resolution in Families." In Mudd, ed., *Conflict Resolution and World Education*, pp. 58–69.

76. See Stephen Flamer (1986). "Clinical-Career Intervention with Adults," *Journal of Community Psychology* 14:224–227.

77. Jody Shachnow (1987). "Preventive Intervention with Children of Hospitalized Patients." *American Journal of Orthopsychiatry* 57:66–77.

78. John Scali (1987). "Backstage Mediation in the Cuban Missile Crisis." In John W. McDonald and Diane B. Bendahmane, eds., *Conflict Resolution,* pp. 73–80. Washington, D.C.: U.S. Department of State; Foreign Service Institute.

79. Perry London (1969). *Behavior Control,* p. 3. New York: Harper & Row.

Chapter 3 Rationale

1. Adrian C. Moulyn (1982). *The Meaning of Suffering,* p. 22, chap. 10. Westport, Conn.: Greenwood.

2. Richard A. Smith (1986). "Argumentation and Decision Making in Government." In Richard R. Lau and David O. Sears, eds., *Political Cognition,* pp. 337–340. Hillsdale, N.J.: Erlbaum.

3. See Mickael Hoffman (1967). "Interindividual, International Conflicts and Cooperation." In Stuart Mudd, ed., *Conflict Resolution and World Education,* pp. 228–237. Bloomington: Indiana University Press.

4. Sheila Kessler (1978). *Creative Conflict Resolution,* pp. 1–8. Fountain Valley, Calif.: National Institute for Professional Training.

5. Anthony de Reuck (1984). "The Logic of Conflict." In Michael Banks, ed., *Conflict in World Society,* pp. 96–111. New York: St. Martin's.

6. Caroline Thomas (1985). *New States, Sovereignty, and Intervention,* pp. 1–33. Aldershot, Hampshire: Gower.

7. See Susan T. Fiske (1989). "Explaining the Role of Intent." In James S. Uleman and John A. Bargh, eds., *Unintended Thought,* pp. 253–283. New York: Guilford.

8. Ernst B. Haas et al. (1972). *Conflict Management by International Organizations,* p. 5. Morristown, N.J.: General Learning Press.

9. Jeffrey Z. Rubin (1981). "Introduction." In Jeffrey Z. Rubin, ed., *Dynamics of Third Party Intervention,* pp. 3–43. New York: Praeger.

10. Donald R. Kinder et al. (1980). "Presidential Prototypes." *Political Behavior* 2:315–337.

11. Susan T. Fiske (1981). "Schema-Triggered Affect." In Margaret S. Clark and Susan T. Fiske, eds., *Affect and Cognition*, pp. 55–78. Hillsdale, N.J.: Erlbaum.

12. Donald R. Kinder (1986). "Presidential Character Revisited." In Lau and Sears, eds., *Political Cognition*, pp. 233–255.

13. See Gabriel Almond and Sidney Verba (1963). *The Civic Culture*, chaps. 6, 7. Princeton: Princeton University Press.

14. Ernest R. Hilgard (1965). *Hypnotic Susceptibility*, esp. pp. 272, 282. New York: Harcourt, Brace and World.

15. Margaret G. Hermann and Nathan Kogan (1977). "Effects of Negotiations' Personalities on Negotiating Behavior." In David Druckman, ed., *Negotiations*, pp. 247–274. Beverly Hills: Sage.

16. See Barry R. Schlenker (1983). "Translating Actions into Attitudes." *Advances in Experimental Social Psychology* 15:193–247.

17. Donald Van De Veer (1986). *Paternalistic Intervention*, p. 346. Princeton: Princeton University Press.

18. Luc Reychler (1979). *Patterns of Diplomatic Thinking*, p. 226. New York: Praeger.

19. Stanley I. Greenspan (1990). "Comprehensive Clinical Approaches in Infants and Their Families." Samuel J. Meisels and Jack P. Shonkoff, eds., *Handbook of Early Childhood Intervention*, pp. 150–172. Cambridge: Cambridge University Press.

20. Theodore Scurletis et al. (1976). "Comprehensive Developmental Health Services." In Theodore D. Tjossem, ed., *Intervention Strategies for High Risk Infants and Young Children*, pp. 305–323. Baltimore: University Park Press.

21. See, e.g., Thomas L. Morrison et al. (1984). "Member Perceptions in Small and Large Tavistock Groups." *Journal of Social Psychology* 124:209–217.

22. See Melanie Killen (1987). "Definitions, Acquisitions, and Sources of Moral Concepts." *New Ideas in Psychology* 5:239–243.

23. Knut Midgaard and Aril Underdal (1977). "Multiparty Conferences." In Druckman, ed., *Negotiations*, pp. 329–345.

24. See William A. Donohue (1985). "Ethnicity and Mediation." In William B. Gudykunst et al., eds., *Communication, Culture, and Organizational Processes*, pp. 134–154. Beverly Hills: Sage.

25. Leonard L. Riskin (1985). "Mediation and Lawyers." In Leonard L. Riskin, ed., *Divorce Mediation*, pp. 25–60. New York: American Bar Association.

26. See, e.g., Karl Mannheim (1936). *Ideology and Utopia*, pp. 136–146. New York: Harcourt, Brace.

27. Alexander L. George (1980). *Presidential Decisionmaking in Foreign Policy*, pp. 64–72. Boulder, Colo.: Westview Press.

28. Wolfgang Fritzemeyer (1984). *Die Intervention vor dem Internationalen Gerichtshof*, p. 179. Baden-Baden: Nomos.

Chapter 4 Timing

1. Eloisa G. E. Lorenzo (1976). "Latin American Perspective." In Theodore D. Tjossen et al., eds., *Intervention Strategies for High Risk Infants and Young Children*, pp. 7–22. Baltimore: University Park Press.

2. Jacob Bercovitch (1989). "International Dispute Mediation." In Kenneth Kressel et al., eds., *Mediation Research*, pp. 284–299. San Francisco: Josey-Bass.

3. See George Maclay and Humphry Knipe (1972). *The Dominant Man*, pp. 69–70. New York: Delacorte.

4. Andrew Rosenthal (1991). "Bush Greeted with Silent Protest at Black College." *New York Times*, May 11, p. A10.

5. See R. De V. Peters and Gary A. Bernfeld (1983). "Impulsivity and Social Reasoning." *Developmental Psychology* 19:78–81.

6. Philips Talbot (1977). "The Cyprus Seminar." In Maureen Berman and Joseph E. Johnson, eds., *Unofficial Diplomats*, pp. 159–167. New York: Columbia University Press.

7. Leonard W. Doob (1971). *Patterning of Time*, p. 84. New Haven: Yale University Press.

8. Leonard W. Doob (1961). *Communication in Africa*, chap. 8. New Haven: Yale University Press.

9. Leonard W. Doob (1968). "Tropical Weather and Attitude Surveys." *Public Opinion Quarterly* 32:423–430.

10. See Doob, *Patterning of Time*, p. 99.

11. See Leonard W. Doob (1990). *Hesitation*, pp. 1–10. Westport, Conn.: Greenwood.

12. Charles E. Lindblom (1990). *Inquiry and Change*, p. 47. New Haven: Yale University Press.

13. Leonard W. Doob (1964). *Patriotism and Nationalism*, pp. 119–127. New Haven: Yale University Press.

14. See Richard Brislin (1986). "Prejudice and Intergroup Communication." In William B. Gudykunst, ed., *Intergroup Communication*, pp. 74–85. London: Edward Arnold.

15. See John Thibaut and Laurence Walker (1975). *Procedural Justice*, p. 7. Hillsdale, N.J.: Erlbaum.

16. Curt Riess (1948). *Joseph Goebbels*, pp. 337–345. Garden City, N.Y.: Doubleday.

17. See William C. Gilmore (1984). *The Grenada Intervention*, pp. 25–31. New York: Facts on File Publications.

18. See Leonard W. Doob (1948). *Public Opinion and Propaganda*, pp. 398–400. New York: Holt, Rinehart, & Winston.

19. See Leonard W. Doob (1987). "Adieu to Private Intervention in Political Conflicts?" *International Journal of Group Tensions* 17:15–27.

20. Human Sciences Research Council (1987). *The South African Society*, pp. 172–173. Westport, Conn.: Greenwood.

21. S. A. Snyman and J. M. Lötter (1988). "On the Road to Equitable and Affordable Social Provision." In H. C. Marais, ed., *South Africa*, pp. 105–123. Pinetown; South Africa: Burgess.

22. Quincy Wright et al., eds. (1962). *Preventing World War III*, p. 9. New York: Simon & Schuster.

23. Doob, *Patterning of Time*, pp. 244–247.

24. Leonard W. Doob (1960). *Becoming More Civilized*, pp. 84–93. New Haven: Yale University Press.

25. Marie Lazarsfeld-Jahoda (1933). *Die Arbeitslosen von Marienthal*. Leipzig: Hirzel.

26. Alexander Abdennur (1987). *The Conflict Resolution Syndrome*, pp. 107–108. Ottawa: University of Ottawa.

27. See Arnold Sameroff and Barbara H. Fiese (1990). "Transactional Regulation and Early Intervention." In Samuel J. Meisels and Jack P. Shonkopf, eds., *Handbook of Early Childhood Intervention*, pp. 119–149. Cambridge: Cambridge University Press.

28. Cited by Julius Stone (1977). *Conflict through Consensus*, p. 42. Baltimore: Johns Hopkins.

29. *Charter of the United Nations*. Articles 34, 35, 39.

30. Boutros Boutros-Ghali. *An Agenda for Peace*, p. 11. New York: United Nations.

31. See Newell M. Stultz (1989). *The Apartheid Issue at the Security Council*, p. 6 ff., Bramfontein: South African Institute of International Affairs.

32. Articles 2, sect. 7; 55, sect. c.

33. See Mark A. May (1943). *A Social Psychology of War and Peace*, pp. 11, 238. New Haven: Yale University Press.

34. See Richard Little (1975). *Intervention*, p. 79. Totowa, N.J.: Rowman and Littlefield.

35. See James S. Fiskin (1982). *The Limits of Obligation*, p. 31. New Haven: Yale University Press.

36. Bibb Latané and John M. Darley (1970). "Social Determinants of Bystander Intervention." In J. Macaulay and L. Berkowitz, eds., *Altruism and Helping Behavior*, pp. 13–27. New York: Academic Press.

37. Stanley Milgram (1974). *Obedience to Authority*, chap. 9. New York: Harper & Row.

38. Cited by Roger Hilsman (1967). *To Move a Nation*, p. 15. Garden City, N.Y.: Doubleday.

39. See Doob, *Patriotism and Nationalism*, p. 6.

40. Arthur R. Jensen (1973). *Educability and Group Differences*, pp. 357, 363. New York: Harper & Row.

41. Herbert Kaufman (1985). *Time, Chance, and Organization*, pp. 42–43. Chatham, N.J.: Chatham House.

42. Fred E. A. Sander (1985). "Varieties of Dispute Processing." In Leonard L. Riskin, ed., *Divorce Mediation*, pp. 1–23. New York: American Bar Association.

43. Benedict S. Alper and Lawrence T. Nichols (1981). *Beyond the Courtroom*, pp. 112–127. Lexington, Mass.: D. C. Heath.

44. William L. Ury (1985). *Beyond the Hotline*, pp. 9, 52. Boston: Houghton Mifflin.

45. See Charles S. Pearson (1985). *Down to Business,* pp. 13, 27, 77. Washington, D.C.: World Resources Institute.

46. Celia A. Dugger (1991). "International Calamities Tax America's Compassion." *New York Times,* May 12, A6.

47. Walter D. Connor (1972). *Deviance in Soviet Society,* p. 31. New York: Columbia University Press.

48. See Joseph H. Himes (1980). *Conflict and Conflict Management,* pp. 242–246. Athens: University of Georgia Press.

49. See Janic A. Roehl and Royea F. Cook (1989). "Mediation in Interpersonal Disputes." In Kressel et al., eds., *Mediation Research,* pp. 31–52.

50. See W. Friedmann (1971). "Intervention and International Law." In Louis G. M. Jaquet, ed., *Intervention in International Politics,* pp. 40–68. The Hague: Institute of International Affairs.

51. Stone, *Conflict through Consensus,* p. 40.

52. See Sherman Kent (1953). *Strategic Intelligence,* pp. 209–215, chap. 10. Princeton: Princeton University Press. See Boutros-Ghali, *Agenda for Peace,* chap. 3.

53. Isaac D. Levine (1969). *Intervention,* pp. 104–105. New York: David McKay.

54. Carol C. Nadelson and Marie Saugier (1989). "Intervention Programs for Individual Victims and Their Families." In Leah J. Dickstein and Carol C. Nadelson, eds., *Family Violence,* pp. 155–178. Washington, D.C.: American Psychiatric Press.

55. Howard B. Levy et al. (1989). "Special Intervention Programs for Child Victims of Violence." In Dickstein and Nadelson, eds., *Family Violence,* pp. 179–211.

56. William Austin and Joyce M. Tobiasen (1984). "Legal Justice and the Psychology of Conflict Resolution." In Robert Folger, Ed., *The Sense of Injustice,* pp. 227–274. New York: Plenum.

57. Jacques Ardoino (1980). "L'Intervention." In Jacques Ardoino et al., eds., *L'Intervention Institutionnelle,* pp. 11–46. Paris: Payot.

58. See Eviater Zerubavel (1981). *Hidden Rhythms,* chap. 1. Chicago: University of Chicago Press.

59. Adam Curle (1986). *In the Middle,* p. 14. New York: St. Martin's.

60. Jessica Pearson and Nancy Thoennies (1989). "Divorce Mediation."

In Kenneth Kressel et al., eds., *Mediation Research*, pp. 9–30. San Francisco: Josey-Bass.

Chapter 5 Method

1. Geoffrey M. White (1985). "Premises and Purposes in a Solomon Islands Ethnopsychology." In Geoffrey White and John Kirkpatrick, eds., *Person, Self, and Experience*, pp. 328–366. Berkeley: University of California Press.

2. Peter Just (1986). "Let the Evidence Fit the Crime." *American Ethnologist* 13:43–61.

3. Jerome Alan Cohen (1967). "Mediation on the Eve of Modernization." In David C. Buxbaum, ed., *Traditional and Modern Legal Institutions in Asia and Africa*, pp. 54–76. Leiden: Brill.

4. Arnold van Gennep (1960). *The Rites of Passage*, pp. 3, 189. Chicago: University of Chicago Press.

5. Sally Engle Merry (1989). "Mediation in Nonindustrial Societies." In Kenneth Kressel et al., eds., *Mediation Research*, pp. 68–90. San Francisco: Josey-Bass.

6. Kwoh Leung and E. Allan Lind (1986). "Procedural Justice and Culture." *Journal of Personality and Social Psychology* 50:1134–1140. Kwoh Leung (1987). "Some Determinants of Reactions to Procedural Models for Conflict Resolution." *Journal of Personality and Social Psychology* 53:898–908.

7. T. Hanami and R. Blanpain (1984). "Introductory Remarks and a Comparative Overview." In T. Hanani and R. Blanpain, eds., *Industrial Conflict Resolution in Market Economies*, pp. 1–20. Deventer, Neverthelands: Kluwer.

8. See Shalom H. Schwartz (1990). "Individualism and Collectivism." *Journal of Cross-Cultural Psychology* 21:139–157.

9. Silvia S. Canetto (1991). "Gender Roles, Suicide Attempts, and Substance Abuse." *Journal of Psychology* 125:605–620.

10. John Naisbitt (1982). *Megatrends*, p. 159. New York: Warner Books.

11. Hanami and Blanpain, *Industrial Conflict Resolution in Market Economics*.

12. See Leonard W. Doob (1961). *Communication in Africa,* chap 5. New Haven: Yale University Press.

13. See Leonard Weiner et al. (1967). *Home Treatment.* Pittsburgh: University of Pittsburgh Press.

14. Barbara Crosette (1991). "Couch Gives Peace Talks a Distinction." *New York Times,* Dec. 21, p. All.

15. See Stanley Milgram (1974). *Obedience to Authority,* chap. 4. New York: Harper & Row.

16. See Carl C. Walton et al. (1988). "The Role of Caucusing in Community Mediation." *Journal of Conflict Resolution* 32:181–202.

17. Richard Smoke (1977). "Analytic Dimensions of Intervention Decisions." In Ellen P. Stern, ed., *The Limits of Military Interventions,* pp. 25–44. Beverly Hills: Sage.

18. See Urs Schwarz (1971). *Abkehr von der Gewalt,* pp. 24–25, 36. Düsseldorf: Econ Verlag.

19. K. J. Holsti (1967). *International Politics,* pp. 338, 340–343. Englewood Cliffs, N.J.: Prentice-Hall.

20. Articles 43, 52.

21. Jacob Bercovitch (1989). "International Dispute Mediation." In Kressel et al., eds., *Mediation Research,* pp. 284–299.

22. K. J. Holsti (1966). "Resolving International Disputes." *Journal of Conflict Resolution* 10:272–296.

23. K. J. Holsti (1988). "Paths to Peace?" In Thakur Ramesh, *International Conflict Resolution,* pp. 105–132. Boulder, Colo.: Westview Press.

24. Paul R. Pillar (1983). *Negotiating Peace,* pp. 18–22, 39, 245. Princeton: Princeton University Press.

25. Herbert Ekwe-Ekwe (1990). *Conflict and Intervention in Africa,* p. 151. London: Macmillan. See Frank C. Zagare (1987). *The Dynamics of Deterrence,* pp. 134–150.

26. Joseph J. Kruzel (1977). "Military Alerts and Diplomatic Signals." In Ellen P. Stern, ed., *The Limits of Military Intervention,* pp. 83–99. Beverly Hills: Sage.

27. Zagare, *Dynamics of Deterrence,* p. 29.

28. Institute of Social Research, Makerere University, Kampala (1987). *Uganda.* London: International Alert.

29. Leonard W. Doob (1988). *Inevitability,* chap. 2. Westport, Conn.: Greenwood.

30. Hugo Prein (1987). "Strategies for Third Party Intervention." *Human Relations* 40:699–719.

31. See Jeffrey Z. Rubin (1980). "Experimental Research on Third-Party Intervention in Conflict." *Psychological Bulletin* 87:379–391.

32. See Marsha R. Shelburn (1984). *Rules for Regulating Intervention under a Managed Float,* pp. 47–48. Princeton: International Finance Section, Department of Economics.

33. Richard Little (1975) *Intervention,* p. 192. Totowa, N.J.: Rowman and Littlefield.

34. Harold H. Kelley (1968). "Two Functions of Reference Groups." In Herbert H. Hyman and Eleanor Singer, eds., *Readings in Reference Group Theory and Research,* pp. 77–83. New York: Free Press.

35. James A. Wall (1981). "Mediation." *Journal of Conflict Resolution* 25:157–180.

36. Charles E. Lindblom (1959). "The Science of 'Muddling Through.'" *Public Administration Review* 19:79–88.

37. See Alan J. Flisher and Gordon M. Issacs (1987). "The Evaluation of a Training Program in Rape Crisis for Lay Therapists." *South African Journal of Psychology* 17:40–46.

38. Ernest Abel and Barbara E. Buckley (1977). *The Handwriting on the Wall,* pp. 17, 44. Westport, Conn.: Greenwood.

39. John C. Hammerback et al. (1985). *A War of Words,* pp. 5–6. Westport, Conn.: Greenwood.

40. Richard K. McGee (1974). *Crisis Intervention in the Community,* pp. 151–163. Baltimore: University Park Press.

41. Bernard M. Dickens (1985). "Prediction, Professionalism, and Public Policy." In Christopher D. Webster et al., eds., *Probability and Prediction, Psychiatry and Public Policy,* pp. 177–207. London: Cambridge University Press.

42. See Jock R. Anderson and Jesuthason Thampapillai (1990). *Soil Conservation in Developing Countries,* pp. 15, 27. Washington, D.C.: World Bank.

43. Peter S. Adler (1987). "Is ADR a Social Movement?" *Negotiation Journal* 3:59–71.

44. Kent M. Weeks (1978). *Ombudsmen around the World*, p. ix. Berkeley: Institute of Governmental Studies.

45. Yehuda Amir (1969). "Contact Hypothesis in Ethnic Relations." *Psychological Bulletin* 71:319–342.

46. Bryant Wedge (1971). "A Psychiatric Model for Intercession in Intergroup Conflict." *Journal of Applied Behavioral Science* 7:733–761.

47. Elliot Aronson et al. (1975). "The Jigsaw Route to Learning and Liking." *Psychology Today* 8:43–50, n. 9. Also (1978) *The Jigsaw Classroom*. Beverly Hills: Sage.

48. Cited by Joseph Schwarzwald and Yehuda Amir (1984). "Interethnic Relations and Education." In Norman Miller and Marilyn B. Brewer, eds. *Groups in Contact*, pp. 53–76. Orlando: Academic Press.

49. Donella Meadows (1989). *Managing the Information Sphere*. Lecture: Yale University, Nov. 28. Leon McClelland and Stuart W. Cook (1979–80). "Energy-conservation Effects of Continuous In-home Feedback in All-electric homes." *Journal of Environmental Systems* 9:169–173. Lawrence Becker and Clive Seligman (1978). "Reducing Air Conditioning Waste by Signalling it is Cool Outside." *Personality and Social Psychology Bulletin* 4:412–415.

50. Mary L. M. Bryan and Allen F. Davis (1990). *100 Years at Hull House*, p. 49. Bloomington: Indiana University Press.

51. Jacob Bercovitch (1984). *Social Conflicts and Third Parties*, p. 147. Boulder, Colo.: Westview Press. See Walter G. Stephan and Cookie W. Stephan (1984). "The Role of Ignorance in Intergroup Relations. In Miller and Brewer, *Groups in Contact*, pp. 229–255.

52. Kelvin J. Keane and Robert E. Kretschmer (1987). "Effect of Mediation Learning Intervention on Cognitive Task Performance with a Deaf Population." *Journal of Educational Psychology* 79:49–53.

53. Debra Shapiro et al. (1985). "Mediator Behavior and the Outcome of Mediation." *Journal of Social Issues* 41:101–114, n. 2.

54. See Theodore Tjossen (1976). "Early Intervention." In Theodore D. Tjossen, ed., *Intervention Strategies for High Risk Infants and Young Children*, pp. 3–33. Baltimore: University Park Press.

55. Walter H. Denenberg (1976). "From Animal to Infant Research." In Theodore Tjossen, *Intervention Strategies*, pp. 85–106.

56. George Tarjan (1976). "The Present and the Future." In Theodore D. Tjossen, *Intervention Strategies*, pp. 773–778.

57. Michael E. Cavanagh (1987). "Employee Problems." *Personnel Journal* 66:35–40, n. 9.

58. Morton Deutsch (1973). *The Resolution of Conflict*, pp. 382–387. New Haven: Yale University Press. See Jeffrey Z. Rubin and Bert R. Brown (1975). *The Social Psychology of Bargaining and Negotiation*, pp. 60–61. New York: Academic Press.

59. Gene Sharp (1973). *The Politics of Nonviolent Action*, pp. xii–xvi, chap. 6. Boston: Porter Sargent.

60. Norbert Elias and Eric Dunning (1986). *Quest for Excitement*, pp. 42, 223. Oxford: Basil Blackwell.

61. Hans Speier (1941). "The Social Types of War." *American Journal of Sociology* 46:445–454.

62. Articles 36, 40–42.

63. Indar J. Rikhye et al. (1974). *The Thin Blue Line*, pp. 3, 5–6.New Haven: Yale University Press.

64. See Paul Lewis (1992). "U.N.'s Fund Crisis Worsens as Role in Security Rises." *New York Times*, Jan. 27, pp. A1, A8.

65. John W. Burton (1969). *Conflict and Communication*, pp. 61–62. New York: Free Press.

66. Leonard W. Doob (1981). *The Pursuit of Peace*, pp. 234–239. Westport, Conn.: Greenwood.

67. Leonard W. Doob (1987). "Adieu to Private Intervention in Political Conflicts?" *International Journal of Group Tensions* 17:15–27.

68. Urie Bronfenbrenner (1975). "Is Early Intervention Effective?" In Marcus Guttenberg and Elmer L. Struening, eds., *Handbook of Evaluation Research*, 2. 519–603. Beverly Hills: Sage.

69. Ibid., p. 595.

70. See Bary R. Schlenker (1983). "Translating Actions into Attitudes." *Advances in Experimental Social Psychology* 15:193–247.

71. See Bercovitch, *Social Conflicts and Third Parties*, p. 147.

72. Harry H. Ransom (1989). "Covert Intervention." In Peter Schraeder, ed., *Intervention in the 1980s*, pp. 101–114. Boulder, Colo.: Lynne Rienner.

73. See John Thibaut and Laurens Walker (1973). *Procedural Justice,* pp. 7–9. Hillsdale, N.J.: Erlbaum.

74. Arthur T. Hadley (1978). *The Empty Polling Booth,* pp. 20–22, 39–41. Englewood Cliffs, N.J.: Prentice-Hall.

75. See I. William Zartman and Maureen R. Berman (1982). *The Practical Negotiator,* p. 78. New Haven: Yale University Press.

76. Ronald J. Fisher (1990). *The Social Psychology of Intergroup and International Conflict Resolution,* p. 163. New York: Springer Verlag.

77. See Glenn H. Snyder and Paul Diesing (1977). *Conflict among Nations,* pp. 227–232. Princeton: Princeton University Press.

Chapter 6 Morality

1. See Phillips Talbot (1977). "The Cyprus Seminar." In Maureen R. Berman and Joseph E. Johnson, eds., *Unofficial Diplomats,* pp. 159–167. New York: Columbia University Press.

2. See Donald Van De Veer (1986). *Paternalistic Intervention,* chap. 1. Princeton: Princeton University Press.

3. See Paul L. Fisher and Ralph L. Lowenstein, eds. (1967). *Race and the News Media.* New York: Praeger.

4. See Robert B. Toplin (1975). *Unchallenged Violence,* p. 277. Westport, Conn.: Greenwood.

5. David Suzuki and Peter Knudtson (1989). *Genethics,* p. 23. Cambridge: Harvard University Press.

6. Esther B. Fine (1990). "Estonia Sends Firmer Signal to Moscow." *New York Times,* April 4, A14.

7. William Austin and Joyce M. Tobiasen (1984). "Legal Justice and the Psychology of Conflict Resolution." In Robert Folger, ed., *The Sense of Injustice,* pp. 227–274. New York: Plenum.

8. G. C. Oosthuizen et al. (1988). *Religion, Intergroup Relations, and Social Change in South Africa,* pp. 15, 67. Westport, Conn.: Greenwood.

9. Prince Bandar bin Sultan (1990). Lecture: Yale University; Dec. 4.

10. Immanuel Kant (1965). *Critique of Pure Reason,* pp. 635–636. New York: St. Martin's.

11. Leonard W. Doob (1987). *Slightly beyond Skepticism,* pp. 3–7. New Haven: Yale University Press.

12. James Rachels (1986). *The End of Life*, pp. 106–108. Oxford: Oxford University Press.

13. David Margolick (1990). "Patient's Suit Says Saving Life Ruined It." *New York Times*, March 18, 1, 24.

14. James S. Fishkin (1984). *Beyond Subjective Morality*, pp. 11–15. New Haven: Yale University Press.

15. Cited by Kyung D. Har (1930). *Social Laws*, p. 63. Chapel Hill: University of North Carolina Press.

16. Leonard W. Doob (1964). *Patriotism and Nationalism*, chap. 10, 11. New Haven: Yale University Press.

17. *New York Times*, March 18, 1991, p. All.

18. Urs Schwarz (1971). "Intervention." In Louis G. M. Jaquet, ed., *Intervention in International Politics*, pp. 29–39. The Hague: Netherlands Institute of International Affairs.

19. Christopher D. Webster et al. (1985). *Dangerousness*, p. 1. London: Cambridge University Press.

20. See Richard L. Rubenstein (1983). *The Age of Triage*, chap. 10. Boston: Beacon Press.

21. Paul A. Neuland (1971). *Traditional Doctrine on Intervention in the Law of Nations*, pp. 96–97, 140. Washington, D.C.: Georgetown University Press.

22. Resolution 2625; Oct. 24, 1970. See Sydney D. Bailey (1972). *Prohibitions and Restraints in War*, p. 16. London: Oxford University Press.

23. Gunnar Myrdal (1944). *An American Dilemma*, p. 558. New York: Harper.

24. Article 5.

25. See John W. Burton (1984). *Global Conflict*, pp. 109–110. Brighton, Sussex: Wheatsheaf.

26. Cited by Robert W. Tucker (1985). *Intervention and the Reagan Doctrine*, pp. 4–5. New York: Council on Religion and International Affairs.

27. See, e.g., Jane Perlez (1990). "U.S. envoy steps in political firestorm in Kenya." *New York Times*, March 6, A13.

28. Cited by John Donnelly (1989). *Suicide*, pp. 33–36. Buffalo: Prometheus Books.

29. Herbert C. Kelman and V. Lee Hamilton (1989). *Crimes of Obedience*, p. 56; chap. 5, 6. New Haven: Yale University Press.

30. Leonard W. Doob (1988). *Inevitability*, p. 5, chap. 5. Westport, Conn.: Greenwood.

31. See Dean E. Peachy (1989). "What People Want from Mediation." In Kenneth Kressel et al., eds., *Mediation Research*, pp. 300–321. San Francisco: Josey-Bass. See Harry Kaufman (1970). "Legality and Harmfulness." In J. Macaulay and L. Berkowitz, eds., *Altruism and Helping Behavior*, 77–81. New York: Academic Press.

32. See Austin and Tobiasen, "Legal Justice."

33. Douglas J. Amy (1987). *The Politics of Environmental Mediation*, pp. 201–212, 220–224. New York: Columbia University Press.

34. Owen Fiss (1984). "Against Settlement." *Yale Law Journal* 93:1073–1090, n. 6.

35. Jack Byles (1983). "The Myth of Preventing Delinquency through Early Identification and Intervention." In John Gandy et al., eds., *Improving Social Intervention*, pp. 122–144. New York: St. Martin's.

36. See Tom Wicker (1990). "Rights and Morality." *New York Times*, April 26, p. A31.

37. Rauf R. Denktash (1990). *A New Pattern of Relationships in Cyprus*, p. i. Nicosia: Public Information Office of the Turkish Republic of Northern Cyprus.

38. George Vassilou cited in *Cyprus Bulletin* 28, April 2, 1990, n. 7.

39. P. K. S. Namboodire et al. (1982). *Intervention in the Indian Ocean*, p. 10. New Delihi: ABC Publishing House.

40. Alan J. Kimmel (1988). *Ethics and Values in Social Research*. Newbury Park, Calif.: Sage.

41. See Leonard W. Doob (1976). "Evaluating Interventions." In G. E. Kearney and D. W. McElwain, eds., *Aboriginal Cognition*, pp. 53–68. Canberra: Australian Institue of Aboriginal Studies.

42. Carol C. Nadelson and Maris Saugier (1989). Intervention Programs for Individual Victims and Their Families. In Leah J. Dickstein and Carol C. Nadelson, eds., *Family Violence*, pp. 155–178. Washington D.C.: American Psychiatric Press.

43. See Diana Wylie (1991). "The Limits of Paternalism." Essay presented at Southern African Research Seminar (Yale), Jan. 9.

44. Cited by Lloyd J. Dumas (1989). "The Promise of Economic Conversion." In Lloyd J. Dumas and Marek Thee, eds., *Making Peace Possible*, pp. 253–263. Oxford: Pergamon.

45. Robert Clausi (1989). *Donor Response to the Environmental Impact of Ethiopian Refugees in Eastern Sudan*. Lecture: Yale University, Dec. 5.

46. See James S. Fishkin (1982). *The Limits of Obligation*, chap. 19. New Haven: University Press.

47. Jonathan Mann (1991). "No Sovereignty for Suffering." *New York Times*, May 12, p. E17.

Chapter 7 Reality

1. Sheila Kessler (1978). *Creative Conflict Resolution*, pp. 15ff. Fountain Valley, Calif.: National Institute for Professional Training.

2. P. H. Gulliver (1979). *Disputes and Negotiation*, p. 214. New York: Academic Press.

3. Anseln Strauss (1978). *Negotiations*, p. 1. San Francisco: Josey-Bass.

4. Leonard W. Doob (1988). *Inevitability*, pp. 77–81. Westport, Conn.: Greenwood.

5. Daniel Dana (1983). "Mediating Interpersonal Conflict in Organizations." In Donald W. Cole, ed., *Conflict Resolution Technology*, pp. 29–39. Cleveland: Organization Development Institute.

6. Robert S. Wyer, Jr. (1974). "Some Implications for the 'Socratic effect' for Alternative Models of Cognitive Consistency." *Journal of Personality* 42:399–419.

7. See Donald R. Kinder and David C. Sears (1985). "Public Opinion and Political Action." In Gardner Lindzey and Elliot Anderson, eds., *Handbook of Social Psychology* 2. 659–741. New York: Random House.

8. John B. McLaughlin (1980). *Gypsy Lifestyles*, pp. 22–24. Lexington, Mass.: Heath.

9. See Norbert Elias and Eric Dunning (1986). *Quest for Excitement*. Oxford: Basil Blackwell.

10. Adam Curle (1986). *In the Middle*, chap. 1. New York: St. Martin's.

11. See, e.g., Kevin C. Brechner (1977). "An Experimental Analysis of Social Traps." *Journal of Experimental Social Psychology* 13:552–564.

12. See David Ehrenfeld (1991). "The Management of Diversity." In F. Herbert Borman and Stephen R. Kellert, eds., *Ecology, Economics, Ethics*. New Haven: Yale University Press.

13. Everett M. Rogers (1962). *Diffusion of Innovation*, p. 254. New York: Free Press.

14. Alex S. Jones (1990). "Television Networks Reported Ready to Form Group to Poll Voters." *New York Times*, Feb. 24, p. 9.

15. See e.g., Ronald W. Perry and Alvin H. Mushkatel (1984). *Disaster Management*, pp. 215–216. Westport, Conn.: Quorum Books.

16. See Richard C. Robertiello et al. (1963). *The Analyst's Role*, chap. 1. New York: Citadel Press.

17. J. Webb (1984). Ph.D. thesis summarized by G. M. Stephenson. "Intergroup and Interpersonal Dimensions of Bargaining and Negotiation." In Henri Tajfel, ed., *The Social Dimension* 2.646–667. Cambridge: Cambridge University Press.

18. Dean G. Pruitt (1989). "Process of Mediation in Dispute Settlement Centers." In Kenneth Kressel et al., eds., *Mediation Research*, pp. 368–393. San Francisco: Josey-Bass.

19. Dean G. Pruitt (1971). "Indirect Communication and the Search for Agreement in Negotiation." *Journal of Applied Social Psychology* 1:205–239, n. 2.

20. Leonard W. Doob (1978). *Panorama of Evil*, pp. 132–134. Westport, Conn.: Greenwood.

21. Alex Kozulin (1991). *Vigotski's Psychology*, p. 88. Cambridge: Harvard University Press.

22. Robert A. Dahl (1971). *Polyarchy*, pp. 3–4. New Haven: Yale University Press.

23. Karl Mannheim (1936). *Ideology and Utopia*, p. 36. New York: Harcourt, Brace.

24. Mary Follett (1924). *Creative Experience*, pp. 156–178. New York: Longmans, Green.

25. See Curle, *In the Middle*, p. 36.

26. Ralph K. White (1984). *Fearful Warriors*, chaps. 10, 12. New York: Free Press.

27. Yousuf J. A. Duhul (1970). "Appraisal by a Somali." In Leonard W.

Doob, ed., *Resolving Conflict in Africa*, 38–56. New Haven: Yale University Press.

28. Flo Conway and Jim Siegelman (1978). *Snapping*, p. 225. Philadelphia: J. B. Lippincott.

29. See Martin Harrow et al. (1971). "The T-Group and Study Group Laboratory Experiences." *Journal of Social Psychology* 85:225–237.

30. Leonard W. Doob and William J. Foltz (1973). "The Belfast Workshop." *Journal of Conflict Resolution* 17:489–512.

31. Richard E. Walton (1970). "Strategic Issues in Designing Workshops." In Doob, ed., *Resolving Conflict in Africa*, pp. 137–161.

32. See Norman R. F. Maier et al. (1975). *The Role-Play Technique*, pp. 2–3. La Jolla, Calif.: University Associates.

33. Adam Curle (1971). *Making Peace*, chap. 18. London: Tavistock.

34. See Walter G. and Cookie Stephan (1984). "The Role of Ignorance in Intergroup Relations." In Norman Miller and Marilyn B. Brewer, eds., *Groups in Contact*, pp. 229–255. Orlando: Academic Press.

35. P. H. Gulliver (1979). *Disputes and Negotiation*, pp. 224–225. New York: Academic Press.

36. Dana, "Mediating Interpersonal Conflict," p. 31.

37. Sigmund Freud (1957). *The Future of an Illusion*, p. 6. Garden City, N.Y.: Doubleday.

38. See Douglas J. Amy (1987). *The Politics of Environmental Mediation*, chap. 4. New York: Columbia University Press.

39. Michael Bond et al. (1985). "How Are Responses to Verbal Insult Related to Cultural Collectivism and Power Distance?" *Journal of Cross Cultural Psychology* 16:111–127.

40. Curle, *In the Middle*, p. 9.

41. See William A. Donohue (1985). "Ethnicity and Mediation." In William B. Gudykunst et al., eds., *Communication, Culture, and Organizational Processes*, pp. 134–154. Beverly Hills: Sage.

42. John W. Burton (1972). "The Resolution of Conflict." *International Studies Quarterly* 16:5–29.

43. See Gordon Lippitt and Ronald Lippitt (1986). *The Consulting Process in Action*, pp. 38–41. San Diego: University Associates.

44. John Dollard et al. (1939). *Frustration and Aggression*, pp. 8–9. New Haven: Yale University Press.

45. Gulliver, *Disputes and Negotiation*, pp. 220–226.

46. William A. Donohue (1989). In Kressel et al., eds., *Mediation Research*, pp. 322–343.

47. Roger Fisher and William Ury (1981). *Getting to Yes*, pp. 31, 62, 63, 70. New York: Houghton Mifflin.

48. See I. William Zartman and Maureen R. Berman (1982). *The Practical Negotiator*, p. 153. New Haven: Yale University Press.

49. See Stanley Schachter and Larry P. Gross (1968). *Journal of Personality and Social Psychology* 10:98–106. James T. Tedeschi and Thomas V. Bonoma (1977). "Measures of Last Resort." In David Druckman, ed., *Negotiations*, pp. 213–241. Beverly Hills: Sage.

50. See Jeffrey Z. Rubin (1981). "Introduction." In Jeffrey Z. Rubin, ed., *Dynamics of Third Party Intervention*, pp. 3–43. New York: Praeger.

51. Jonathan M. Feldman (1989). "Converting the Military Economy through the Local State." In Lloyd J. Dumas and Marek Thee, eds., *Making Peace Possible*, pp. 139–159. Oxford: Pergamon Press.

52. Indar J. Rikhye et al. (1974). *The Thin Blue Line*, chaps. 5, 6. New Haven: Yale University Press. Boutros Boutros-Ghali (1992). *An Agenda for Peace*, chap. 4. New York: United Nations.

53. See Judith Rodin (1981). "Current Status of the Internal-External Hypothesis for Obesity." *American Psychologist* 36:361–372.

54. Shelley E. Taylor (1986). *Health Psychology*, chap. 4. New York: Random House.

55. Robert Jervis (1986). "Cognition and Political Behavior." In Richard R. Lau and David O. Sears, eds., *Political Cognition*, pp. 319–338. See Ulf Himmelstrand (1960). "Verbal Attitudes and Behavior." *Public Opinion Quarterly* 24:224–250.

56. Leonard W. Doob (1990). *Hesitation*, chap. 2. Westport, Conn.: Greenwood.

57. Leonard W. Doob (1987). "Adieu to Private Intervention in Political Conflicts?" *International Journal of Group Tensions* 17:15–27.

58. Christopher C. Joyner (1989). "International law." In Peter Schraeder, ed., *Intervention in the 1980s*, pp. 191–204. Boulder, Colo.: Lynne Rienner.

Chapter 8 Evaluation

1. Ernest B. Haas et al. (1972). *Conflict Management by International Organizations*, pp. 10, 14, 43–44. Morristown, N.J.: General Learning Press.

2. Glenn H. Snyder and Paul Diesing (1977). *Conflict among Nations*, chap. 6. Princeton: Princeton University Press.

3. Douglas J. Amy (1987). *The Politics of Environmental Mediation*, pp. 1–3, 125–127. New York: Columbia University Press.

4. See Clark Kerr (1954). "Industrial Conflict and Its Mediation." *American Journal of Sociology* 60:230–245.

5. Leslie McCain and Richard McCleasy (1979). "The Statistical Analysis of the Simple Interrupted Time-Series Quasi-experiment." In Thomas D. Cook and Donald T. Campbell, eds., *Quasi-experimentation*, pp. 233–293. Chicago: Rand McNally.

6. Roslyn H. Corney (1987). "Marital Problems and Treatment Outcomes in Depressed Women." *British Journal of Psychiatry* 151:652–659.

7. See Alice R. Gold et al. (1976). *Fists and Flowers*, pp. 195–196, chap. 10. New York: Academic Press.

8. Henk A. Becker and Alan L. Porter (1986). *Impact Assessment Today* (2 vols.). Utrecht: Van Arkel.

9. Robert M. Browning and Donald D. Stover (1971). *Behavior Modification in Child Treatment*, chap. 8. Chicago: Aldine-Atherton.

10. See Leonard W. Doob (1960). *Becoming More Civilized*, pp. 84–93. New Haven: Yale University Press.

11. Richard J. Gerrig and Deborah A. Prentice (1991). "The Representation of Fictional Information." *Psychological Science* 2:226–240.

12. Thomas L. Wright et al. (1985). "Satisfaction and Things Not Said." *Small Group Behavior* 16:565–572.

13. Philip D. Stewart (1987). "The Dartmouth Conference." In John W. McDonald and Diane B. Bendahmane, eds., *Conflict Resolution*, pp. 21–26. Washington, D.C.: Foreign Service Institute.

14. J. Rotblat and W. I. Goldanski (1989). *Global Problems and Common Security*, p. 254. New York: Springer-Verlag.

15. See Alexander Abdennur (1987). *The Conflict Resolution Syndrome*, p. 124. Ottawa: University of Ottawa.

16. Cited by Adam Curle (1971). *Making Peace,* p. 275. London: Tavistock.

17. Lawrence Klippenstein (1979). *That There Be Peace,* p. 92. Winnipeg: Manitoba CO Reunion Committee.

18. E. Allan Lind and Tom R. Tyler (1988). *The Social Psychology of Procedural Justice,* pp. 213–214. New York: Plenum.

19. See Tom R. Tyler (1990). "Justice, Self-interest, and the Legitimacy of Legal and Political Authority." In Jane J. Mansbridge, ed., *Beyond Self-interest.* Chicago: University of Chicago Press. See Pauline Houldin et al. (1978). "Preference for Modes of Dispute Resolution as a Function of Process and Decision Control." *Journal of Experimental Social Psychology* 14:13–30.

20. Ruth Leger Sivard (1983). *World Military and Social Expenditures 1983,* p. 5. Washington, D.C.: World Priorities, 1983.

21. Townsend Hoopes (1969). *The Limits of Intervention,* pp. 7–24. New York: David McKay.

22. Jon Hurwitz (1987). "How Are Foreign Policy Attitudes Structured?" *American Political Science Review* 81:1099–1120.

23. See Raymond Breton (1991). *The Governance of Ethnic Communities,* chap. 1. Westport, Conn.: Greenwood.

24. Michael Billig (1987). *Arguing and Thinking,* p. 256. New York: Cambridge University Press.

25. Joel Shor and Jean Saiville (1978). *Illusion in Loving,* p. 107. Los Angeles: Double Helix Press.

26. See Howard Leventhal (1980). "The Smoking Problem." *Psychological Bulletin* 88:370–405.

27. See Urie Bronfenbrenner (1975). "Is Early Intervention Effective?" In Marcus Guttentag and Elmer L. Struening, eds., *Handbook of Evaluation Research.* 2.519–603. Beverly Hills: Sage.

28. Thelma E. Lobel et al. (1985). "Guilt Feelings and Locus of Control of Concentration Camp Survivors." *International Journal of Social Psychiatry* 31:170–175.

29. Herbert Kaufman (1985). *Time, Chance, and Organizations,* pp. 49, 67. Chatham, N.J.: Chatham House.

30. Leonard W. Doob (1981). *The Pursuit of Peace,* pp. 167–168. Westport, Conn.: Greenwood.

31. Stephen M. Berk (1985). *Year of Crisis, Year of Hope,* pp. 139–140. Westport, Conn.: Greenwood.

32. Cited in John L. Gaddis (1987). *The Long Peace,* p. 49. New York: Oxford University Press.

33. Karl Kaiser (1971). "The Political Aspects of Intervention in Present Day International Politics." In Louis G. M. Jaquet, ed., *Intervention in International Politics,* pp. 76–87. The Hague: Netherlands Institute of International Affairs.

34. Irving L. Janis (1989). *Crucial Decisions,* chaps. 3 & 4. New York: Free Press.

35. Roger Fisher (1964). "Defects in the Governmental Decision Process." In Roger Fisher, ed., *International Conflict and Behavioral Science,* pp. 248–253. New York: Basic Books.

36. Philip E. Tetlock (1986). "Psychological Advice on Foreign Policy." *American Psychologist* 41:557–567.

37. Kenneth Kressel and Dean G. Pruitt (1989). "Conclusion." In Kenneth Kressel et al., eds., *Mediation Research,* pp. 394–435. San Francisco: Josey-Bass.

38. Marc Miller (1986). "Legal Constraints on Intervention Programs in Public Schools." In Peter W. Greenwood, ed., *Intervention Strategies for Chronic Juvenile Offenders,* pp. 123–147. Westport, Conn.: Greenwood.

39. Josef Cardinal Glemp (1991). "A Pastoral Letter on the Jews." *New York Times,* Jan. 20, p. E19.

40. Joan McCord (1978). "A Thirty-Year Follow-up of Treatment Effects." *American Psychologist* 33:284–289.

41. Paul H. Nitze (1989). *From Hiroshima to Glasnost,* pp. 376–389. New York: Grove Weidenfeld.

42. Leonard W. Doob (1971). "The Impact of the Fermeda Workshop on the Conflicts in the Horn of Africa." *International Journal of Group Tensions* 1:91–101.

43. Landrum Bolling (1987). "Strengths and Weaknesses of track two." In John W. McDonald, Jr., and Diane B. Bendahmane, eds., *Conflict Resolution,* pp. 53–64. Washington, D.C.: Foreign Service Institute.

44. Robin Toner (1989). "Americans Much Warmer toward Soviets, Poll Finds." *New York Times,* Dec. 3, p. 29.

45. A. M. Levi and A. Benjamin (1977). "Focus and Flexibility in a

Model of Conflict Resolution." *Journal of Conflict Resolution* 21:405–424.

46. Jeffrey Z. Rubin (1981). "Integration and Commentary." In Jeffrey Z. Rubin, ed., *Dynamics of Third Party Intervention*, pp. 272–292. New York: Praeger.

47. Francis C. Byrnes (1965). *Americans in Technical Assistance*, p. 35. New York: Praeger.

48. See K. J. Holsti (1988). "Paths to Peace?" In Ramesh Thakur, ed., *International Conflict Resolution*, pp. 105–132. Boulder, Colo.: Westview.

INDEX

The page numbers in *italics* indicate the text pages on which a reference note is made without mention of the author's name.